SIEGES

A Comparative Study

Bruce Allen Watson

Westport, Connecticut
London

Library of Congress Cataloging-in-Publication Data

Watson, Bruce A.
    Sieges : a comparative study / Bruce A. Watson.
      p. cm.
    Includes bibliographical references and index.
    ISBN 0–275–94034–9 (alk. paper)
    1. Siege warfare. I. Title.
  UG444.W33 1993
   355.4'4—dc20   92–46422

British Library Cataloguing in Publication Data is available.

Library of Congress Catalog Card Number: 92–46422
ISBN: 0–275–94034–9

First published in 1993

Praeger Publishers, 88 Post Road West, Westport, CT 06881
An imprint of Greenwood Publishing Group, Inc.

Printed in the United States of America

∞™

The paper used in this book complies with the
Permanent Paper Standard issued by the National
Information Standards Organization (Z39.48–1984).

10 9 8 7 6 5 4 3 2 1

In memory of my father
George Hughson Watson

He left a life at sea in 1914 to serve as a cavalry officer in Britain's New Army, then, in 1917, was sent to the United States, where, as a liaison officer, he helped shape a still newer army. He never went home.

Contents

Illustrations and Maps   ix

Preface   xi

1   Sieges: Overview and Method   1

2   Jerusalem, 1099   11

3   Malta, 1565   35

4   Sebastopol, October 1854 to September 1855   57

5   Kut-al-Amara, December 1915 to April 1916   83

6   Singapore, 7 December 1941 to 15 February 1942   107

7   Five Sieges: Constants and Variables   129

8   The Ongoing Story   145

Selected Bibliography   165

Index   169

Illustrations and Maps

Illustrations follow page 81.

ILLUSTRATIONS

1   The Capture of Jerusalem

2   Departing for the Crusades

3   An Artist's Interpretation of the Fall of Sebastopol

4   Three Gurkhas in a Trench at Kut-al-Amara

5   British Home-made Weapons at Kut-al-Amara

6   Smoke Rising Above Singapore

7   A Japanese Zero Fighter

8   U.S. Sherman Tank

9   German Tiger Tank

10   Two U.S. Abrams M1A1 Tanks in the Kuwait Desert

11   U.S. F-117A Stealth Fighter

MAPS

1   Eastern Mediterranean   16

2   Syria and Judea   23

3	Jerusalem	25
4	Malta	37
5	Grand Harbor Area	44
6	Crimean Coast	62
7	Sebastopol Region	67
8	Sebastopol	69
9	Lower Mesopotamia	89
10	Kut-al-Amara	93
11	Malayan Peninsula	115
12	Singapore Island	118
13	Dien Bien Phu	148
14	Kuwait and Lower Iraq	158

Preface

The purpose of this book is to present a comparative study of sieges. I shall articulate the constants and variables they exhibit regardless of time and place. I have chosen five examples for initial close examination: Jerusalem from the First Crusade, Malta from the late sixteenth century, Sebastopol in the mid-nineteenth century, Kut-al-Amara during World War I, and Singapore from early in World War II. My choices were predicated on the conceit that, if they interested me, then they would interest others. I hope so. But my selection was also based on finding sieges that spanned the historical periods I was interested in exploring, that reasonably demonstrated the development of fortifications and weapons technology, and, most importantly, represented the issues I thought needed discussion.

Sieges are a fascinating aspect of military history and many have been studied individually. Such studies are customarily limited to narratives of what happened or are investigations of weapons technology or fortress building. But I think sieges have additional features that need exploration. First, most sieges have been conducted in confined spaces that bring armies to a grinding halt. Limited space has important implications for the manner in which sieges are fought. Second, that confined space, so often taken for granted, and the static relationship between the opponents during sieges change human conduct, norms, expectations, and even perceptions. This study explains why.

My approach has been very much influenced by the ideas of the British military historian John Keegan, who gives us an insightful re-shuffling of long-held assumptions in military history in his book *The Face of Battle*. The results have proven useful in my presentation of the five sieges. Central to my discussion of each siege and of my chapters is Keegan's notion of categories of combat, those man-to-weapons equations that emerge within each battle and the will to combat that either sustained or failed the soldiers.

Specific comparisons between the five sieges are developed in a chapter devoted to the analysis of the constants and variables that play such an important role in siege warfare. Here, again, I utilize Keegan's approach. My comparative framework was adapted from his discussion of sieges in *The Nature of War* with commentaries on war art by John Darracott. My final chapter is a discussion of post–World War II developments. Dien Bien Phu and Kuwait are analyzed under the light cast by our knowledge of sieges. I end with a few speculations about the future of sieges.

The sieges discussed here place emphasis on Western European armies. Sometimes these armies fought in exotic places, but the backgrounds of the conflicts were distinctly Western. Even so, I have knowingly ignored many important Western sieges. But siege warfare, by its very nature, usually follows certain patterns and takes similar shapes. I have identified, and made more evident, the nature of those patterns and the character of those shapes.

ACKNOWLEDGMENTS

The Bodleian Library, Oxford University, and the Doe Library of the University of California, Berkeley, provided valuable assistance. And I never cease to be amazed at the gems contained in the library of my home institution, Diablo Valley College. Although appropriate photo credits are given, I should like to thank the staff members of the collections involved for their courtesy and efficiency. I must thank Terrance Masterson, Bill Brandt, and Siska Cushman for reading the manuscript and for their comments and suggestions. Last, but always first, I thank my wife, Marilyn, for her patient, critical reading and for editing of the numerous manuscript drafts. I could not have done the job without her.

Chapter 1

Sieges: Overview and Method

SELECTED HISTORICAL OVERVIEW

Siege: catapults hurl stones into the medieval castle as battering rams hammer the gates; great siege towers bridge the parapets; knights and men-at-arms struggle up ladders placed against the castle walls as defenders rain rocks, arrows, and boiling water on them.

Television and motion pictures have bombarded our senses with this picture. Siege via MGM and Paramount Pictures! Justifiably, we may choose to believe that such visual imagery is distorted by an overly romantic view of the Middle Ages. Ironically, this same picture would be familiar to any resurrected soldiers we might find from ancient Greece and Rome. Costuming excepted, the setting of the siege, the machinery used, and the hand-held weapons altered very little between those ancient civilizations and the Middle Ages. The basic problem faced by besieging forces for all those intervening centuries was to get under, through, or over the defensive walls. Manpower was the energy of sieges. Men hauled battering rams and catapults into place. Men dug mines under the walls. Men wielded swords and axes. The reliance on manpower gave sieges a static character that did not significantly change until the fourteenth century and the advent in Western Europe of gunpowder weapons.

Sieges in the Gunpowder Era

The introduction of gunpowder and, with it, cannon, brought an end to medieval warfare, but the change was an evolution rather than a revolution. Men-at-arms did not suddenly appear with cannon and muskets to bring down the venerable castle and pot some errant knight who had the bad luck to stray across their muzzles. Cannon were first introduced in Western Europe during the early fourteenth century; however, it would be more than a hundred years before they were considered a common weapon. Problems of safety, accuracy, and unreliable range had to be overcome. Also, and most significantly, cannon were very expensive. Usually, only kings could afford them in sufficient numbers to make a difference in battle. That resulted in more real firepower against local lords who resisted the growing centralization of authority in Europe's incipient nation-states.

The adaptation of gunpowder was less a rational choice than one forced by events. In 1494, Charles VIII of France invaded Italy. His siege train included forty bronze cannon with barrels eight feet long. These guns were easily elevated or depressed because they moved on two prongs or trunnions just forward of the barrels' balancing point. Except for the heaviest, these cannon were easily moved by lifting the trail of the gun mount and shifting it to one side or the other. They fired iron balls at ranges equal to those of earlier cannon that were three times the calibre. Charles's guns were transported on carriages, increasing their mobility. No wonder, then, that Christopher Duffy, in his book *Siege Warfare*, considers the French invasion a kind of blitzkrieg warfare. One Italian fortress after another fell to the French bombardments. As Duffy notes, the fortress of San Giovanni, once besieged for seven years, was reduced by French gunners in only eight hours. The garrison was then slaughtered. Indeed, the medieval castle was now obsolete.

Not to be overlooked was the introduction in the early sixteenth century of hand-held gunpowder weapons. These were available in the 1521 war between Francis I of France and the Holy Roman Emperor Charles V. The guns had six-foot barrels and one-inch bores. Francis's infantry, positioned in their trenches, raked the parapets of Charles's castles with fire, forcing the defending infantry to take cover. But defensive volley fire from hand-held guns could disorganize attacking masses of enemy troops. Such weapons both increased the distance at which soldiers often fought and increased the destructive capacities of siege warfare.

New fortress designs were created to counter the effects of gunpowder weapons. Most of the early works were Italian. Artists such as the Sangallo family working out of Rome, Leonardo da Vinci, and Michelangelo brought their fertile imaginations to fortress design. And in Germany, the painter and printmaker Albrecht Dürer contributed new designs. The military engineer would soon be a specialist in his own right.

The medieval square castle design with corner towers gave way to the square fort with corner bastions. At first, the bastions were simple triangular works that projected from each corner so that their facings would cover all approaches to the main walls. Later they were heart-shaped, to increase the areas covered. By changing the basic square to a polygon—pentagons, hexagons, and octagons were all used—architects could multiply the number of bastions. Another wall or at least an earthwork was constructed around and outside the main defenses, giving the complex the overall appearance of a multi-pointed star. A sloped ditch was then dug around the entire perimeter. This already intimidating fortification was further reinforced toward the end of the sixteenth century with the addition of ravelins—triangular, free-standing works positioned between the bastions. Next, so-called covered ways were added to the surrounding ditch so that defending infantry could lay down enfilading fire against approaching enemy infantry. Some of the finest examples of these new designs are the Castel Sant'Angelo in Rome, to which bastions were added, the Citadel de Basso built for the Medici, the Citadel Ancona designed by Antonio Sangallo the Younger, and the Turin Citadel.

The new ideas rapidly spread into northern Europe, where they were much elaborated. Maurice of Nassau's plan for re-building Coevorden, Holland, by adding bastions, turned into a 14-point star. During the English Civil War the Royalists planned to double-wall Oxford, a scheme possibly inspired by Dutch examples. Likewise, Palmanova, Italy, was planned as an 18-point star.

These new forts were constructed both to withstand sieges and to support active, punishing defenses. Christopher Duffy lists three requirements for a fortress to withstand bombardment and mount its own defense. First, walls had to be built lower to reduce the target surface, be thick enough to absorb bombardment, and have enough strength to support the fort's own gun platforms. Second, the main wall had to be radically sloped to prevent any attempts to climb it. Third, the fortress could have no "dead ground," that is, areas where the besiegers could reach the walls unharmed. Every approach had to be a killing ground.

How could an attacking army overcome such multi-layered defenses? Duffy notes that even the "provisional" log and earthwork fortress at Santhia, attacked by the Spanish in 1555, absorbed 6,300 artillery rounds in three days without much damage. New offensive methods were needed.

Because new fortresses were so elaborate and formidable, the leader of the attacking forces had to select one point for his main attack. Preparations included constructing redoubts for artillery and trenches for infantry. Saps, or narrow zigzag trenches, were dug from the main trenches toward the defenses by special digging teams appropriately known as sappers. When the saps were within a few feet of the defensive perimeter ditch, grenadiers threw hand bombs into the ditch, clearing it of defending infantry. The sappers cut through the berms, laid down bridges or causeways, and the assault force moved to the walls. In the early days of gunpowder, miners dug under the walls and used gunpowder merely to ignite the supporting timbers, causing the wall above to collapse. By the sixteenth century, properly set explosives could actually bring down the walls. This is exemplified by the 1522 siege of Rhodes, where the Knights of St. John, holding one of the strongest fortresses ever built, were defeated by Turkish mining.

The possibility of bringing down walls with cannon fire increased as artillery improved. Bombardment was thought safer and more certain than mining, there was less risk of being repulsed trying to cross the perimeter ditch because of covering fire by one's own guns, and, if the bombardment was correctly directed, much time was saved. There was also the psychological advantage that a bombardment, supplemented by howitzers and mortars that could fire over the walls, could shatter the defenders' desire to hold out. Advantage to the besiegers was given an added boost when, in the seventeenth century, Menno van Coehorrn developed a small, light, and mobile mortar that enabled the besiegers to fire over the walls at any point desired, shift position, and fire again.

Sébastien le Prestre de Vauban, Louis XIV's chief military engineer, was probably the most influential siege theoretician and practitioner of his time. His ideas and plans are accessible through Duffy's *Siege Warfare* and *Fire and Stone*, so they do not need repeating here. Suffice it to say that Vauban, absorbing lessons from Turkish operations against Vienna and other contemporary sieges, systematized siege warfare. He insisted that the digging of saps proceed from trenches that paralleled the fortifications and that artillery be placed in the forward-most parallel trenches. Those guns could fire at the fort's ramparts, making sapping operations safer and more efficient. Simultaneously, artillery was to breach the walls and bastions at selected spots. That meant concentrating artillery bombardments rather than simply having the guns fire along the expanse of wall and hoping something collapsed.

Nonetheless, fortresses remained difficult to subdue, largely because artillery technology soon stagnated. Consequently, in the eighteenth century, a counter-trend surfaced to siege warfare. Mobile warfare, symbolized by the campaigns of Frederick the Great of Prussia, became the norm. Strong fortresses were by-passed. There was nothing novel in the idea. The Duke of Parma, in the 1570's, had used by-pass as an integral part of his campaign tactics. But in the eighteenth century and beyond, the Peninsular sieges of the Napoleonic Wars notwithstanding, battle was dominated by mobile infantry formations. These were not just massive human chess games, Wellington trying to checkmate Napoleon. Inevitably, the armies stood face-to-face, each trying to annihilate the other in battles of attrition.

New fortresses were constructed to interrupt the mobility of an enemy army, causing a campaign to falter or a grand strategy to collapse. This, of course, had been done before, when European castles were first constructed to circumvent the mobility of the swiftly moving Goth invaders. The new late eighteenth century forts were, like the castles of yore, refuges for the defending forces against the hellish world of open field battle. But the new forts could not simply be larger versions of old designs. Frederick the Great, not especially known as a fortress builder, introduced the technique of building free-standing strongpoints beyond the fortress perimeter to stall direct assault on the main fort. Their coordinated fire was designed to enfilade attacking infantry. Then, in 1777, the Marquis de Montalembert created a design that influenced fortress building through the nineteenth century. This was the *caponiere*, a heavily walled structure three stories high and at a right angle to the main wall. Each story was a great gun platform, multiplying in a stroke the number of cannon facing an assault force. The guns were no longer exposed along the parapet but were sheltered, or casemented, by partition walls and by roofs. The casements diminished casualties among the gunners and lowered the possibility of the guns being easily dismounted by enemy bombardment.

The caponiere idea spread over Europe to sites from Sebastopol in the Crimea, to Toulon in southern France, to Portsmouth, England, and then across the Atlantic to Fort Sumter in Charleston Harbor, South Carolina, and Fort Point at the mouth of San Francisco Bay. These were all harbor facilities. The invention of steam ships and then iron-clad ships made siege from the sea more possible than in the age of sail, when vessels had to rely on the vagaries of wind and tide to maintain station for their bombardments.

Paradoxically, the siege of Sebastopol during the Crimean War and the sieges of the American Civil War, such as Vicksburg and Petersburg, demonstrated how wrong military theorists could be. For, although fortresses once again had become powerful defensive weapons, offensive technology and tactics did not keep pace. The widely approved land-based assault technique against the new forts was the frontal infantry attack. As Major Matthew Steele concludes in *American Campaigns,* infantry assaults against such fortifications were attritional, a senseless waste of life. Starvation, Steele further concludes, that most ancient siege weapon, remained the most successful means of forcing a defense to surrender.

Sieges in Modern Warfare

If the futility of frontal attacks against strong fortifications had been a lesson absorbed by subsequent military planners, then World War I might have been a different affair. What began in 1914 as a mobile war, the Germans on the Western Front striking quickly through Belgium and south toward Paris, became static trench warfare after the Battle of the Marne. A siege mentality gripped both sides, each looking for a breakthrough of the enemy lines. Tragically, the waves of soldiers sent "over the top" of their trenches against rapid fire artillery and machine guns resulted in millions of casualties but only a few dents and bends in the 700-mile trench line. Not until the British introduced the tank at Cambrai and at Amiens was a breaching tool found. But in neither battle were the advantages of the new machine really understood or exploited. Infantry continued to be slaughtered in frontal attacks.

The potentialities of the tank were fully realized in World War II. Unfortunately, that realization was first expressed by the Nazi war machine in blitzkrieg warfare, involving the close coordination of infantry, armor, artillery, and air power. The German Pz Mark III, mounting a 50mm gun, and Pz Mark IV, mounting a 75mm gun, were the early workhorses of the German army. They were later replaced by the formidable Tiger tank with heavy armor plating and armed with the deadly 88mm gun. British tanks such as the Matilda, much used in the Western Desert, were good enough at the beginning of the war, but it was not until 1944 that the Cromwell tank was introduced. Heavily enough armored to stand up to the German Tigers, it was nonetheless outgunned. The Allied armies came to depend on the American Sherman tank with its single molded body, good speed, and its 75mm gun. The Soviets built the T-34, armed initially with an 85mm gun and later with a 100mm gun. Despite the development of some good armored weapons, the Allies did not learn blitzkrieg-type coordination until later in the war, through the terrible lessons of battle.

Sieges, as such, were relatively few in World War II. Tobruk, Malta, and Singapore were, for instance, each important, but the vast arena of the war, the impact of air power, and the rapid movement of armies enhanced by the formation of full tank corps, mechanized infantry, and mobile artillery rendered siege warfare seemingly irrelevant. Thus, the infamous French Maginot Line became a symbol of the French tendency to prepare for the last war. But the Germans did not assault the line; instead, they outflanked it. The German assault on the Belgian fort of Eben Emael, 11 May 1940, was more a portent of the future. The Germans landed only seventy-eight paratroopers on the fort's roof and, in twenty-eight hours, piercing the roof with explosives, they shocked the garrison into submission. The advent of bombers capable of delivering heavy loads added a new dimension to sieges. J. B. Bell makes a convincing argument in his book *Besieged* that the Nazi bombing of London was essentially an aerial siege, as it were, a massive attempt to jump over the British defenses and pulverize the people into surrender.

The Germans failed in that attempt, and they would fail again and again when, on 22 June 1941, they invaded the Soviet Union. They unleashed Operation Barbarossa, a blitzkrieg advance by 3 million troops with 7,000 guns and 3,300 tanks along a 2,000-mile front. The Soviets, however, forced the Germans into sieges at Leningrad, Moscow, Sebastopol, and Stalingrad that forestalled the German's rapid thrusts, consumed time, weapons, supplies, and ground up German manpower as quickly as it could be advanced.

Barbarossa involved a three-pronged German attack. Army Group South, commanded by Gerd von Runstedt, broke through the Stalin Line between Cherniov in the north and Odessa on the Black Sea. Army Group Center, under Fedor von Bach, charged toward Minsk and Smolensk. Beyond lay Moscow. Army Group North, commanded by Ritter von Leeb, burst out of East Prussia toward Leningrad. The purpose behind taking Leningrad was simple. As Franz Halder, chief of the German general staff, wrote in his private journal, Adolf Hitler wanted to level the city, making in uninhabitable, so that the Germans would not have to feed the population during the winter months. Then he would cede the land to Finland. By the end of September, the Germans advanced over 300 miles in the south, taking Kiev and Novgorod. Army Group Center advanced 200 to 250 miles, and Army Group North nearly cut off Leningrad.

Nearly was not good enough. A major problem was that the steel tip of the German blitzkrieg was blunted before it started. When the Germans invaded France, four tank battalions were assigned to each panzer division. At the beginning of Barbarossa, that number was reduced to three and would be reduced again to two battalions. Then Hitler, self-proclaimed master strategist, declared that some of Army Group Center's tanks should be diverted to other battle zones, the 41st Panzer Corps being sent north, weakening the thrust toward Moscow. Meanwhile, although considerable success was experienced in the south, the Eleventh Army of Erich von Manstein ran into stubborn resistance at Sebastopol. Despite the German's use of "Gustave", an 80cm gun that fired a projectile six feet long and required a battalion to operate, the fortress city held out for almost a year.

Leningrad held out for 900 days and was never taken. The Nazi forces pounded the city. The Russians counter-attacked again and again, experiencing heavy casualties. By early July 1941, twenty-one out of thirty-one Russian divisions had lost at least 50 percent of their manpower, and remaining units had little ammunition, fuel, or food. By 8 August 1941, the Germans moved through the suburbs and were directly assaulting the city. In September, the Germans bombarded Leningrad 200 times with artillery and launched 23 major air raids. Civilian casualties numbered 4,000 each day. On 16 September, Communist Party secretary Andrei Zhdanov declared in the Leningrad *Pravda* that "The enemy is at the gates." Regardless of the devastation heaped on the city by the German offensive, despite the killing and the suffering, the Germans could not penetrate the city's main defenses. There were many reasons for this, a few of which are useful to this survey.

First, the Soviet authorities conscripted a half-million civilians, many of them women, to construct defense lines in depth around the city. As John Keegan notes in *The Second World War*, the workers dug 620 miles of earthworks, 420 miles of anti-tank ditches, built 5,000 pillboxes, and strung 370 miles of barbed wire. Second, the Germans could not completely encircle the city. They tried but failed to force passage of the Neva River to join their Finnish allies, who stopped their advance north of Lake Ladoga and far short of German expectations. That left Lake Ladoga open, a veritable roadway which, when frozen over, allowed evacuees to leave the city and supplies and reinforcements to enter. Third, the German armored units taken from Army Group Center were recalled from Leningrad in the middle of an assault that was making good progress. So depleted were the remaining units that, once the 41st Panzer Group was gone, only twenty tanks were left for the final attack.

The attack sputtered, and the Germans dug in around the city. When, on 13 September, Marshall G. K. Zhukov assumed command, he ordered immediate and massive artillery and aerial bombardment of the German positions. Then the first snows of October fell. The Germans were broken and never again attacked in full force. Great battles lay ahead at Moscow and Stalingrad but, in each instance, German armor and air power were stopped by Soviet tenacity and their strong defensive lines.

The United States and the Soviet Union emerged from World War II as the world's two great super-powers, their relationships characterized by a long period of stalemate in which neither was willing to risk direct confrontation lest the situations get out of hand and turn into nuclear holocaust. Instead, maneuvering was through client states where one or the other power could stand aside and let the other blunt its prestige in some minor faraway war, the military outcome of which was less important than the propaganda value derived from it.

Then, in 1989, with unexpected abruptness, Soviet domination of Eastern Europe collapsed with the emergence of a profound anti-communist resentment and a movement, however economically enfeebled, toward democratization. With equally unexpected abruptness, the Soviet Union itself unravelled as old nationalisms and ethnic identities were asserted beyond the Kremlin's protective walls. All-out nuclear war seemed less possible as geographers scrambled to keep pace with the world's changing political configurations. What was overlooked in the euphoria over the Soviet demise was that new battlefields were being drawn with each line added to the maps.

WRITING ABOUT SIEGES

The foregoing survey alerts us to the seemingly endless variety of sieges. It is no wonder that the mountain of literature devoted to siege warfare shows similar variety. In order to better demonstrate where this study sits on the mountain, I wish to briefly survey the literature, grouping it into three convenient and very general categories.

The first category of siege literature includes those works authored by eyewitnesses to sieges—the tradition of the chronicler, a tradition unbroken since the beginning of written history. In the context of this study we shall see that Fulcher of Chartres wrote accounts of the sieges at Nicaea, Antioch, and Jerusalem. Francisco Balbi di Corregio authored a vivid account of the Malta siege. S.J.G. Calthorpe chronicled the siege of Sebastopol, and F. Spenser Chapman portrayed the tragedy of Singapore.

The full list is very long because many soldiers would as soon pick up a pen as a sword, an affliction particularly widespread among Queen Victoria's officers. However personal and poignant, these eyewitness accounts must be carefully scrutinized. That is not because the authors intentionally lied or distorted truth, but for the simple reason that no one person can see everything that is happening in a battle. Thus, as John Keegan concludes, in *The Face of Battle*, an observer's subsequent reminiscences are conditioned by his "personal angle of vision," where he was as the battle unfolded. What could he see and what did he see? Francisco Balbi, for instance, for all the seeming authority of his account, was, in fact, a minor Spanish infantryman bottled up for most of the Malta siege in Fort St. Michael and probably saw very little.

The second category of siege literature is composed of works that are concerned with changes in fortifications and weapons technology. The works by I. V. Hogg, *A History of Artillery* and *Fortress: A History of Military Defense*, are among the more accessible books in this category. Some works, especially those written between the sixteenth and nineteenth centuries, are more technical. Vauban's famous *Manual of Siegecraft and Fortifications* is a prime example of the type.

The third category, and the most consistently popular, is the historical narrative tradition that tells us who did what to whom and when. Alistair Horne's *Fall of Paris* in the Franco-Prussian War, and Russell Braddon's *The Siege* about Kut-al-Amara are illustrative of this trend. Closely related are works that cover sieges in a particular area or during a period. Frederick Myatt's *British Sieges of the Peninsular War* and the book about English Civil War sieges by Brigadier Peter Young and W. Emberton are two fine examples. There are also narrative studies that cover even broader areas of siege warfare. J. B. Bell's *Besieged* is a study of seven modern cities under siege, from Madrid during the Spanish Civil War to the London Blitz to Stalingrad. William Seymour's *Great Sieges of History* describes seventeen sieges from Acre in the Third Crusade to Khe Sahn during the Viet Nam War. I selected these last two works for special mention because their narratives can be compelling and because there is some overlap in coverage with my study. There are also some significant differences that need to be explained.

TOWARD A COMPARATIVE METHOD

This study begins with analyses of five sieges: Jerusalem, Malta, Sebastopol, Kut-al-Amara, and Singapore. Although, like Bell and Seymour, I am interested in who did what to whom and when, I go beyond those elements of the narrative tradition. I begin the analysis of each siege with a description of the campaign within which it took place, then depict either the attacking or defending army, depending on which viewpoint I adapt. That is supplemented by commentary on the leadership and the impact on the siege of their experiences, expectations, and perceptions. Following a description of the siege itself is an analysis of its components, or what Keegan refers to as "categories of combat." These include the man versus weapons relationships that shape the siege. What, for instance, was the impact of artillery on infantry, or of armor against artillery and against infantry? What was the influence of air power? Another important category is the will to combat that either kept the soldiers going during the sieges or failed them. Consideration is also given to how prisoners and the wounded were handled and to the aftermath of the siege.

These categories of combat, establishing a common framework for the presentation of each siege, become the bases for the comparative analysis that follows in Chapter 7. There I discuss sieges as a form of battle, a unique feature in this study, which emphasizes the ingredients necessary to develop commitment to siege. That is followed by a discussion of the siege as defense, then as offense, in both instances identifying the constants and variables that can be found in sieges regardless of time and place. For example, how have offenses gone under, through, and over the defensive wall—whatever shape it may take? By what means have defenses repelled the offense? The product of that comparative analysis is then applied to the two modern sieges at Dien Bien Phu and Kuwait.

No other study is so premeditatedly comparative in approach. That intellectual conceit, harmless enough, nonetheless has value. For if this exercise is to end with something more than another general statement of how some sieges were conducted in different periods—yet another list of favorite and decisive sieges—if the reader is to end with more than another stack of loosely related historical facts, and if we are to make useful comparisons between our recent and future history on the one side and our past on the other, then a systematic comparative study is a timely addition to that mountain of siege literature.

Chapter 2

Jerusalem, 1099

In 1099, the First Crusade arrived before the gates of Jerusalem after a gruelling three-year campaign during which they besieged Nicaea and Antioch. They laid siege to Jerusalem for six weeks, finally penetrating the defenses and pouring into the city. An infamous slaughter of the survivors ensued.

THE FIRST CRUSADE BEGINS

Europe in the eleventh century was not a nice place to live. The earlier Carolingian political hegemony had been shattered by the Treaty of Verdun that divided the empire, by the inability of remaining ostensible authority to stem the rising tide of regionalism, and by the Viking invasions. Secular life was dominated by local lords—earls, barons, and counts—who battled one another endlessly, seeking to enhance their power, prestige, and property. What they created was institutionalized violence, rooted on the one side in the ancient and traditional prerogatives of European tribal warrior classes and equally rooted on the other in their own arbitrary, if not capricious, understanding of those traditions. As for the sacred life, the Roman Catholic Church, despite all peaceful pretensions, adapted its own violent pattern. The world and man were sinful, and that sin had to be purged. Unbelievers of all sorts, real and imagined—heretics, Jews, Moslems, and those full-fledged Christians whose piety was judged lax—were periodically burned, hanged, chopped, squashed, flogged, branded, drowned, and flayed. And more than one cleric, such as Odo, Bishop of Bayeaux and brother of William of Normandy, took up sword and mace and charged into battle—all in the name of God.

But Western Europe faced a challenge more tangible than mortal sin: the great force of Islam. The Moslems invaded Spain in 717, extending their power into the western Mediterranean and to most of its islands. By the end of the tenth century, however, the Christian armies took back León and Navarre in northern Spain and Sardinia. The Normans, meantime, re-took Sicily. Successive popes called for holy wars against Moslem Spain. The time had come, as Steven Runciman stated, for a Christian counter-attack.

In March 1095, Pope Urban II held council at Piacenza, where he received envoys from Alexius I, emperor of Byzantium. Urban was told that a decisive counter-offensive against the Moslems was needed in the east because, despite some gains in Romania, the Turks were losing their resolve. To exploit that lapse, Alexius needed more troops than he could recruit. Without help from Western Europe, the Moslems could not be driven from formerly Christian lands, and Christians would continue to suffer under Moslem rule. And more: If the Turks recognized Alexius's troop shortage, they might find new energy and threaten more Christian territory.

Urban saw Alexius's request as a dual opportunity to cement Western Europe and enhance papal power. Yet Urban was a cautious man. He spent the next months travelling through southern France and the Midi, soliciting opinions about aid to Alexius. Among those he visited was Adhémar, bishop of Le Puy, sitting in his tiny church atop its needle rock. From there Urban called for another council to be held at Clermont on 18 November 1095.

The Clermont council did not initially address Alexius's request for assistance. Then, on 27 November, Urban spoke to a large gathering outside Clermont's gates, enjoining them to partake in a holy war to save Eastern Christians from Moslem rule. An indulgence would be granted to all those who helped free Jerusalem. Urban promised grants of land from within the conquered territories. There was also the implied promise of loot. Quite cleverly, as the modern historian Frederic Duncalf puts it in Baldwin's *The First Hundred Years*, Urban had masterminded a way to replace European feudal war with a foreign war. And who should step forward as the first enlistee but Adhémar of Le Puy. He was immediately appointed the Crusade's papal legate and its vicar. On 1 December, Raymond, marquis of Provence and count of Toulouse, sent word that he and several of his lords would take up the cross. This may have been a pre-arranged enlistment, the fruit of Urban's travels in southern France. The First Crusade, with Jerusalem its final goal, was launched.

Historians like to point out that Urban wanted a trained fighting army, for his Clermont speech explicitly discouraged the aged, women, children, and the poor from participating. He could not have anticipated the torrent of enthusiasm that would not be dammed as thousands of commoners joined his holy crusade. Nor could Urban have anticipated the charismatic impact of the peasant priests, such as Peter the Hermit, whose own poverty, fundamentalistic piety, and visions communicated to the poor, the dis-enchanted, and the dispossessed promises of redemption and paradise with the certainty of a modern televangelist. From Denmark to Sicily, from Britain to Germany, people of all sorts, wanted or not, were on the move. Once in process, the Crusade was a movement that no single authority could control.

THE CRUSADER ARMY

Any discussion of the Crusader army involves difficulty. None of the First Crusade's chroniclers describes the army's organization or its weapons; nor does any of them give accurate numbers of men. A primary reason for the last problem is, as August Krey points out, that there were no enlistment rolls; there was as well a blurred distinction between who was and who was not a combatant. Furthermore, none of the chroniclers, much less anyone else associated with the Crusade, had experience estimating numbers. Thus, Fulcher of Chartres's belief that Kerbogha's Turkish army at Antioch numbered 300,000 is nonsense. As both Krey and Runciman note, such estimates probably meant only that the Turkish army was very large. Modern historians generally agree that the Crusader army that reached Jerusalem numbered around 13,500. This was the same number given by the chronicler Raymond of Aguilers. The consensus among historians to believe him, given their doubts of other estimates, may seem a contradiction, but the figure does seem reasonable. Based on his review of all the numbers given by the chroniclers, Runciman estimates that between 60,000 and 100,000 people crossed into the Byzantine Empire and of these the non-combatants represented about 25 percent. With every man counted who could in any way be considered a combatant, the ratio of cavalry to foot soldiers was about one-to-seven. That only 13,500 reached Jerusalem seems a severe reduction; but the long and exhausting marches, exposure, disease, the battles first against the Byzantines and the constant campaigning against the Turks severely reduced the Crusader ranks. Moreover, there were periodic individual and mass defections. Stephen of Blois, for example, tired of the campaign, packed it in and went home, taking his army with him. The wonder, then, is not that the number who reached Jerusalem was so small, but that any of them at all reached their goal.

Perhaps one of the reasons that there are no precise descriptions of the Crusader army is that it lacked any formal structure. Historians use such designations as "battalions" and "regiments" to describe certain formations, but they are words of convenience rather than accurate descriptions. Any organization was informal, temporary, more a response to the conditions of battle than a permanent structure. What can be said with certainty is that the army was intensely regional, for the Crusade was really an amalgamation of several armies representing Flanders, Lorraine, Normandy, Provence, Toulouse, and Norman Sicily. It was from these regions that the majority of the Crusaders came, led by the feudal lords to whom they owed fealty.

The knights and foot soldiers were viewed collectively as Franks by the Byzantines, but it was a designation that had little meaning within the Crusader army. How much more important that the warrior was a Norman or a Fleming. The concept "France," the king notwithstanding, was vague at best—thus Urban's appeal to regional lords rather than to a central government. But no individual lord had overall power within the army. Consequently, the Crusader army can be politely described as a diffuse organization. In more concrete terms it was little more than a mob.

The Crusader army was hierarchal in character. Knights were the elite fighters. Separated from common soldiers by ritual accolade, blessed by the Church, trained to use a variety of weapons, mounted on a fine charger, the knight was a force to behold. He was the quintessential heavy cavalryman, the medieval version of the tank that could hit his enemy with great force and run into the ground any poor foot soldier who got in his way.

The knights were not without their shortcomings. As Sir Charles Oman points out, arrogance and stupidity were rife. At the Battle of Hastings in 1066, the Norman knight Taillefer, supposedly singing of Roland and Oliver, went to the Duke of Normandy and asked a favor—that he be allowed to strike the first blow. The boon granted, Taillefer charged the English ranks, killing a foot soldier before he himself was killed. From a romantic viewpoint, this was a grand gesture, *une beau geste*, the essence of knightly valor. Slightly less noble is the view that the Normans may have needed a visible example of courage and Taillefer appointed himself that role. Or, more cynically, the good knight may have realized he was going to die anyway, so why not go in a manner that guaranteed some immortality? Courageous, yes; arrogant, no doubt; but the act probably had little military value. Trading his life for that of an English foot soldier was a bad bargain.

The knights were not the equivalent of the modern field officer nor even of later cavalry. They did not command x-number of fledgling knights or foot soldiers. The knight was an individual warrior who, mostly at his convenience, was part of a larger mass. This creates an enormous gap in our understanding of the Crusader army (or any other medieval army) because we simply do not know how orders were transmitted and who led whom into battle. But that a gap existed between leaders and led is unquestionable. Knights were notoriously undisciplined. They could be arrayed for a charge; yet if one or more decided to go in a different direction, there was no one to stop them. Any charge that did take place was bereft of tactics. The impact of sheer mass was expected to scatter the enemy. What happened after that was a matter of chance. A lord might try to rally his knights for another charge, but that was difficult to achieve because there was a lot of milling about and there was seldom a follow-up plan.

Foot soldiers were, indeed, the pawns of medieval warfare. They were considered less valuable than knights, were scantily armored if armored at all, armed with a variety of weapons, and were usually un-trained. They were thought necessary for establishing and guarding camps, but their appearance on the battlefield, at least in the eleventh century, did little to discourage the enemy.

The most important roles for a foot soldier emerged during a siege. These were the men who built the great siege machines, who pushed and pulled them into place, who filled the perimeter ditches, and who mined beneath the walls. Because they were at the attack points, the soldiers were often the first to reach the walls. Their efforts cleared the way for the knights, now cast as heavy infantry, to bludgeon their way into the fortress.

Trailing behind the fighting men was a cloud of non-combatants. These included the wives and children of several lords, their retinues, clergymen, various artisans, and a conglomeration of men, women, and children, the old and the very young, healthy and infirm, moral and otherwise, who hoped to find whatever they were looking for—riches, simple booty, freedom from a host of European social and economic ills, adventure, and salvation. Urban did not want them to go, but he was powerless to stop them.

Peter the Hermit's Peasant Crusade demonstrated the depths of enthusiasm for the enterprise. Not waiting for the mighty lords to assemble, Peter led some 20,000 rather common people, together with some knights and foot soldiers, toward Jerusalem. They descended on the Balkans like a herd of locusts, shocked Alexius by their appearance at Constantinople, and were quickly hustled across the Bosphorus by the emperor, who was glad to see them go. Six months after leaving Cologne, Germany, the Peasant Crusade camped at Civetot, a short distance from Nicaea. On 21 October 1096, they marched toward the great city. They had gone only three miles when the Turks ambushed them. Those who survived the trap ran back to their camp, where they were either massacred by the pursuing Turks or taken into slavery.

Raymond of Toulouse, the first great lord to take up the cross, did not leave home until that same October. As with the other regional lords marching south toward the Dalmatian coast, as with Peter the Hermit who went before him, Raymond was to join a heterogeneous, largely undisciplined mass called the Crusader army and march into a cruel environment that most did not understand against an enemy most had never seen. Faith and personal goals may have driven them all. Their feudal lords would have to lead them.

LEADERSHIP OF THE FIRST CRUSADE

Raymond of Toulouse expected Urban II to appoint an overall military commander. And Raymond's further expectation, not entirely unfounded, was that Urban would select him. He was, after all, the most powerful lord in southern France and was the first to volunteer. He would supply the largest force, numbering about 10,000 knights and men-at-arms. He vowed

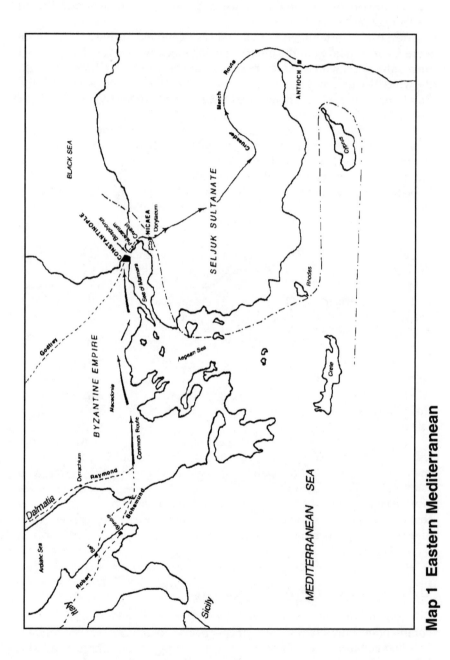

Map 1   Eastern Mediterranean

to spend the rest of his life—he was in his 50s—in the Near East. He renounced his claim to the abbey and lands of St. Gilles, transferring as well several personal holdings to the abbey. However, as Runciman notes, Raymond may have hedged a little because he left sizeable holdings in care of his natural son but did not renounce his claim to them.

What Raymond was like, as is often the case, depends on whom one reads. Runciman concludes that Raymond's actions during the Crusade revealed a "vain, obstinate, and somewhat rapacious"personality but, Runciman quickly adds, the Byzantines found him honest, reliable, and pious. Perhaps their opinions of Raymond were based on comparisons with some of the other Western lords with whom they had to deal.

Raymond's ambition to lead the Crusade may seem vain and self-serving, and his transference of lands to the Church more a bribe than an act of piety. Yet, since his envoys were in Clermont a few days after the papal exhortation, it is fair to conclude that Raymond knew what Urban was going to say and was a willing participant in the council's orchestrated events. Who else had a better right to think he would be the leader? But Urban kept silent. Raymond chafed under the papal neglect.

The only formal appointment made by Urban was to declare Adhémar of Le Puy papal legate and vicar of the Crusade. Adhémar was not only a churchman but also a trained warrior who distinguished himself in battle more than once. Popular with the army at large and respected by the lords, he could have assumed secular command without any serious objections. Unfortunately, at a critical juncture of the campaign, just when a strong leader was needed to unify the various army factions, Adhémar fell ill and died.

Raymond, in the meantime, took his time organizing his army and did not leave Toulouse until October 1096, some two months later than the pope's desired departure date of 15 August. Raymond led his troops across the Alps and along the Dalmatian coast, where they were frequently ambushed by Slavic tribesmen. Sending his main army ahead to the imperial border, Raymond stayed behind with his rearguard, butchered what prisoners they had taken, gouging out their eyes and cutting off their hands and feet. He left the wretches wriggling helplessly on the road as a warning to their fellow tribesmen.

At Dyrrachium, his army was met by imperial envoys and an escort of imperial police, Pecheneg mercenaries from north of the Baltic Sea. The march to Constantinople was long and the Crusaders, as their supplies dwindled, grew wary of the imperial police. About a hundred miles from the capital, Raymond's men attacked the town of Roussa, pillaging it and simultaneously confirming the Emperor Alexius's worst fears about the Frankish knights who came to rescue him. The Crusaders, their appetites whetted, raided the countryside to within forty miles of the capital. But imperial troops were sent out, and they soundly defeated Raymond's men.

Raymond was not with his army. Rather, he was already in Constantinople, meeting with Alexius. When news arrived that the imperial army had scattered Raymond's men to prevent further raiding, mutual accusations were made, both men growing very angry. But tempers soon cooled and Alexius asked of Raymond, as he had of other lords already in the city, that he take an oath of fealty to him. Raymond refused. A compromise was reached, Raymond swearing he would do nothing during the campaign that would harm the emperor and that he would return to Alexius any imperial lands he might win back from the Moslems. In the end, Raymond became one of Alexius's favorite lords.

Godfrey of Bouillon arrived in Constantinople earlier than Raymond. He was duke of Lorraine, an office given him by the Holy Roman Emperor Henry IV. His real holdings were the county of Antwerp and Bouillon in the Ardennes region. He was a handsome man, tall, fair, and well built. His looks were augmented by charm and good manners.

Yet, this picture of a storybook knight who traced his ancestry to Charlemagne was marred. Although Godfrey served his emperor loyally, Henry was dissatisfied with his administration of Lorraine, and a rumor spread that he would get sacked. Additionally, Cluniac reforms were rife in Lorraine, a movement Henry resisted because of their strong and competing papal loyalties. It may be, as Runciman suggests, that the ensuing contest pricked Godfrey's conscience, placing him in a moral dilemma. Distracted, feeling his future in Lorraine was doubtful, seeing the opportunities for a new life offered by the Crusade, he packed up his wife, his children and, joined by his two brothers, Baldwin and Eustace, marched east.

The Lorrainers camped outside Constantinople. Godfrey met with Alexius but refused to take the emperor's oath. When Alexius tried to influence him by cutting off promised supplies, Baldwin retaliated by raiding Constantinople's suburbs. The situation deteriorated further until, by Easter week 1097, Godfrey determined to attack the city. On 2 April, there was a battle that the imperial troops won handily. Godfrey submitted and took the oath.

Another Western lord who awaited Raymond's arrival was Bohemund of Taranto. In his mid-forties, he was a tall Norman with blond hair, a fair complexion, and a solid build. The Normans had ruled much of southern Italy and Sicily since the 1040s. Bohemund was the eldest son of Robert Guiscard, who, twenty years earlier, cemented the region into a small but important kingdom. But when Robert died intestate, Bohemund and his brothers fell to fighting among one another. Bohemund then heard about the Crusade from French troops waiting for sea transport at Bari. Realizing his prospects in Sicily were bleak, seeing the opportunity to carve out his own Eastern kingdom, he gathered his family together and joined the Crusade.

Alexius feared Bohemund more than any other Western lord. Bohemund had twice met armies led by Alexius in Macedonia during the 1080s, and the emperor was all too familiar with the rapaciousness that lurked beneath the Norman's knightly bearing. But Bohemund did not want trouble with Alexius so, true to his own agenda, he willingly took the imperial oath as well as the gifts and money offered him. No wonder, then, that Alexius's sister, Anna Comnenus, saw cynicism lurking behind the knight's gracious smile.

Bohemund harbored an ambition more immediate than carving out his own kingdom. He wanted to be leader of the Crusader army, the same position coveted by Raymond of Toulouse. Only Bohemund realized that Alexius, not Urban, could determine the Crusade's leader; for it was Alexius who was paying the bill, it was Alexius whom the lords were helping, and it was in his capitol that the lords for the first time had met as a group. But Bohemund was served no better by the emperor than was Raymond by the pope. Alexius appointed no one. The Crusade proceeded without a designated leader.

There were a number of other lords who marched east. Robert of Normandy, the oldest son of William the Conqueror, mortgaged his lands to his brother William Rufus, the English king, to afford the venture. He was accompanied by his cousin Robert, Count of Flanders, and his brother-in-law Stephen of Blois, one of the richest men in France. Baldwin, brother of Godfrey of Bouillon, also wanted a kingdom for himself and his family. Even Hugh of Vermandois, son of Henry I of France, took the cross. An obsequious man, he may have done so to impress Urban, but he had no hesitation about embracing Alexius.

Despite their varying personalities, despite their different geographical origins, and despite their individual goals, the Western lords shared one common leadership trait. In battle, they would commonly be at the point of attack. That was where they were expected to be by virtue of their training, knightly tradition, and lordly rank. That positioning allowed for some self-indulgences along the road of Jerusalem but, on the whole, it served the army well.

I make no pretense that these brief sketches give great insight into the leadership of the First Crusade. But I would argue that, overall, the composite picture seems rather grim. There was an almost universal self-seeking quality to the newly found obligation to crusade. That is unattractive enough to make us suspect the depth of their faith and to view the whole venture with a certain skepticism. Yet, such judgments, if they are necessary at all, may be too quick, colored perhaps by our own expectations of chicanery in high places. We must instead see these adventurers in their own context and be no less generous for having done so. The Oxford historian Robert Southern points out that these were men used to exchanging land for military service, so that the desire of someone like Bohemund to create his own kingdom, perhaps a little excessive, was business as usual. Urban had promised them as much. The conflict resided in Alexius's demanded oath, whereby the lords were required to return to him any imperial lands they freed from the Moslems. The oaths were sworn but, to a man, the lords must have had their fingers crossed. That implicit conflict would cause great strain at times, evoke considerable mistrust on both sides, and even endanger the Crusade.

THE CAMPAIGN

Nicaea and Dorylaeum

Once ferried across the Bosphorus and camped at Pelacanum on the shore of the Sea of Marmara, the Crusaders could look forward to a 1,100-mile march across Turkey and south through Syria and Lebanon, across mountains and deserts, through extremes of cold and heat they never imagined. They would have to fight Moslem armies almost the entire distance.

The more experienced Byzantine generals advised the Crusade leaders to besiege Nicaea, located on the east shore of Lake Ascanian. This was a Seljuk Turk capitol and stronghold ruled by Sultan Kilij Arslan, and it was his troops that ambushed the Peasant Crusade. Nicaea was looped on the landward side by a wall four miles long and reinforced by 240 towers.

Between 6 May and 3 June 1097, the Crusader army gathered around Nicaea's walls. Arslan was away from his city at the time, but he was informed by a messenger of the siege. He sent a small relieving column, but it was readily defeated by Raymond's men. On 21 May, Arslan arrived with his main army and immediately attacked Raymond's forces gathered at the south wall. But Raymond, reinforced by Robert of Flanders, beat back the Turks. The Franks then decapitated many of the Turkish dead and catapulted the heads over the city wall. Other heads were impaled on spikes and paraded below the city gates.

Nicaea's walls were too strongly defended for quick penetration. Raymond tried mining but that, too, proved fruitless. The garrison did not suffer because they were supplied regularly from the lake side until, at long last, Alexius established a naval blockade. Yet, it still took five weeks for the garrison to reach the point of surrender. Rather than surrendering to the Crusaders, the Turks negotiated with the Byzantine general Manuel Bustimites. How shocking to the Crusaders when, on 19 June, the day of a planned all-out assault, they awakened to find Alexius's banner flying over the city and the gates guarded by the hated imperial police. Runciman states that the Crusaders were probably informed of the emperor's intentions and that they doubtless approved. But it may be that the Crusaders were not privy to final negotiations, an omission that helps explain why the Crusaders became increasingly mistrustful of Alexius. Not entirely insensitive, Alexius sent the Frankish lords gift and money and even had small sums distributed to the common soldiers.

By 26 June, the Crusaders were headed for Dorylaeum, about sixty-five miles south of Nicaea. The army was divided into two columns under

Bohemund and Raymond. On 30 June, Bohemund's men camped near Dorylaeum. At dawn the next day they were attacked by forces of Kilij Arslan, who was waiting to spring a trap. Bohemund sent a messenger to Raymond, requesting help.

The Turks thought they had surrounded the entire army as they sent volley after volley of arrows into the camp. Fulcher of Chartres said that the Crusaders were huddled together like sheep ready to die. Around noon, Raymond's column arrived and joined with Bohemund's men to form a single front. The Turks tried to maintain their showers of arrows against the armored line, but they were running short. The historian Ernle Bradford makes the important point that the Crusaders' waiting tactic was an important lesson for them. Individual knights or small groups charging about on their own, as if they were fighting in France, were routinely killed by the highly mobile mounted Turkish archers. Now the knights waited until the arrow volleys slackened, then charged. At that moment, a column led by Adhémar arrived on high ground behind the Turks. Arslan could not contain his men. They panicked and ran from the field, abandoning their camp, all its contents, and Arslan's treasury.

The campaign, it was now obvious, was going to be a series of sieges. The Turks held several urban strongholds, like so many stepping-stones, between Nicaea and Jerusalem that had to be taken as sources of supplies and loot. To the Turks it was equally obvious that the Frankish army represented a terrible enemy when met en masse in the open field. True, the Turks had the initial advantages of speed and mobility, but once the knights charged their lightly armored opponents, the tactical advantage quickly swung to the Crusaders. The Turks in the open field henceforth relied more on entrapments of foraging and scouting parties whose small numbers were easily overcome. For major confrontations, they would wait behind their fortified walls.

Antioch

The Crusaders pushed on, elated by their two recent victories. By October that elation had turned to despair. Harassed by the Turks, alternately beset by mountain cold and desert heat, tired, hungry, and thirsty, the Crusader army was unravelling. Desertions increased. Tancred, nephew of Bohemund, and Baldwin simply left the army for independent raiding. Somehow, by 20 October, the army stood at Antioch's gates.

Antioch was governed by Yaghi-Siyan and was considered the strongest fort in the region. Positioned on a fertile plain, it had an ample water supply and was protected by a heavy curtain wall with 400 towers. Starving the garrison would take forever, and a direct assault, Raymond's wishes to the contrary, was considered too costly.

Toward the end of December, Yaghi-Siyan received news that a relief column was coming from Damascus, but Bohemund and Robert of

Flanders, leading 20,000 Crusaders, defeated them. Another relief column, commanded by Ridwan of Aleppo, was sent in February. Again under Bohemund's leadership, the column was defeated.

On 4 March, an English convoy off-loaded supplies for building siege machines and artisans to build them. By this time, the Crusaders had completely blockaded the city. Their conditions also improved because merchants who previously dealt only with the Turks, now unable to get into the city, found a ready market with the Crusaders. Perhaps Antioch could be starved out after all.

Enter Bohemund's ambitions. He wanted Antioch for himself and, having convinced most of his fellow lords of this, he connived with a disaffected Armenian named Firouz to betray the Turks. Firouz was captain of a city gate in the south wall. Perhaps he wanted revenge on his Moslem oppressors, perhaps he had been cuckolded by a Turk or, as Fulcher of Chartres believed, he had a vision of Christ—whatever the reason, Firouz agreed to let Bohemund's men invade his gate tower. Thus, at dawn, 3 June, sixty knights scaled ladders, took Firouz's tower, quickly took two others, and opened the city gates. The Crusaders rushed into the city and, aided by local Christians, butchered every Moslem they could find. Bohemund planted his banner over the city.

The victory was short-lived, as a relief column led by Kerbogha, ruler of Mosul in northern Iraq, arrived on 7 June and had the city surrounded in three days. The Moslems besieged Antioch for twenty days. The Crusaders were getting desperate. Bohemund once again showed his military prowess. On the morning of 28 June, he led the Crusaders out of Antioch, some of the knights walking because their horses were dead, in a relentless attack that routed Kerbogha's army and saved the campaign.

Bohemund used the victory to further press his claim to rule Antioch. But Raymond, his hatred and envy of Bohemund growing, continued to resist the demand. Complicating the issue was the death of Adhémar, the one man who might have found a point of reconciliation. During the fall months, the Crusader army scattered as the lords argued, went on raids, pursued individual conquests, occasionally skirmished with the Moslems, and otherwise dissolved. The situation was so depressing that many common soldiers swore that if some accord was not reached, they would burn Antioch and march to Jerusalem on their own. In the end, Bohemund literally abandoned the Crusade, walling himself inside Antioch. Raymond headed for Jerusalem, walking barefoot, his troops trailing behind. His example shamed the other lords into following him. At last, Raymond led the army.

THE SIEGE OF JERUSALEM

On 7 June 1099, nearly four years after Urban's call for a holy war, the Crusaders saw the domes of Jerusalem. The medieval city was going to be

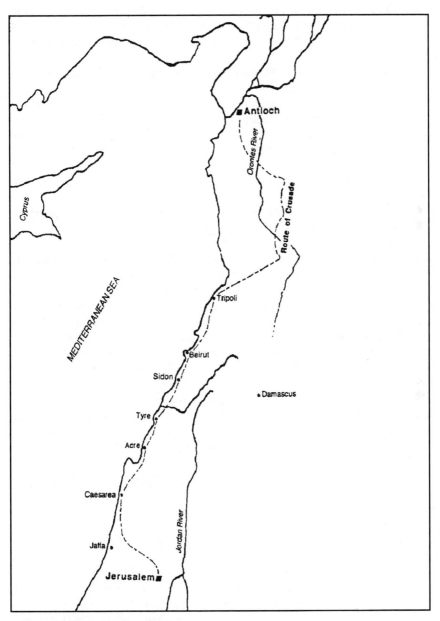

Map 2 Syria and Judea

difficult to attack. The main walls, nearly three miles long, were forty feet high and surrounded by a ditch sixty-two feet wide and twenty-three feet deep. The Gehenna Valley offered protection along the southeast perimeter. Another valley paralleled the west wall, and a ravine made access from the east difficult. Although the north wall cut across Mt. Sion, the land was level enough to support an attack.

Jerusalem, recently taken by the Egyptians from the Turks, was governed by Iftikhar-ad-Dawla. With the approach of the Crusaders, he ejected all Christians from the city and gleaned all standing crops and livestock from the countryside. Water supplies were ample, and the old Roman drainage system was a safeguard against disease. But realizing his fighting garrison of Arabs and Sudanese was not large enough to defend all the walls, Iftikhar sent for reinforcements.

The Crusader army numbered about 1,300 knights and 12,000 foot soldiers. Their supplies were running short, a situation made worse because Iftikhar had the outlying water wells poisoned. One available well was the Pool of Siloam, but it was dangerously close to the city wall, and anyone seeking water was shot with arrows or pelted with rocks. There were some wells six miles from the city, but Iftikhar made certain that the journey was hazardous by setting ambushes along the road. The siege, the Western lords concluded, would need to be brief.

Robert of Normandy placed his troops around Herod's Gate on the north wall. Robert of Flanders took position opposite the Damascus Gate. Godfrey of Lorraine's men, reinforced by Tancred's column, were around the Jaffa Gate. Raymond of Toulouse positioned his men on Mt. Sion.

On 12 June, egged on by the prophecies of a hermit preacher but against their own best judgments, the lords ordered an attack against Jerusalem. It was badly planned, poorly executed and, despite fierce fighting, a failure. The Crusaders had no siege engines—those built earlier at Antioch were abandoned as the army moved south—and too few scaling ladders. They were simply a lot of men throwing themselves against the walls.

This failure, coupled with all the shortages they were experiencing, brought the Crusaders once again to the brink of despair. They felt deserted by their European brethren and by the Byzantines. Morale plummeted and many were ready to give up and go home.

Whatever prayers for deliverance may have been cast up were answered when, on 17 June, six ships arrived at Jaffa loaded with food, weapons, and materials needed to build new siege engines. Three siege towers were built, one for Raymond, another for Godfrey, and the third positioned near the Jaffa Gate. A battering ram was also constructed, together with catapults and a large number of scaling ladders.

The work was slow and difficult, the heat intense, and the newly arrived provisions were quickly consumed. Tempers flared, desertions increased, and for yet another time the lords quarreled over who would get what. Just as collapse was near, Peter Desiderius, a priest known for his visions,

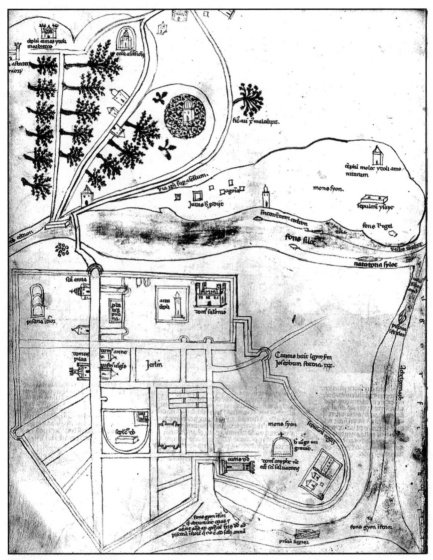

Map 3 Jerusalem
Drawn about the time of the First Crusade. From Bodleian Library, MS
Tanner 190, fol. 206v. (By permission of the Bodleian Library, Oxford.)

proclaimed that he had witnessed the presence of the dead Adhémar who commanded that there be a feast and a solemn procession around the city walls. The vision was believed. Priests carrying crosses, icons, and relics led the ragged, half-starved, barefoot army. They prayed and sang as trumpets sounded. Gathering on the Mount of Olives, they heard sermons by Peter the Hermit (who survived the ambush of his Peasant Crusade) and other zealots who encouraged the army to forget their differences and fight their common enemy. Religious fervor had fuelled the Crusade in the first place; now it kept the movement going at a crucial moment. Crusader lords, knights, and soldiers, joined by a host of non-combatants, returned to the siege.

Meeting as a council, the lords determined to attack Jerusalem on the night of 13 July. As catapults hurled stones and archers showered the parapets with arrows, the great perimeter ditch was filled at those points where the siege towers were to be placed. The defenders fought back with catapults and arrows and hurled liquid fire on the battering ram and the siege towers.

Raymond's tower was the first in place, but his men could not gain the wall top. But the men in Godfrey's tower were successful. Scaling ladders enabled more men to top the wall. Godfrey's men, closely followed by Tancred's column, poured into the city. Tancred accepted the surrender of Moslems who sought refuge in the mosque of Al-Aqsa. Meantime, the Moslems fighting Raymond's force saw at once that they were outflanked by the successful escalation by Godfrey and Tancred. They quickly abandoned their positions, allowing Raymond's troops into the city. Iftikhar and his personal bodyguard took refuge in the Tower of David and, from there, successfully negotiated with Raymond for their safe passage out of Jerusalem. Raymond took control of the tower, together with a handsome treasure.

Iftikhar and his guard were about the only survivors. Running amok, the Crusaders killed everyone left in the city. Jews hiding in a synagogue were killed when it was burned down around them. Tancred's captives did not survive the day but were butchered in the mosque. The blood flowed, depending on which chronicler is believed, ankle high, knee high, or as high as a horse's bridle. Some modern historians have tried to discount the number killed in the siege and its aftermath, noting that Iftikhar reduced the population by evacuation. But that was the Christian population. The Jews and Moslems stayed and died. As the anonymous author of the *Gesta Francorum* wrote, "Indeed, it was a just and splendid judgment of God that [the temple] would be filled with the blood of the unbelievers." The siege of Jerusalem was over.

CATEGORIES OF COMBAT

Regardless of the enthusiasm that greeted Urban's plea for a holy war, the First Crusade consistently leaned toward failure. The bickering between the feudal lords and their independent attitudes more than once threatened to end the campaign. The lack of a single commander who could unify the half-dozen armies was an added threat. Poor logistics, the resulting deprivations, and feelings of abandonment also threatened the campaign. Nor was the ambiguous relationship between the Western lords and Emperor Alexius a harbinger of success. Yet, the Crusaders persisted, taking stronghold after stronghold until Jerusalem itself fell to their swords. The answers to the question of why they achieved their military goal are both ideological and technical, answers best understood by referring to the various categories of combat.

The Will to Combat

There can be little doubt: Faith sustained the Crusaders and, at crucial junctures during the campaign, unified the diverse armies so that victory was possible.

But the Moslem defenders were also of one faith, fighting infidels, and dedicated to preserving their holy relics within Jerusalem. But a series of non-religious differences forestalled their unity. The Moslem world was deeply divided by dynastic rivalries, and jealousies between and within families were common. When Kerbogha, for instance, marched against Antioch, he led an army that was already fractured by internal family feuds. When the Crusaders soundly defeated him, Kerbogha made the unpopular declaration that he believed the Christians were unstoppable. His worth in the Moslem world dramatically ended. Also the Turks, as a people, did not like the Fatimid Egyptians for taking Jerusalem and other territories from them. Consequently, they were not much motivated to rescue the Jerusalem defenders. The Moslems, however much they wanted to stop the Crusaders, could not find enough common ground between themselves to create a coordinated defense. Consequently, the Moslem cities were plucked by the Christians one by one.

In contrast, most Crusaders shared a common goal—Jerusalem. As long as they could keep that goal at the forefront of their campaign, shaky at times, the Crusaders could believe God was on their side. A little guilt and fear added zeal to their quest. Any warrior who did not go to Jerusalem would have an account to settle. "Oh what reproaches will be charged against you by the Lord Himself," Pope Urban intoned at Clermont, "if you have not helped those who are like yourselves of the Christian faith." Fulcher of Chartres tells us that Jesus Christ delivered the city of Antioch into the hands of the faithful. God fought beside the Crusaders. God provided, God guided, God brought victory.

The Crusaders' will to combat emerged from something more than repeated hosannas. Certainly hatred of the Moslems came easily enough. They were nothing more than vile, worthless desecrators of Jerusalem's holy places. First and foremost, however, a will to combat had to manifest itself within the army, not as so many religious fanatics marching into an unknown future, but as soldiers. Given the hierarchal nature of the medieval army, we must look to the Frankish lords as the source of that will. To be sure, they were an independent lot who, like Tancred and Baldwin, might go a-raiding with no one to stop them. Yet, meeting in council, these same lords often found consensus. Adhémar, whilst he lived, was usually ex officio chairman, and his good sense and practicality brought more agreement about tactics than discord. His death was untimely, but his processes of decision-making remained intact. The priests might go on endlessly about God's will, sending up thankful prayers when things went right, castigating convenient scapegoats when they did not, and proclaiming convenient visions and miracles, but it was the council of lords, making tough pragmatic decisions that, in the long run, brought the army to Jerusalem.

Faith buoyed the Crusaders, and their leadership worked often enough to prevail over their deprivations. But how the Crusaders functioned in battle determined whether they would survive the campaign. Therefore, attention must be given to the man versus weapons relationships that forged the Crusader battles.

Cavalry versus Cavalry

The mounted Crusader knights were ineffective during siege operations. Horses might bring a man to a wall, but until a breach was made or a gate opened, a horseman was useless. Having stated the obvious, it must be acknowledged that it was those same knights that enabled the Crusaders to win many of their victories. To accomplish that, the knights had to first defeat the Moslem cavalry.

The mounted Moslem warriors were a potent weapon. Typically, multiple waves of mounted archers assaulted the Crusaders, each wave retiring after loosing their arrows. These successive attacks were designed to wear down the Crusaders from a distance, a point nearly reached at Dorylaeum, where Fulcher's observation that the Crusaders huddled like sheep was appropriate. Moslem heavy cavalry, armed with lances, swords, and maces, would have finally charged and killed whoever remained. But the Turks erred, believing they had surrounded the entire Crusader army, a lamentable intelligence lapse. Thus, at the eleventh hour, the remaining Crusader cavalry came to the rescue, joining the survivors to form a single line of armored heavy cavalry that was too formidable for the Turks. The sudden appearance of Adhémar's troop behind them converted an already disorderly Turkish withdrawal into a complete rout. Again at Antioch, the heavily armored knights prevailed against two strong Turkish relief forces. But simply saying the knights won, or narrating what happened, does not explain these victories. To do so we must look at the various weapons used by the cavalry of both sides.

The Turkish archers used little armor, relying more on speed, overall superior horsemanship, and maneuverability to avoid direct confrontation with the knights. Their bows were of the highest quality. Short and re-curved, they had a 100-pound pull with a resulting high velocity that allowed their arrows to puncture chain mail. The knight might not be killed—there were some who took several direct hits and kept going—but the harassing effect could break the knights' ranks and lessen confidence. Of course, the poorly armored foot soldiers bore the brunt of such attacks, and their casualty rates were proportionally higher.

If the knights outlasted the arrow barrages and closed on the Moslems, the advantage then shifted to the Crusaders. The knights' horses were larger, more like solid jumpers than the stereotypical Percheron, and their shields, swords, and lances were heavier than those used by the Turks. The Turkish scimitar was a fine weapon, light and deadly in the down-stroke. But the three-foot Crusader sword could equally hack, slash, and thrust. Wielded by a powerful man, it could sever hands and legs, cleave skulls and, as Godfrey of Lorraine allegedly did, cut an armored Turk in half, leaving the lower half of the body still mounted. Consequently, what the knights lacked in numbers they made up in the weight of their attack.

Although some cooperation among the lords was necessary for victory, their tactics, especially in open field fighting, were makeshift, born of the moment's needs. For example, the late arrival of Raymond's troops surprised the Turks. The appearance of Adhémar's column at their rear routed the Turks, but it was a maneuver that was doubtlessly the bishop's invention, executed without any pre-planning.

Artillery versus Artillery

Of course there was no artillery at Jerusalem as we think of it today. But if artillery is any weapon that hurls a projectile by means of mechanical propulsion, then catapults by whatever name and design were the stuff of medieval artillery. It was rare that catapults were used in open battle. Offensively, their immobility left them too vulnerable to attack and, defen-sively, their targets were too mobile for accurate hurling. Siege brought the weapon into its own. Offensively, the catapult had two functions: first, to breach the walls and, second, to clear the parapets of defenders. There were also two defensive functions: first, to cripple the siege weapons of the assaulting army and, second, to prevent escalation of the walls.

Even though catapults changed in design and propulsion method over the centuries, they all shared common principles. A beam was pulled back under great tension. At the end of the beam was a cup into which the projectile—usually a stone—was placed. When the beam was released, the projectile was hurled toward its target. Because sighting the weapon was inexact and because velocity and trajectory were dependent on the size, weight, and shape of the projectile—which might vary from shot to shot—the word *target* includes anything within a wide scope of possibilities.

Although stones were the common catapult ammunition, firebrands made of wood dipped in pitch, wax, and sulphur were also used. One chronicler, Raymond, canon of Le Puy, states that straw and hemp were bound by iron bands, ignited, and catapulted over the walls. The bands kept the bundles together, so that they kept burning after impact. Ideally, they would land on rooftops within the city, causing fire and panic and perhaps destroy some supplies.

On the whole, the catapulted projectiles were ineffective. The catapults did not breach the walls, which, despite constant bombardment, were continuously defended. Their greatest value may have been psychological. Not unlike the V-1 rocket bombs over London in World War II, the projectiles were going to hit someplace and would do damage; but no one knew where. That uncertainty may have counted for something among the remaining civilians, but the seasoned garrison appeared able to handle the barrage.

The artillery used to defend the city was more effective than that used by the offense. Raymond of Le Puy wrote that "the Saracens had constructed so many machines that for each one of ours they now have nine or ten" (quoted in Krey, p. 260). Raymond further complained that many Crusader siege engines were "shaken apart by the blows of many stones," indicating some defensive accuracy. This was no mean task. The defenders had to select a target and see whether they could hit it and then hit it again. Repeating the hit was a severe test because they functioned without sights, using stone projectiles that certainly varied in size, weight, and shape. Further, material fatigue altered the tension exerted on the propelling beam, and that influenced range and accuracy. A hit posed other problems. Depending on the weight and velocity of the stone and the relative density and thickness of the wood in the target, the stone projectile could break apart on impact or hit and bounce off. If, for instance, a Crusader catapult was hit once, it might shake, quiver, or even splinter. Little apparent damage was done. Successive hits would wear binding ropes or loosen them, spring pegs, and break nails until, with just one more hit, the machine came untethered and collapsed.

Soldiers and camp followers were killed by defensive missiles, most incidentally. Raymond of Le Puy mentions two women who were trying, for whatever reasons, to bewitch a Crusader catapult as a stone shot from a Moslem catapult hit and killed them, together with some slaves. Witchcraft or not, the stone must have followed a fairly flat trajectory and the victims must have been hit in a row. But such hits, causing multiple casualties, were probably rare. The real danger to the Crusaders was when they were in close proximity to the walls from which the defenders dropped stones and other lethal missiles.

Infantry versus Infantry

Since Crusader artillery did not penetrate the walls, men on foot had to climb over them. That meant the construction of siege towers and scaling ladders. Under a rain of arrows, stones, fire bundles, and flaming pitch, men moved forward without much overhead protection to fill the perimeter ditch so that the towers could be rolled against the wall. Once against the wall, the forces led by Godfrey and Tancred successfully bridged the parapets and entered Jerusalem.

Their success transformed the function of the knights from that of heavy cavalry to heavy infantry. That they moved so adroitly runs counter to our modern expectations. These, I submit, may be conditioned by the picture of knights from later in the Middle Ages, clad in great armored suits that left them helpless when dis-mounted. The eleventh-century knight, wearing sixty pounds of chain mail, was quite capable of running, jumping, and climbing. Thus, scrambling up a siege tower or a scaling ladder was not a great problem. Crashing into their lightly clad opponents with shields, swords, and maces, they rapidly gained the upper hand.

Because the Moslem defenders did not have a secondary defense line, the Crusaders needed only one point of entry to win the city. The troops led by Godfrey and Tancred made that necessary penetration. The defenders facing Raymond, recognizing they were outflanked, fled. Lacking organization, will, discipline, and leadership, the defensive infantry disintegrated before the attacking Christians.

AFTERMATH

In the Jerusalem siege, the process of disintegration and the aftermath are inextricably bound together.

The defenders took flight into the city. This was panic behavior, an escape from a situation over which they had diminishing control. They erroneously believed that distance, any distance, from the source of danger equalled safety. But, as John Keegan pointed out in *The Face of Battle*, turning one's back on the enemy is an invitation to disaster. Self-defense is rendered ineffective, and organizational support rapidly disappears. Discipline is lost as an "every man for himself" psychology takes over that is caused by a rapidly declining confidence in the military organization's ability to provide means of survival. This feeling among the defenders probably was like a flash point because there was little or no sub-organization within the Moslem army. They had no battalions or regiments to bind their loyalties. The defending troops most likely shared the expectation, not uncommon in the medieval world, that their leaders would sell them out in order to save themselves. And that is exactly what happened when Iftikhar negotiated his own safe passage out of the city, abandoning his garrison.

The survivors could not escape the walls that were their first and only defense. Many were cut down as they ran away. Many huddled together in buildings, hoping that the proximity of others would make them safe from the disaster unfolding around them. The feeling was an illusion. Gathering in buildings simply made it easier for the Christians to find them and to slaughter everyone.

The Crusaders are often condemned in history for the terrible, un-Christian acts they perpetrated. Horrible as they were, the slaughter, looting, raping, and burning did not result from a momentary loss of faith, from hypocrisy, or temporary madness. Rather, these acts emerged from the conditions of battle, as certain a form of panic behavior as the flight of the defenders. The conventions of medieval warfare held that the governor of a city could justifiably defend his domain for an unspecified time. Some defense was always expected. And there was always the possibility the attackers might go away. But if the siege persisted, then a delicate and un-stated timing was invoked. We need only remember the words shouted by Shakespeare's Henry V to the governor of besieged Harfleur:

> If I begin the battery once again,
> I will not leave the half-achieved Harfleur
> Till in her ashes she lies buried.
> The gates of mercy shall be all shut up.
>
> (3.3.7–10)

Nicaea, where the siege lasted five weeks, was sensibly surrendered to the Byzantines who had not participated. The city's population survived. At Antioch, the Byzantines were nowhere to be seen. The city held out until Bohemund arranged a betrayal and the gates were opened to him. The population was slaughtered. At Jerusalem, Iftikhar held out in expectation of being rescued. No relief column came. The magic moment passed when surrender was possible. The defenders would pay for their continued resistance with their lives. There was something more: The Crusaders rushed into the city, toward the source of their long suffering, for the defenders were visible and tangible representatives of the causes of that suffering, and they had to be eradicated. Thus, the slaughter was a terrible consequence of both the traditions of medieval warfare and the specific conditions of the siege.

The conquest of Jerusalem resulted in the establishment of Western kingdoms in the Near East. Baldwin was elected king of Jerusalem. Bohemund retained sovereignty over Antioch, and Tancred took Edessa. Raymond of Toulouse continued to fight Moslems, becoming more a soldier of fortune with each passing year. Godfrey held the decorative title of Advocate of the Holy Sepulcher and carved out a small holding for himself in southern Palestine. These and other Crusader principates did not quell the forces of Islam. They only set the stage for future intra-mural feudal warfare and for the Crusades that followed.

Chapter 3

Malta, 1565

During the summer of 1565, the Turkish army of Suleiman the Magnificent invaded the Mediterranean island of Malta, their purpose to annihilate the Knights of the Order of St. John. The siege was confined to the Grand Harbor area and rapidly became a battle of attrition that anticipated many following slaughters.

PRELUDE TO SIEGE

The Knights of St. John, also known as the Hospitallers, were organized at the end of the First Crusade to tend the wounded, sick and, later, pilgrims in the Holy Land. Their base was a Jerusalem hospital named for John the Baptist. After the pope gave them the status of a religious order in 1143, the order grew, establishing hospitals along the pilgrimage routes, training doctors, and generally advancing medical knowledge. But the order also had a military side, assisting in Jerusalem's defense against the Moslems. Thus were born the order's twin functions as healers and perpetual Crusaders.

The Moslems prevailed, however, and forced the order from Jerusalem in 1291. They eventually landed on Rhodes. Patiently they honed their fighting skills and built swift galleys that searched the Mediterranean for Moslem ships, quickly becoming the nemesis of the Turks. In 1522, Sultan Suleiman the Magnificent besieged Rhodes, successfully mining the order's stronghold. Suleiman, in an act of generosity he lived to regret, allowed the order to depart, thinking their importance was at an end.

Suleiman was nearly right. The knights wandered, a homeless band, for eight years, their devotion and discipline slipping as the order's value in the European power market diminished. The incipient rise of nation-states did not bode well for the continuation of what was essentially an international brotherhood whose allegiance was to Rome. Kings and princes were at best apathetic to pleas for some place to found a new headquarters.

There was one exception. Charles V of Spain thought being generous to the order might be useful, so he offered them Malta as their new operational base. For Charles, the order would become a new fighting force in the central Mediterranean, guarding against Barbary pirates and defending Sicily and southern Italy from Moslem raids and outright invasions. The order reluctantly accepted the offer and occupied Malta in 1530.

Malta is the largest of five islands covered by that name and is fifty miles south of Sicily. Gozo, to the northwest, is the most fertile of the group. About 5,000 people lived there in 1530. Its main drawback was lack of an adequate harbor. Malta itself is only eighteen miles long and half that wide. A large horseshoe-shaped bay is at Marsaxlokk at the south end of the island. The rocky west coast has no harbors. On the east side is the spacious Grand Harbor that, with its inlets, provides deep-water anchorages for the largest ships. About 12,000 people, mostly peasants, lived on the island. Mdina, the capitol of the island group, was in the center of Malta, but only a few nobility lived there. The other three islands are very small and play no real part in this narrative. The Knights of St. John did not settle in Mdina but instead chose Birgu, a cramped finger of land poking into Grand Harbor. Birgu was protected, a euphemism at best, by Fort St. Angelo, a deteriorating structure built centuries before.

During the next thirty years, the knights strengthened Malta's defenses. The walls around Mdina were refurbished, Fort St. Angelo was given additions and new forts were built: St. Elmo commanding the entrance to the Grand Harbor and Marsamxett and Fort St. Michael at the landward end of the Senglea Peninsula. The knights also took to sea, raiding Moslem shipping.

Despite the building program, the order grew lax, especially among the older members who knew there had to be a better place for them than the rock-bound island on which the fates cast them. As if to spite the knights, Moslem pirates raided Malta eight times during the initial decades of residence. The famous corsair Dragut even landed 10,000 men on Malta and, although repelled by the knights, sailed to Gozo and packed off a large segment of the population into slavery.

Then, in 1557, everything changed. Jean de La Valette-Parisot was elected grand master of the order. Devout, clever, intelligent, disciplined and, above all, a soldier of considerable experience, he brought to the order renewed purpose. He disciplined his wayward knights and forbade gambling and drinking. He insisted revenues owed the order be paid, using the funds to undertake an ambitious fortification program. La Valette sent his fleet into the very heart of Suleiman's empire, raiding the eastern Mediterranean from Syria to Egypt. But the fleet was most effective in the waters

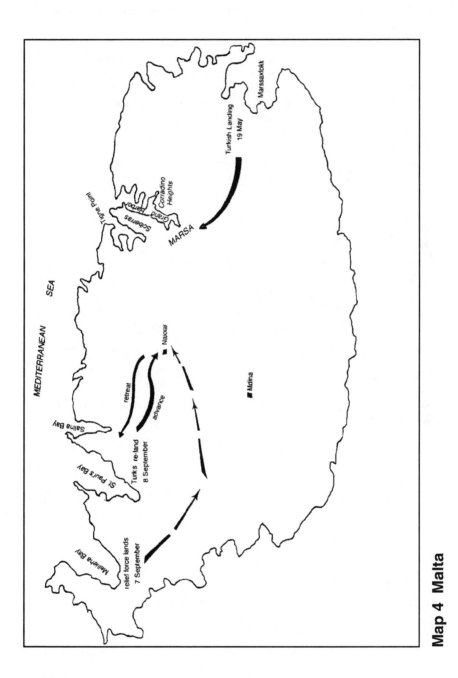

Map 4 Malta

between Africa and Sicily and within the Adriatic Sea, blocking Moslem commerce with Venice.

Suleiman was advised from all sides that Malta had to be taken and the order destroyed once and for all. But Suleiman realized Malta's value exceeded any revenge against the provocations La Valette offered him. He knew, as had Charles V, that Malta was a springboard to Sicily and Italy and that Grand Harbor afforded his fleet a base for incursions further west. Eradication of the order would make firm allies of the Barbary pirates whom Suleiman needed if his forces were to effectively probe the western Mediterranean.

Thus, in October 1564, Suleiman decided to invade Malta and finally destroy those "sons of dogs"whom he had spared at Rhodes more than a generation before.

PREPARATIONS FOR SIEGE

Suleiman's preparations to attack Malta could not be kept secret for long. La Valette concluded that more defensive works were necessary. New walls were constructed and earthworks were built and reinforced with fascines—large bundles of sticks. Artillery batteries were placed near the slave prison and below Fort St. Angelo. St. Elmo was given an outer rampart made of gabions—wooden stick cylinders filled with earth. Houses beyond the defensive perimeter of Birgu were destroyed. A steady stream of ships from Sicily brought provisions, weapons, and munitions. The Maltese were ordered to bring all their animals and crops into either Mdina or Birgu. That portion of the population unfit for service was evacuated to Sicily. Then La Valette appointed a knight to supervise the hospital, another to control water rationing, and another to oversee the making of gunpowder (about 900 pounds each day). A knight was placed in overall command of the artillery, and others were placed in command of the forts and various strong-points.

La Valette was now ready for the siege he expected—the siege he provoked.

THE ARMIES

The Defenders

The Order of the Knights of St. John was grouped into several so-called Langues—groups representing the principal languages or "nations" from which they were recruited. These included England, Germany, Italy, Castile, Aragon, France, Auvergne, and Provence. The French were the largest group. Except for a single member, the English were a defunct Langue because of their split with the papacy. If knights in general were considered the elite soldiers of medieval warfare, then the Order of St. John, by virtue of skill, experience, and sheer survivability, became the elite of the elite. Membership was based on family nobility. Few candidates survived the close investigation that followed application for membership, resulting in bruised egos, tarnished reputations, and lawsuits against the various Langues. This may seem rather too precious today, but the feelings were quite genuine in the sixteenth century. The limitations on membership meant that when La Valette sent out a call for all knights to come to Malta, the total number who responded did not exceed 700.

Even though gunpowder weapons were quite common by 1565, knights still used armor. That worn by the Knights of St. John was plate armor weighing 100 pounds. The breastplate alone, used to deflect gunshots, weighed eighteen pounds. Ernle Bradford points out that this armor was literally tailor-made to the user, carefully balanced so that movement, although slow, would not be entirely encumbered. The knights still used shields, swords, axes, and maces. The main difference between the Knights of St. John and those of an earlier age was that they fought dis-mounted. They had some cavalry, but their life at sea and their island existence transformed them into infantry.

In addition to his knights, La Valette had a corps of professional soldiers, consisting of 400 Spaniards, 800 Italians, and another 500 men who manned the order's galleys. These men were lightly armored with helmets and leather jerkins covered with thin metal strips. Besides carrying the usual medieval weaponry, many of the soldiers also were armed with hand-held gunpowder weapons, an early form of musket called an harquebus or arquebus. The gun had a matchlock ignition and fired a round ball. The earliest versions were heavy and unwieldy, equipped with a short, turned-down stock resembling a pistol grip that was used to swivel the barrel on a forked support. Some improvements were made, mostly by German gunsmiths, so that by the time of the Malta siege the weapon was lighter and could be held against the shoulder or cheek. Despite the inherently elementary character of the arquebus, it could be a deadly weapon.

Native Maltese formed the mass of La Valette's defensive force. Although many were experienced fighters from skirmishes against Moslem raiders, they were neither trained nor organized. Unarmored, except for gleanings from the battlefield, the Maltese used swords, axes, bows, halberds, pikes, and knives. No one knows exactly how many Maltese fought in the siege, but their numbers brought La Valette's total force to between 8,000 and 9,000. Un-counted and often un-sung were those un-armed civilians—men, women, and children—who formed the work parties that repaired walls, built earthworks, and carried water, gunpowder, and supplies to the fighting men. The defenders could not have survived without them. The number of cannons used to defend Malta is not known. There were some 48-pounders and the galleys were stripped of their 8-pounders. If the forts were armed in the manner of continental models, then a safe guess would be that 18-pounders and 24-pounders were also used.

La Valette's force was certainly international in makeup. It lacked uniform training and experience. The only organization it had was that imposed by La Valette. The one factor that brought them together was hatred of the Moslems. The Maltese did not appreciate their islands being occupied by the knights, nor did they appreciate being pawns in Charles V's plans. But they liked the Moslems less and, although Malta provided little in the way of creature comforts, it was their home and they meant to defend it. On that La Valette could rely.

The Moslem Army

In contrast to many other sieges about which information may be more plentiful concerning one side but not the other, knowledge of Suleiman's army, hardly precise, is sufficient and noteworthy. The total force numbered between 30,000 and 40,000 men, the exact number on the island varying as the weeks passed. This included some 9,000 Spahis or irregular cavalry from Romania, Turkey, and North Africa. Two-thirds of the Spahis were archers, according to Francisco Balbi, the Spanish infantryman who wrote a chronicle of the siege. Another 10,000 volunteers and levies formed almost a third of the army. The elite force, the spearhead, was a contingent of 6,300 Janissaries. The Janissaries were formed in the 1300s as a special hand-picked troop. Most were the sons of Christian captives who were then trained in the Moslem faith and in the skills of warfare. Theirs was a Spartan existence. Their only purpose was to serve Allah and the sultan. At Malta, they wore loose-flowing robes rather than armor, depending more on movement for safety. They were well armed with scimitars and the arquebus. In addition to these troops, there were 3,900 Iayalars, religious fanatics who, allegedly stimulated by hashish, had little regard for their own lives and none at all for those of their enemies. Their principal weapon was the scimitar. Engineers and sappers came from Egypt. Most of the manual labor was done by numerous slaves whom the Moslems sacrificed to the defender's guns without hesitation.

Naturally enough, Suleiman provided his army with heavy siege guns: Two culverins, heavy, long-barreled cannon that fired 60-pound shot; ten 80-pounders; a gun that, according to Balbi, fired 160-pound shot and another that fired 300-pound shot. Beyond these guns, it is very difficult to assess the number of artillery pieces brought to Malta because the amount varies with time and circumstance; also, many batteries were moved about. One contemporary writer estimated that between 6,000 and 7,000 rounds fell on Fort St. Elmo each day. This meant that the Turks had a sizeable artillery train. We read about a thirty-eight-gun battery on Mt. Salvatore and another of fifty guns dragged up Mt. Sciberras to reinforce those already in position. The corsair Dragut brought guns ashore from his ships, and the Turks added to their land-based artillery with bombardments from their naval vessels. But whatever their number and size, the Turks had more cannon of heavier calibre than the defenders. The Turkish gunners were also trained and experienced in siege warfare.

DEFENSIVE LEADERSHIP AND CHANGES IN MILITARY ORGANIZATION

Western military organization underwent some fundamental changes from the time of the First Crusade to the Malta siege, regardless of the persistence of noble titles and pretensions toward knightly ideals. Whereas the medieval army was little more than a crowd, those of the sixteenth century were more permanent, better organized, and more professional. Rather than being a gathering of local lords and their men-at-arms, armies were more often an extension of the central authority of kings. The reasons for these changes are clear. The increasing development of the nation-state and central authority weakened the power of local lords. Warfare became tremendously expensive, a burden better borne by a king than a baron. The new gunpowder weapons were not cheap, and the necessity of training men to use them demanded time and training provided only by full-time soldiers. The aristocracy could not provide the manpower necessary to fill the ranks of such armies; nor could they consistently supply the officers necessary to lead them. Even though titled men continued to be officers, there was a new trend developing to dip into the ranks of seasoned and knowledgeable soldiers who viewed military life as a career. This trend was transforming military service from an obligation of class into a profession.

Gunpowder weapons not only necessitated specific training for loading and firing; they required, as well, that the troops learn to handle them in coordinated fashion, firing artillery in planned barrages and the arquebus in volley fire. That meant there had to be battlefield supervision of relatively small units working together. Thus, armies were broken down into units that could be controlled in battle, giving birth to regiments, battalions, and companies. The old individualism enjoyed by the medieval knights perished under the requirements for teamwork. Commanders of these small units were expected to lead at the point of attack, to be sure, but the leaders of larger units, divisions and corps, were more likely to be found at the rear.

This descriptive model of organizational change had relative application to the Malta siege. First, the Knights of St. John retained much of the chivalric and spiritual code thought fundamental to a Christian knight but which was becoming excess baggage in the sixteenth century. How the Knights of St. John fought consequently seems closer to how their ancestors in Jerusalem did battle. Second, the Malta knights, although an elite, did not fight as a unit but were sent as unit leaders or formed small and determined cadres of fighting excellence at various posts throughout the defensive system, unifying the diverse elements of the defense.

In principle, the order's grand council made all decisions. These were knights of long military, religious, and administrative experience. These men were nominated to their positions and elected by the order. Although final approval was given by the pope and the Holy Roman Emperor, it was about as democratic a system as could be found at the time.

As the inevitability of an attack against Malta dawned, one man's presence dominated the grand council: It was the Provencal Jean de La Valette. He was seventy years old in 1565, a fifty-year veteran of the order.

La Valette saw his first action at the siege of Rhodes. He subsequently joined his grand master in the quest through various European courts for a new operational base. Over the next several years La Valette became an accomplished sailor, finally commanding his own galley. But, at age forty-seven, his ship was sunk in an engagement with the Barbary pirates. Wounded, Valette was taken prisoner and made a galley slave. Only a prisoner exchange a year later freed him. He returned to the order a much harder man.

La Valette rose to important positions within the order, among which were lieutenant to the grand master and general of the fleet. Under his command, the order's ships raced after Moslem shipping with a vigor not seen since their days on Rhodes.

Physically, La Valette was tall and considered handsome. He spoke several languages, including Greek, Italian, Spanish, and Arabic. He was a stern disciplinarian, largely responsible for restoring order among the dispirited and wayward knights. A soldier of proven ability, experienced in all areas of the order, much respected, La Valette was elected grand master in 1557. He dominated his council, guided the defensive buildup, turned the order to his will, and gave the defenders a sense of common purpose.

LEADERSHIP AMONG THE MOSLEM BESIEGERS

Suleiman, the Lawgiver, the Magnificent, inherited the Turkish throne from his father at age twenty-six. He immediately reformed his government and campaigned from the Near East to the gates of Vienna, creating a vast empire.

But forty years of the order's mounting harassment led Suleiman to regret his gentle handling of the knights at Rhodes. He wanted to squash these impudent Christians, take Malta, and open the door to the West. Suleiman chose two commanders to lead his invasion force. Mastapha Pasha was his army commander, and Piali Bassa commanded the navy. They would equally share the powers of leadership. Thus, Suleiman made a fateful division of responsibility.

Mustapha Pasha was ambitious, cruel, and an experienced soldier. From one of Turkey's most respected families, he long served his emperor in Persia, Hungary, and Rhodes. Since the available histories of the siege were written by Christians, Mustapha is typically portrayed as heartless and a religious fanatic. Yet, in historical context, his behavior was not really much different than that of his enemies. One man's fanaticism was usually another man's faith; one man's cruelty was another's pragmatism.

One thing is certain: Mustapha did not get along with Piali. Piali was born to Christian parents but was abandoned as an infant in 1530 near Belgrade. He was taken to the sultan's court and raised there with all the privileges of royal birth, eventually wedding one of Suleiman's grand-daughters. At age thirty-five, he possessed a considerable reputation as a naval commander.

Suleiman, probably realizing that a divided command might lead to divided purpose, ordered that Mustapha and Piali not begin any major operations on Malta until a third commander arrived, the corsair Dragut Rais, also known as Torghud.

Dragut was born in 1485 and was one of those individuals upon whom the accidents of life confer rewards. He was born into a poor Turkish family, but a governor passing through Dragut's home village took a liking to the boy, and together they went to Egypt. Dragut was sent to school and eventually joined the Mameluke Turkish army, becoming an accomplished artilleryman. But his interest turned to the sea, where his teacher was the pirate Khair-ad-Dein, better known as Barbarossa. With his master's death in 1546, Dragut became the most powerful Barbary pirate, raiding Malta and the Italian coast, and enslaving thousands. Ironically, Dragut encountered La Valette twice. They first met when the knight was captured and sent to the galleys. They met again when Dragut, himself, was captured and made a galley slave of the Christians.

Suleiman's plan was for Dragut to act on his behalf as a buffer between Mustapha and Piali, overseeing their councils, and lending his experience to their deliberations. Unfortunately for the sultan's cause, Dragut did not arrive until after the siege began. He found much to criticize.

But the Mustapha-Piali conflict was not on anyone's mind as the Moslem fleet, an armada of between 170 and 200 ships, departed Constantinople for Malta.

THE SIEGE OF MALTA

The Assault on Fort St. Elmo

On 18 May 1565, the Turkish fleet sighted Malta and scouted the coast, landing the next day at Marsaxlokk, an undefended bay on Malta's south coast. With only skirmishers to oppose them, the Turks marched to Marsa at the head of Grand Harbor and established their base camp. On 22 May, they moved onto the Sciberras Peninsula, preparing to attack Fort St. Elmo.

Apparently Mustapha wanted to attack the Bigu-Senglea fortifications first, but Piali insisted that the St. Elmo attack take precedent. There was a

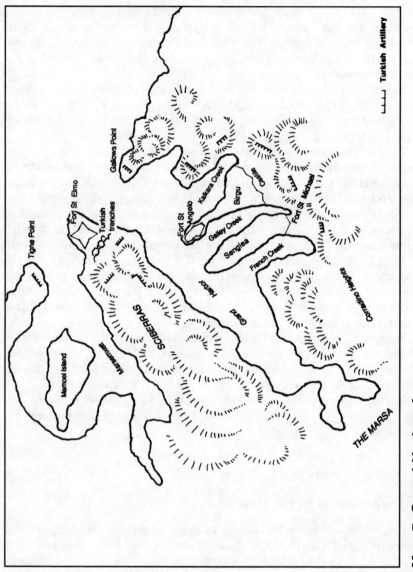

Map 5 Grand Harbor Area

Turkish Artillery

Tigne Point
Fort St Elmo
Turkish trenches
Gallows Point
Kalkara Creek
Fort St Angelo
Castile
Birgu
Galley Creek
Senglea
Fort St Michael
French Creek
SCIBERRAS
Manoel Island
Marsamxett
Grand Harbor
Corradino Heights
THE MARSA

certain logic to his argument because the reduction of the fort would give Piali's fleet access to Marsamxett, an excellent anchorage on the opposite side of Sciberras. That would shorten the Turkish supply lines and mini-mize their use of Marsaxlokk which, with a six-mile coastline, was open to attack by Christian ships. Additionally, taking St. Elmo would give the Turks undisputed control over the Sciberras Peninsula, the heights of which command the entire Grand Harbor and the Senglea Peninsula with Birgu and Fort St. Angelo at the sea end and Fort St. Michael on the landward side.

Whether or not Piali got his way because he was part of Suleiman's family or whether the two leaders reached a tactical consensus is not known. More importantly, both commanders overlooked the possibility, indeed the necessity, of attacking Mdina, whose small garrison was to play a vital role in the siege.

Fort St. Elmo was designed by the Spanish engineer Pedro Pardo and was built on low ground at the end of the Sciberras Peninsula. It was a simple four-pointed star, the defensive perimeter totalling about 900 yards. The walls, constructed of sandstone and limestone, rested on a solid rock foundation and were surrounded by a ditch. A ravelin was built on the landward side with 300 yards of open ground in front of it. Dominated by the Sciberras cliffs, the fort's position had its dangers, but these were compensated for by covering fire from Fort St. Angelo.

By 31 May, the Turks had twenty-four guns aimed at Fort St. Elmo, and on 2 June, Dragut arrived with 1,500 men and siege guns. He was very angry that Mustapha and Piali chose to ignore Suleiman's order not to begin a major operation without him. Dragut immediately saw that the attack on St. Elmo was a mistake and that Mdina should have been assaulted instead. At age seventy, the old corsair knew a thing or two about sieges, and his advice might have significantly altered the siege's outcome. But it was too late; the army was committed to attacking St. Elmo. All Dragut could do was hope for the best.

On 3 June, Dragut had all the Turkish guns aimed at the St. Elmo ravelin. After a preparatory bombardment, the Janissaries attacked and took the position. Dragut ordered a gun platform built higher than the ravelin's ramparts. The two cannon mounted on it began an immediate frontal bombardment of St. Elmo's wall.

The Turks threw a bridge across the perimeter ditch and the Janissaries swept forward. Two defensive cannon cut swaths in their ranks, but they were not stopped and finally placed ladders against the wall. The defenders responded with arquebus fire, but more effective were the incendiary projectiles hurled at the massed infantry. One such weapon was wildfire, a concoction of saltpeter, pitch, sulphur, ammoniacal salts, resin, and turpen-tine packed into thin-walled pots and sealed. The pots were laced with four lighted cords soaked in sulphur. These incendiary bombs were thrown down into the Janissaries, exploding and showering them with flame.

Trumps, or hollow metal tubes tied to long poles, were also used. The tubes were stuffed with a mixture similar to wildfire and, once ignited, spewed flames fifteen to twenty feet. Firehoops were wooden rings dipped in liquor, gunpowder, and saltpeter. Layers of the stuff were built up, ignited, and tossed over the walls using fire tongs. Francisco Balbi thought the firehoops created the most havoc among the Janissaries because their loose, flowing robes were easily ignited, and the fires spread quickly among the closely packed troops. When Mustapha called off the attack, 2,000 Janissaries lay dead. The defenders lost ten knights and seventy soldiers.

The bombardment of St. Elmo went on and on. Each night the wounded were transported across Grand Harbor to the hospital at Birgu. Each night supplies and reinforcements, 100 to 200 men, were sent to St. Elmo. La Valette needed help and sent a message to the imperial viceroy in Sicily, asking for 15,000 troops. He knew he would not get that many; indeed, in the privacy of his own thoughts, he did not believe any help would be forthcoming. He did not give his men empty promises, telling them bluntly that they had to give their lives for the order and their faith and that no position would be surrendered.

On the night of 10 June, the Janissaries once again attacked St. Elmo, pitching their own incendiary bombs into the ramparts. Anticipating such an attack, the defenders placed large water tubs behind the walls so that anyone ignited could jump in and douse himself. It worked. The defenders held their position, and another 1,500 Janissaries lay dead.

The bombardment raged on, with 160-pound shot hurled against the walls. Guns on Sciberras, Tinge Point, Gallows Point, guns on the captured ravelin and on Piali's ships off shore all belched shot at the fort. On 16 June, under cover of a massive bombardment, 4,000 Turkish arquebusiers opened fire, pinning down the defenders. Then the Turkish infantry rose from their positions and ran forward. First came the Iayalars, dressed in animal skins, then the Janissaries in their beautiful robes. With them were Dervishes, crying for the blood of the infidels. But an artillery battery at Fort St. Angelo raked the flank of the advancing enemy. After seven hours, 1,000 invaders were strewn across the battlefield. St. Elmo had withstood yet another attack.

And still the bombardment continued.

Dragut, meanwhile, decided that a screening wall should be built along the east side of Sciberras down to the water's edge. That would protect work parties, gunners, and arquebusiers. On 18 June, while supervising the work, a rock cannon ball fired from St. Angelo shattered nearby, and some splinters mortally wounded the old pirate. The next day, the Turkish master general of ordinance and the aga of the Janissaries were killed.

St. Elmo had to be taken quickly. On 21 June the Janissaries overran the fort's cavalier, and the next day Piali arrayed his ships tightly around the fort, their bow chasers firing at point-blank range. Hand guns were of little value in the hand-to-hand fighting that followed. Swords, axes, daggers, clubs, and maces seemed to transport the contest back to the First Crusade. But the Turks could not prevail.

By 23 June, only 100 defenders were left in St. Elmo. The Turks attacked again, this time easily penetrating the fort and overcoming those left. Dragut's pirates took some prisoners, mindful of ransom, but most were killed. Only a few Maltese swam to Birgu.

The cost of taking St. Elmo was high—higher than Mustapha and Piali anticipated. Eight thousand were killed. The defenders lost 1,500 but, unlike the Turkish forces, these men would probably not be replaced.

Mustapha ordered the heads of the principal knights severed and impaled, their bodies hung in mock crucifixions. La Valette coldly observed this desecration, then ordered all the Turkish prisoners decapitated. Their heads were stuffed into cannon and fired into the enemy camp. This was to be a fight to the death.

The Assault on Senglea

The defenders' morale leaped when news came that four galleys commanded by the Chevalier de Robles had arrived off the coast of Gozo. De Robles was ordered by the viceroy not to land on Malta if the Turks had captured St. Elmo. But the messenger de Robles sent to Birgu withheld from him the news of the fort's demise. The reinforcements, about 700 strong, landed on Malta's north coast and marched west around the Turkish patrols to Kalkara. From there they crossed the inlet to Birgu.

Mustapha, furious at the successful landing, manufactured a surprise for the defenders. Eighty boats were hauled on rollers over the Sciberras peninsula for an amphibious attack on Senglea. But a Turkish deserter, a Greek nobleman named Lascaris, revealed Mustapha's plan to La Valette: Once the boats were in place, Mustapha was going to attack both Fort St. Michael and along the peninsula. La Valette had a stake palisade driven into the inlet bed. Another stake palisade was put into Kalkara Creek.

Two Turkish attacks against the stake palisade at the inlet failed. At that juncture, Dragut's son-in-law Hassem, together with the viceroy of Algiers, arrived on Malta and decided that Mustapha's tactics were too timid. They would show him how to achieve victory. So, on 15 July, Hassem led the first attack on Senglea. One contingent of Algerians attacked from the water, heaving their boats onto the palisade. Their commander, Candelissa, jumped into the water and, followed by his troops, struggled to shore. The withering arquebus fire did not stop them as they rushed the walls. Just then a powder magazine behind the wall exploded and breached it. Candelissa's men surged forward.

In concert, with Candelissa's charge, Hassem attacked Fort St. Michael at the base of the peninsula. Defensive artillery shredded the Algerian ranks, but they pushed recklessly forward, gaining the ramparts. Attackers and defenders merged into a formless mass, neither side gaining advantage in the terrible hand-to-hand fighting.

Now the commanders tried to tip the scales of battle. La Valette sent reinforcements from Birgu to Senglea by a boat bridge he had constructed some weeks before. Seeing their comrades rushing to help gave the defenders renewed vigor. At the same time, Mustapha launched ten boats filled with a thousand Janissaries. The plan was to land around the northern tip of Senglea and outflank the defenders.

What Mustapha did not know was that the Chevalier de Guiral commanded a five-gun battery at the water's edge just below Fort St. Angelo. When it was obvious what the Turks were going to do, de Guiral ordered his guns to open fire. They could not miss at such close range. The first salvo blew nine boats out of the water. The second showered the survivors with shrapnel. Those that were still alive struggled ashore where they were killed by Maltese who dashed among them with swords and knives.

Nor could Candelissa sustain his attack. His men fell back from the breach, swimming out to their ships. But many were caught on the beach, where they were cut down by the Maltese. Likewise, Hassem's men were beaten back from St. Michael's walls, chased by a vengeful garrison that poured through the gates. The battle for St. Michael's lasted five hours. The defenders lost 250 men. The Turks and Algerians lost 3,000.

Mustapha was torn by the results. He was not displeased with Hassem's failure—at least there would be no more bravado from that quarter. But the consistently high losses for so little gain were profoundly discouraging. He decided to re-double his effort against the Senglea Peninsula. Another eighteen guns were put on Mt. Sciberras, including two basilisks capable of firing, however slowly, 300-pound shot.

By 2 August, Mustapha had seventy guns firing continuously at Fort St. Michael and the Senglea positions. Then he launched his infantry but, after five attacks, not an inch of ground was taken. The bombardment rained down for another five days. On 7 August, the Turkish infantry advanced, and troops under Piali swept into the fort's cavalier. Victory was theirs—or so they believed. Actually, they fell into a trap, for inside they were confronted by a hastily built secondary wall. Crowded in from the rear, unable to advance or retreat, the Turks were slaughtered by cannon and arquebus fire.

Not knowing the fate of Piali's men, Mustapha personally led an attack against Fort St. Michael. But the unexpected happened. At the point where the defenders seemed to be weakening, the Turks panicked. A moment later, they were in full retreat. A message had arrived at the Turkish camp that the viceroy Don Garcia de Toledo had landed with a large relief force from Sicily. But no such force existed. The report was utterly false.

With the Turkish army fully committed to the siege, the small garrison at Mdina seized the opportunity to strike the base camp at Marsa. Commanded by the Chevalier de Lugny, about a hundred cavalrymen, supported by a hundred arquebusiers and Maltese irregulars, charged the Turkish camp, burning tents and supplies, killing the sick and wounded and the few camp guards.

In desperation, Mustapha tried two new tactics. First, utilizing Egyptian engineers and sappers, the castile at Fort St. Michael was mined. Second, two large siege towers were erected and hauled toward the walls. By 18 August, a coordinated attack was launched against St. Michael. The mine under the castile exploded and the wall crumbled. An infantry column commanded by Piali ran into the breach, and soon their banners were flying from the fort's ramparts. To counter that thrust, La Valette, age seventy, personally led a counter-attack, his presence a rallying point. The defenders held out through the night.

The next day Mustapha ordered a siege tower to be rolled against a bastion of the castile. La Valette, foreseeing the maneuver, had ordered a hole cut in the wall at ground level. As the siege tower was brought to the wall, the hole was punched through, and a cannon drawn forward. Firing chains, the gun soon brought the tower crashing down.

Mustapha then ordered a long wooden barrel constructed, banded by iron, and loaded with gunpowder and shrapnel. The Turks laboriously dragged it to the top of a wall and dropped it among the defenders below. But the fuse failed. So the defenders hauled the barrel to the ramparts they controlled, relighted the fuse and, bouncing the barrel off the side of the perimeter ditch, sent it flying among the Turks, where it exploded with frightful results.

On 20 August, 8,000 Turks again attacked Fort St. Michael, bringing forward the second siege tower. Rather than destroying the tower, the defenders captured it and turned it into an external strongpoint from which they sniped at the Turks with arqebus fire.

Another massive assault was launched on 1 September with no more success than the earlier attacks. The Turks were now demoralized by their losses and by their inability to make significant progress despite their continual bombardment. Also, disease, poor water, and hunger were beginning to take a toll.

On September, a relief convoy of twenty-eight ships commanded by Viceroy Don Garcia de Toledo reached Gozo. The next day the force of 8,000 men landed unopposed on Malta. A Moslem galley slave was purposely released and given misinformation that 16,000 had landed. He made his way to Mustapha's camp and reported what he was told. Mustapha, not seeing through the ruse, ordered an immediate withdrawal from the island.

Don Garcia's force marched inland from Mellieha Bay, completely unaware that the Turks were leaving. When scouts reported to Mustapha the actual size of the relief force, he realized he had been tricked and ordered 9,000 to re-land at St. Paul's Bay very close to where the relief force had landed. They intercepted one another near Naxxar, a ridge behind and above Senglea. The eager Christian soldiers charged. Mustapha ordered his men to higher ground, but it was too late. The new troops would not be denied. They quickly outflanked the Turks and overwhelmed them. The Turks broke and ran north to St. Paul's Bay, where they were caught on the beaches. When the hand-to-hand fighting ended, another 3,000 Turks were dead.

The survivors of the Turkish army struggled back to Constantinople, entering the harbor under cover of night. Suleiman swore revenge and vowed to renew the siege, but he never did. Instead, his attention was drawn to the Austrian frontier, where he died a year later directing another siege.

CATEGORIES OF COMBAT

The conflict between Mustapha and Piali may well have doomed the Malta siege. Divided command, leading to divided purposes, seldom brings victory. In contrast, La Valette's single-minded control over his forces, his ability to see what needed doing, and his courage to live or die by his decisions unified the Malta defenders to a degree the Moslem invaders could not have anticipated. From the perspective of generalship, this contrast in leadership provides some satisfying answers as to why the defenders won and the besiegers lost. Yet, like the Jerusalem siege, the various categories of combat suggest further answers that are both ideological and technical in nature.

The Will to Combat

The history of the Malta siege was written mostly by Europeans who frequently attempted to glorify Christianity over Islam or, short of that, to glorify the Order of St. John. Thus, it is not difficult to tell the heroes from the villains. And heroes abound from La Valette to the humblest Maltese, their names repeated again and again in history books and Maltese legends. From one point of view, such heroes are an essential part of the story because what they did was often crucial to the outcome. Additionally, heroes de-objectify the siege, making it less an academic excursion and more the emotionally charged battle it was.

But I think that once the ideological baggage is sorted out and the various rationales are penetrated, one conclusion stands out above the rest: The two sides killed each other with a determination, almost a joy, seldom found in military history. This is not to be confused with numbers of casualties; for, certainly, there have been battles, sieges, with greater numbers lost. There have been longer battles. One could argue that there have been more savage battles. But for sheer delight in slaughter, Malta must rank near the top of the list. Granted that the soldier just killed cares little whether his enemy did him in with relish or regret. Dead is dead. Glory and heroism are more often ex post facto judgments.

The extraordinary acts that habit and language force us to call heroic or valorous cannot be easily dismissed. When the Turks ran their boats onto the Senglea stake palisade, native Maltese, armed with little more than knives, leaped into the water to kill the invaders. When the Senglea wall collapsed, the knight Zanoguerra and Father Roberto, a cross in one hand and a sword in the other, together led a counter-attack. The knight was shot dead, but not before rallying his men. As St. Elmo was about to be overrun, Juan de Gueras and Captain de Miranda, both badly wounded, had themselves put in chairs, swords at their sides, and awaited death. Nor can we overlook the willingness of leaders from both sides to expose themselves to extreme danger. Dragut boldly appeared on the Senglea heights, not to cheer the slaves building his screening wall but to put some spine in his flagging soldiers. He was killed. Mustapha, Piali, and La Valette led attacks and counter-attacks, demonstrating to their men that they were willing to take the same risks, validating their leadership roles.

Such actions and the intense dedication of the soldiers of both sides are usually explained by appeals to faith. The Christian defenders were fighting for God, the Church, and their order. How easy to enshrine them as knightly martyrs. The only missing element is thunderous organ music. The Moslem forces are often seen as religious fanatics, catapulted into battle by drugs, religious frenzy, and an Eastern disregard for life. The truth is that both sides were perilously close to each other in their willingness to die for whatever cause.

Doubtlessly, religion was an important element for both sides. But Christians and Moslems had been at war with each other for a long time, and Suleiman had even fought the Knights of St. John on Rhodes. Circumstances on Malta, however, changed the character of battle, making it more intense. No quarter was given. What happened?

A finality was manifest in the Malta siege. Suleiman, Mustapha, and Piali, beyond individual differences, shared the common belief that the knightly order was to be destroyed once and for all. Suleiman, when he allowed the order to leave Rhodes, did not anticipate the fresh aggressiveness with which their ships would raid his trade lanes. After all, the order was severely wounded, and it seemed as if their traditional European backers were reluctant to see the patient recover. But attack they did, and with such vigor that their actions could no longer be endured. For the knights, the finality was more direct and simple: They had nowhere else to go. It was survive on Malta or perish.

Such finality was a direct response to the physical conditions of the siege. Malta provided special conditions. It was an island—but so was Rhodes. The difference is size. Rhodes is 540 square miles, but Malta is only 95 square miles. That smaller size compressed the area within which the battle could be joined. Except for Mdina, La Valette practically surrendered the island to the Turks, reducing the battle zone to the area immediately around Grand Harbor, a space only a couple of miles in each direction, and that is being generous. Crowded into that zone were between 40,000 and 50,000 men of both sides with all the firepower of musket and cannon. There could be little or no advance of consequence, and there was certainly no room for retreat.

Given that constricted space, the Malta siege created its own environment of battle. Thus, the Turkish gunners on Tinge Point were only 500 yards from St. Elmo, and Turkish arquebusiers were about the same distance from the ramparts of St. Elmo and sometimes much closer. Piali's ships bombarding Senglea were at point-blank range. The gun batteries on Sciberras overlooked not only St. Elmo but also Fort St. Angelo, St. Michael, the length of the Senglea Peninsula, and Birgu. Typically, when the Turks attacked, the defenders counter-attacked, the two forces tenaciously clinging to what had been taken or needed defending until, like some giant multi-celled organism, they merged into each other, swaying, heaving, fighting, and dying for some fragment of fortification.

The spatial restrictions evoked their behavioral consequences in the slaughter that followed. But saying that is not enough; otherwise we are left with too many rats in one small box, an analogy quickly exhausted. The battle conditions suggest another approach.

Literally no one was exempt from participation in the battle. For the Turks, there were continuous preparations to be made and, when attacks developed, thousands were involved. Support troops were always close at hand and often were as exposed to defensive fire as the assault troops. There was no let-up for the defenders. Constant bombardment became a way of life. With death so close at hand, as it were a daily companion, no one escaped into the luxury of a rest area. No one could let down his guard.

Additionally, there was on both sides a sense of common fate—live or die, kill or be killed. St. Elmo, for example, was consistently reinforced by volunteers who knew there was no chance of survival, only of delaying the inevitable final Turkish attack. That may be faith to some, but it was also a reconciliation with the realities of the battle. Everyone was trapped in the same cauldron. There was no relief, there was no escape. All that a soldier could hope to do was fight, perhaps die, and try to take as many of the enemy with him as possible.

Such feelings of inevitability or fatalism or reconciliation with the situation were expressed at various levels of action. A soldier might silently volunteer for duty in St. Elmo. Once there, he might voice his feelings by calling on God's will, just as the Turks would call on Allah. But verbal expression pales before the unrestrained physical relief of tension. Historians have hit the mark when they describe the Turks "surging forward" or "swarming" through a breach, or when they describe the tremendous élan of the defenders. Such behavior was not necessarily called for by pre-designated leaders or by military norms. It was behavior conditioned by the battle situation in which informal roles of leadership were probably assumed by some of the soldiers, pushing their comrades forward in ways none could have foreseen before the battle. Such behavior emerges in crowd situations where normative organization and expectations give way when confronted by intense stress, such as in battle. The constricted space of the Malta siege increased interaction between the soldiers of both sides that was paralleled by an increase in feeling-states, the subsequent interaction building on itself. Thus, the siege created its own norms that were expressed in unremitting slaughter and the mutual refusal to give quarter.

The men caught in the Malta siege did not need any artificial stimuli behind the will to combat. Both sides willingly died because dying became the normative, if final, behavior.

Artillery versus Infantry

Turkish artillery created a hellish environment for the defenders. The bombardment of 2 August was so massive that the sounds allegedly could be heard in Syracuse, Sicily, sixty-five miles north. But just what did all the sound and fury actually accomplish? Certainly the Turkish guns killed some defenders and wounded many more. Buildings caved in, and walls were occasionally breached. But, given the length and intensity of Turkish artillery fire, and given the continued ability of the defenders to repel infantry attacks, it must be concluded that Turkish artillery was less effective than its intensity would imply.

The Turkish artillery was also ineffective against the defensive artillery. Despite the bombardments, the smaller defensive guns kept working. But, some dramatic shooting aside—such as the killing of Dragut or when the St. Angelo battery blew the Janissary boats out of the water—the defensive artillery did not stop nor seriously diminish the enemy artillery fire or impede their work parties.

Rather, defensive artillery was most effective against attacking infantry. During each attack, the Turks left relatively protected areas to rush across open ground. Fully exposed, packed together like a human juggernaut, the infantry entered a killing zone in which grape shot and chain shot fired at them rapidly diminished their ranks. We read of a hundred defenders killed at one post or 250 killed at another, but we also read of 2,000 or 3,000 Turks felled in a single attack. The siege, consequently, became more than the attempt to take one fort after another; it became a battle of attrition.

Infantry versus Infantry

Artillery can create rubble and blow holes in walls. Artillery may bring a garrison to its knees. But if a siege is to be successful, the offense must occupy the fortress or town, and that usually involves a battle between infantry formations. Infantry encounters on Malta were of two types. The first was confrontations at a distance and the second, hand-to-hand fighting.

The infantry of both sides measured their effective distance by the range of the arquebus. Ranges of 200 yards were common, but accuracy suffered at distances over 50 yards. The well-trained and disciplined Janissaries used the gun with considerable skill and could fire frequently and accurately. They also used volley fire, exemplified at St. Elmo when 4,000 shot volleys cleared the walls of defenders. Of course, the defenders could not match that volume of firing, but their shooting was good enough to help frustrate any attack. Even more efficient was their sharpshooting, a potent capability demonstrated after they captured the siege tower at Fort St. Michael.

The Turks who waded through the carnage of the killing zone always faced two problems once they reached a fortress wall. First, they usually had suffered heavy casualties getting to the wall, lessening the impact of their charge. Second, if 2,000 Janissaries reached a wall and carried with them 200 scaling ladders, then only 200 men at one time could reach the wall top at the same time. That reduced the impact of the charge still further. Going through a breach in a wall was little better because the spaces were narrow, and any formation the attackers tried to maintain was broken by the rubble over which they had to clamber.

The denial of full strength to the offense gave the already smaller defensive force tactical advantages. The massive firepower of the enemy's arquebusiers was muted once they reached the wall. At that point, they engaged in hand-to-hand combat. The arquebus was too awkward and slow firing for such a situation. Once in close proximity, both sides needed weapons that could kill quickly and were easily handled. Swords, knives, clubs, and maces met those specifications. The hand-to-hand encounters were consequently a survival of medieval warfare, a function of technological lag.

Wounded and Prisoners

There is no body of consistent ample evidence to indicate what the Turks did with their wounded. If conditions at the Marsa camp were any indication, those wounded who were retrieved from the fighting were sent to the camp and attended by some retainers and slaves. There were probably doctors about, but how many no one knows.

In contrast, the order possessed a regular hospital, and the staff was medically skilled and experienced. The major problem facing the Malta hospital was overcrowding. This was gradually diminished as the siege progressed because many wounded refused to leave their posts. Soldiers suffering puncture wounds were difficult to treat because the wounds were hard to clean and infection was always possible. Shredded limbs were often amputated. Cuts were the most easily treated. If a wounded man made it to the hospital and received reasonable care, he probably had a good chance of surviving.

Prisoners were another matter. Those taken by the defenders were made slaves or, with La Valette's brutal decision, were decapitated, their heads shot into the Turkish camp. Some prisoners were taken by the Turks, mostly by Dragut's men who sought ransom. Many other prisoners were first tortured for information and then executed.

In fact, neither side was particularly interested in taking prisoners. They were an inconvenience, given the restricted battle zone. Crushed together, with no time to regard the life of an enemy, with no way of handing prisoners to the rear, the quickest solution was to kill everyone in reach.

AFTERMATH

No quarter! These words penetrate the character of the Malta siege. It was a slaughterhouse. The gunpowder weapons not only increased the casualties, they also made it possible to kill more people in less time than with bladed weapons. No longer did one man have to face another. Of course, the troops engaged in hand-to-hand combat at times and under specific conditions (such as on the walls of St. Michael's), but whole companies could be felled with a single cannon salvo or by an arquebus volley.

Siege warfare was re-defined. Now, small contingents of well-armed, well-supplied, and determined defenders could bring a larger army to an abrupt halt and even defeat it. As Christopher Duffy notes in *Siege Warfare*, a defensive position did not have to be some enormous structure to accomplish such a victory. Dirt and logs would do the job if the defenders were bold, imaginative, and dedicated. It will be remembered from the survey of sieges that Major Matthew Steele concludes in his *American Campaigns* that frontal assaults against such installations, citing several examples from the American Civil War, were senseless slaughter. Thus, having sustained enormous casualties on Malta from just such attacks, the Turks quit. They could do no more.

It seems that not many future generals—and in that company of the missing would be those who led the British and French armies against Sebastopol nearly 300 years later— can have studied such sixteenth-century sieges as Malta. Thus they ensured that when their turn came, the carnage would continue.

Chapter 4

Sebastopol, October 1854 to September 1855

The British, French, and Turks besieged the Russian fortress seaport of Sebastopol during the Crimean War to end the threat of the Black Sea Fleet to Turkey and the Mediterranean Sea lanes. The siege lasted nearly one year with much blood-letting that brought both sides to exhaustion.

The Crimean War was a dirty little affair, badly planned if planned at all, and frequently poorly executed. Had it not been for the desperate bravery of some field officers and the men they led, the outcome would have been quite different.

Most historians of the war have concentrated on the character of such leaders as Fitzroy Somerset, Lord Raglan, the British commander-in-chief, or James Thomas Brudenell, Lord Cardigan, who led the infamous Charge of the Light Brigade. And most historians have written about the criminal neglect under which the British army fought the battles that shaped the conflict. What is sometimes lost in the parade of vanities, ineptitude, and outright stupidity is that, rather than being just another battle in a string of battles, the siege of Sebastopol was the focus of the war. How that siege was conducted depended not only on the personalities guiding it but also on the traditions of siege warfare the opponents carried with them.

ON TO THE CRIMEA

On 1 September 1854, a great convoy of 900 ships—the largest convoy of then modern times—set sail from Varna, a Bulgarian Black Sea port, and headed for the Russian Crimean Peninsula. The convoy carried 65,000 troops—27,000 British, 30,000 French, and 8,000 Turks.

A variety of events created this invasion force. Czar Nicholas I earlier used a religious pretext to pounce on the Turks so that he could extend Russian influence into the Mediterranean. Announcing that the Turks were mistreating their Christian minority population, Nicholas proposed that the Turkish sultan anoint him protector of the Orthodox church. That was an ill-timed slap in the face of Napoleon III. He quickly reminded the sultan that France, dating back to the Crusades, was and should remain the declared Protector of the Faith. The sultan agreed with the new French emperor who, matters of faith aside, wanted to re-establish the old glories of his namesake. Now Nicholas felt insulted. Two Russian army corps crossed the Danube into Moldavia and Wallachia. The French were again affronted. The British, trying to negotiate a peace, were alarmed lest the Russians gain access to the Mediterranean. The war was on.

British and French forces gathered at Constantinople, then moved to Varna in early May 1854. From there they could help the Turks in the invaded territory. Their assistance was not needed. The Turks held the Russians. Discouraged, threatened by Austrian intervention, the Russians pulled back across the Danube. Although the war seemed to be over, neither London nor Paris was satisfied. Not only were the Russians escaping punishment for their bad treatment of the Turks, but their Black Sea Fleet, an instrument of further intimidation, rode safely at anchor in the fortified harbor of Sebastopol.

On 15 June, the London *Times*, although initially opposed to war, did an editorial turnabout: "The grand and military objectives of the war could not be attained as long as Sebastopol and the Russian fleet were in existence."

Henry Pelham, duke of Newcastle, informed Lord Raglan that peace was impossible without taking Sebastopol and, with cabinet authorization, empowered him to undertake an expedition to the Crimea, "unless you [Lord Raglan] should be decidedly of the opinion that it could not be undertaken with a reasonable prospect of success." Thus, the final responsibility was handed Raglan, and history would judge him either another Wellington or a goat.

Lord Raglan and Marshal Le Roy de St. Arnaud, the French commander, decided to invade the Crimea based on no more knowledge of the area, as Alexander Kinglake wryly comments, than that the Russians owned it. One reconnaissance was made of the coast, and a landing site was selected at Calamita Bay north of Sebastopol. So, on the first day of September, the great fleet glided across the Black Sea, propelled by the ill-conceived hopes of a bemused cabinet on one side of the English Channel and the blatant ambitions of a self-seeking emperor on the other.

THE BRITISH ARMY: AN ORGANIZATIONAL SKETCH

The story of the British army in the Crimea has been told over and over to the near-exclusion of the French. The main reason for this is that the high drama of the war resides in the British story. Since that drama is relevant to understanding sieges, I shall follow convention and continue that emphasis.

The British army sent to the Crimea was nurtured by little else than ill-conceived hope. Garnett Wolseley, then a captain, likened the British expeditionary force to "a steam engine whose boiler is in Halifax, its cylinders in China, and its other machinery distributed in bits wherever the map of the world is colored red, and for which machine neither water nor coals nor oil nor repair tools are kept at hand" (*The Story of a Soldier's Life*, vol. I, p. 98). The modern historian Corelli Barnett essentially agrees with Wolseley when he writes that the force was little more than a "dusted down" version of the army that fought Napoleon's armies in Spain nearly a half-century earlier.

The army's administrative system was a morass of overlapping and out-of-date departments. The commissariat was still run, as in the Napoleonic Wars, by civilians and had not supplied such a large overseas force since Waterloo. The medical department was responsible to the secretary for war but drew supplies from the commissariat. Lord Henry Hardinge, the commander-in-chief of the British army and headquartered at the Horse Guards in London, could assign officers to any regiment in the army but could not command any forces beyond the British Isles. And so on and on into a bureaucratic maze.

The British expeditionary force comprised four infantry divisions and one of cavalry. Each division contained two brigades of three regiments each. There were three problems and/or peculiarities. First, brigades and divisions were organized only during wartime; consequently, most of the regiments never before served together and certainly never trained together because there was no imperative to do so. In fact, many officers considered training exercises to be a waste of time. Second, divisional and brigade commanders were usually strangers to their troops, having been assigned to their posts at the same time the larger units were organized. Third, regiments were not (and still are not) regiments. This bit of English logic rejects the notion that a regiment should be made up of two or three battalions. Instead, British regiments were battalions, most often one and only occasionally two. The uniqueness of each "regiment" was encouraged. Each had its own history, its own traditions, and even unique features in its uniforms.

The regiments were led by men who, for the most part, purchased their commissions, a system that initially guaranteed that only gentlemen of wealth and title would lead the army. As the nineteenth century unfolded, however, more of the affluent and occasionally not so affluent middle class managed the sums necessary to purchase commissions for their sons. In many instances, that was as far as financial assistance could go, with the result that many officers found themselves stagnating in rank without hope of promotion.

Yet, even if funds were available and a higher rank was purchased, there was no guarantee that the newly promoted officer would find a posting. That was decided by the army hierarchy at the Horse Guards. Social connections, nepotism, and political influence were often the deciding factors. Colin Campbell, commanding the Highland Brigade in the Crimea, earlier in his career managed to purchase a lieutenant colonelcy but waited three years on half-pay before being given a regiment. He had no connections, only talent. Captain Anthony Sterling, Campbell's brigade major, went on half-pay after eighteen years of service. He tried unsuccessfully to purchase the rank of major. The Horse Guards told him that no such vacancy existed. But Lord Hardinge, then commander in India, saw to it that his nephew was made a major and was assigned to his staff. A bitter Sterling was convinced the Guards regiments held a virtual monopoly on promotions and, because of in-bred regimental connections, created a promotion machine that locked out anyone with talent but little social and financial backing. He was almost right.

The purchase system was not rational but, then, neither was British military organization. It was traditional, basing decisions on what had been done during the forty years in which the Duke of Wellington ruled. He had kept the army in low profile, making few demands of Parliament and thus avoiding its scrutiny. The purchase and regimental systems flourished. Simultaneously, the administrative system languished, tangled in its own bureaucratic maze. If challenged, it was enough for the Horse Guards to reply that the British army triumphed at Waterloo, that officers were, after all, gentlemen, and that the common soldier, with his usual pluck and loyalty to both regiment and queen, would steadfastly do his duty.

THE LEADERS OF THE BRITISH EXPEDITIONARY FORCE

Given the traditional character of the British army in 1854, how reasonable it must have seemed that Lord Raglan was made its commander. Earlier in his life, as Lord Fitzroy Somerset, he was the protégé of Wellington. He was Wellington's military secretary during the Peninsular War. At age twenty-three he was made the lieutenant colonel of the 1st Foot Guards even though he never led so much as a platoon into action. He was beside Wellington at Waterloo, where he lost his right arm (the Raglan sleeve was named after the loose-fitting jacket he used thereafter). When the duke became master general of ordnance, he took Fitzroy Somerset with him as his secretary. At Wellington's death, Fitzroy became master general of ordnance and assumed the title Lord Raglan. After thirty-five years at the Horse Guards, at age sixty-seven, he was given his first field command.

London *Times* correspondent William Howard Russell shared a common belief that Raglan's role would be that of negotiator between the various allied commanders and that military decisions would be left to others. To whom? For, if Russell was correct, there would be no unified British

command, only the division commanders left very much on their own—
and what a mixture that would brew.

The Duke of Cambridge, at age thirty-five the youngest divisional
commander, was the queen's cousin, a relationship thought suitable com-
pensation for a total lack of experience. Sir George Brown, commanding the
Light Division, last saw action at Blandesburg in the War of 1812. He then
spent twenty-five years at the Horse Guards where, in 1851, he was
promoted to lieutenant general. Sir Richard England, leading the Third
Division, was a Canadian. He saw little action during the Napoleonic Wars
but served during the 1830s along India's Northwest Frontier and was
appointed commander of the Bombay Division of the Indian Army. Sir
George de Lacy Evans was the most experienced divisional commander.
He had served forty-seven years, much of it on active service from the Battle
of Victoria to Blandesburg and Washington, D.C., where his company
seized the Congressional Building. Then he commanded the British Legion
in the Carlist Wars, earning a reputation for daring leadership. Charles
Bingham, Lord Lucan, led the cavalry division. Written off as an ill-
tempered nincompoop for his part in the ill-fated Charge of the Light
Brigade, he was, nonetheless, the logical choice. He was a brilliant horseman who, when twenty-six, commanded the prestigious 17th Lancers. In
1828, he took leave to serve in Russia on Prince Woronzoff's staff, leading
a cavalry division at the Battle of Adrianople. It was granted that he
understood both the Russians and the Turks. If he did, no one on Raglan's
staff cared.

The brigade leaders were a mixed lot. For example, both Sir Henry
Bentink, commanding the Guards Brigade, and William Codrington, who
commanded a brigade in the Light Division, enjoyed meteoric careers. Both
were Coldstream Guardsmen and had not one day of battle experience
between them. Codrington, in fact, arrived at Verna completely unattached.
Yet, he was shortly promoted to major general and offered a brigade by
Raglan. Sir George Buller had not seen action for two decades when, in 1847,
he went to the Cape colony to serve in the Kaffir War. Sir Colin Campbell,
commanding the Highland Brigade, was doubtlessly the most experienced
soldier in the Crimea. He entered the army in 1808 at age sixteen and, within
a few months, was a lieutenant serving in the Battle of Vimeiro. Then he
fought at Corruna, Badajos, Victoria, San Sebastian, where he was
promoted to captain on merit, and Bidassoa. He subsequently served in
Gibraltar, Barbados, Demerarra, and Ireland. During the Chartist troubles
he commanded the 98th Regiment and kept peace in the Newcastle area.
He took his regiment to China for the First Opium War and became military
governor of Hong Kong and Chusan. He led a division in the Second Sikh
War and commanded the Peshawar Field Force along the Northwest Frontier. Loved by his troops, Campbell nevertheless carried a reputation for
being troublesome and temperamental. Lord Panmure would label him
"the fiery old Scot."

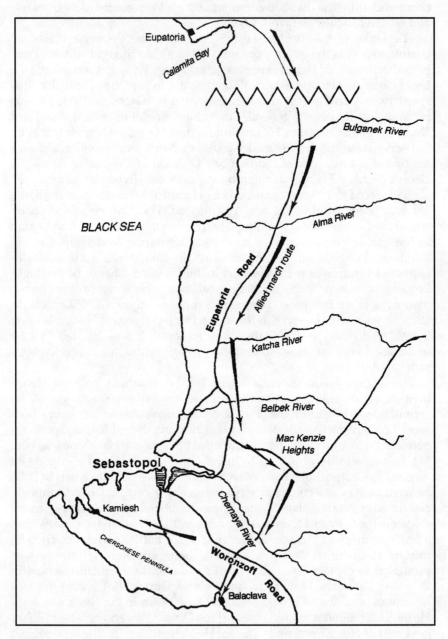

Map 6 Crimean Coast

This mixed leadership, favoring inexperience over experience and privilege over talent, was satisfactory under ordinary circumstances. But given the stresses of war and given the terrible conditions in the Crimea, the mixture proved friable.

THE CAMPAIGN UNFOLDS

The Allied landing at Calamita Bay was without incident, the Russian army conspicuous by its absence. Once ashore, the allies were in a muddle about what to do and when. The French landed abundant supplies and weapons and their Spahis—irregular native Algerian cavalry—drove herds of sheep and cattle into their lines. The British had a transportation problem. They were short 700 wagons because they left theirs in Varna. They managed to commandeer less than a third of what they needed from Russian peasants. It took five days to sort things out but, even as the army gathered in marching order, the British were hauling supplies and equipment, including tents, back to the beaches. Much of that material was either abandoned or thrown into the sea. Thus, the British expeditionary force went to war with what they could carry on their backs.

On 19 September, a bright and clear day, the invasion force lurched forward. They reached the Bulganak River by early afternoon. Many men were already dropping from the line of march, suffering from heat exhaustion, dehydration, diarrhea, dysentery, and cholera, so carts were sent back to pick up the stragglers. A large Russian contingent was later sighted, but no action was taken.

The Battle of the Alma

The first engagement was fought beginning at noon the next day at the Alma River, seven miles beyond the allied camp. Naval observers sighted a large Russian force strung along the heights south of the river. The allied generals agreed to an attack. The Turks anchored the allied line near the river mouth. The French deployed from the river mouth to the Russian center. The British aligned against the Russian right. No more specifics were offered. There was only a consensus that they would battle the Russians.

What the allies saw as they descended into the little river valley were vineyards, a long low stone wall paralleling the river, gardens, scattered houses, and Bourliouk, a village astride the Sebastopol-Eupatoria post road. The French faced steep cliffs, the highest being the so-called Telegraph Hill. On the left opposite the British were the Kourgane Heights. Between the two elevations was a bowl-shaped down.

Prince Menschikoff, the Russian commander, spread his army along the heights. An artillery battery overlooked the post road. Left center, as the British viewed the positions, was the Great Redoubt, containing 14 heavy guns. This was supported by some smaller cannon and four battalions of the Kazan Regiment. The so-called Lesser Redoubt was about a half-mile further left. The Russians opened fire with their artillery at 1:30 P.M. The allied gunners replied.

The French attacked first, following a narrow undefended road leading toward Telegraph Hill. But the élan of their attack collapsed when they could not get their artillery up the road. Menschikoff, seeing the gap in his defenses, ordered some artillery re-positioned. Their shelling slowed the French advance even more. Prince Napoleon's infantry division moved forward in support of their comrades, but they got tangled in the vineyards and suffered heavy casualties from Russian artillery.

The French sent a plea to Lord Raglan that he must advance his troops, or the French attack would fail completely. Raglan ordered a general advance. The troops dressed their ranks and moved forward, clambering through the vineyards, scampering over the stone wall, and wading across the shallow river. Their organization broke down with every step. De Lacy Evan's division stalled in Bourliouk, apparently confused by the smoke and flames from a fire set by the Russians. Brown's division disintegrated into ragged clusters. Codrington's brigade, their leader charging back and forth on his horse, shouting encouragement, made it up the Kourgane Heights to the Great Redoubt. They were thrown back in disarray. But the brigade soon reformed and again attacked the Great Redoubt.

The Duke of Cambridge came across Brigadier General Buller and wondered aloud what he should do. "Why, your Royal Highness," Buller replied, "you had better advance, I think." The duke's division moved forward, the Guards Brigade deploying to reinforce Codrington. Colin Campbell, leading the Highland Brigade, took a point twenty yards in front of the Black Watch. He turned in his saddle and called, "Forward, the Forty-Second." Up the hill went the Black Watch, the 93rd Regiment (Sutherland Highlanders), and the 79th (Cameron Highlanders), advancing in echelon and firing as they marched. The packed Russian infantry columns that rose to meet them were shot to pieces, especially after two British horse artillery batteries came up to support the advance. The Russian flank was turned. Menschikoff retired to Sebastopol.

Balaclava and Inkerman

Colonel Franz Eduard Todleben, a Latvian German, was assigned to strengthen Sebastopol's defenses. Ships were sunk across the harbor entrance, their crews sent ashore with the ships' guns. Earthworks were hastily thrown up on the town's north perimeter but, in September, they contained no artillery.

Marshal St. Arnaud was put off by the Russian activity and announced the French would not attack the north side, even though General Sir George Cathcart and other British officers thought an immediate assault timely because they could force entry into the town. At the urgings of Sir John

Burgoyne, the senior British engineer, Raglan agreed with St. Arnaud's assessment and also agreed to a march around Sebastopol to two small harbors below the great seaport. The French settled into Kamiesh and the British into Balaclava, a dingy little notch six miles from Sebastopol. A narrow muddy road to the fortress snaked uphill over the Chersonese Plateau. All British supplies to their troops engaged in the siege would have to pass along that road.

Meanwhile, the Russians defeated at the Alma marched through Sebastopol and out into the countryside to prowl the allied flank, hoping that as long as they posed a threat, the allies would not attack Sebastopol. To emphasize that threat, the Russians subsequently fought two actions, the Battle of Balaclava on 25 October and the Battle of the Inkerman on 5 November.

Early in the morning of 25 October, Menschikoff sent a large force under General Pavel Liprandi along the Woronzoff Road. This ran the length of a ridge on which the allies established six artillery redoubts manned by Turkish gunners. The Russians quickly took four redoubts, but Lucan moved his cavalry to a flanking position, stopping the Russian advance. The Russians then started hauling away the captured artillery. Raglan sent a message to Lucan to advance and re-capture the guns. Lucan was confused, not knowing exactly what guns Raglan meant because he could not see along the Woronzoff Road. But Captain Edward Nolan, the staff messenger, waved grandly toward Russian guns positioned in a valley northwest of the road. "There, my Lord, is your enemy. There are your guns." Lucan gave Lord Cardigan the order to attack. Of 673 troopers of the Light Brigade who charged, 195 returned. The brigade was destroyed.

Two other related actions were more successful.

Colin Campbell, with about 500 men from the 93rd Highlanders and others from an invalid battalion, stood on a hill, guarding the road to Balaclava. Campbell watched Liprandi's advance and withdrew his men to the reverse slope. Then a massive Russian cavalry column came down the Woronzoff Road. An estimated 400 left the main column and headed for the 93rd. Campbell brought his little force to the forward slope, supported by two artillery batteries. He told his soldiers, "There is no retreat from here, men. You must die where you stand!" The Highlanders fired an ineffective volley at 800 yards and another at 350 yards. The Russians swerved just as Captain Ross brought his grenadier company around to cover the 93rd's flank. They fired yet another volley, and the Russians galloped away. This action, reported by correspondent Russell, became known as "The Thin Red Line."

The main Russian cavalry column, meantime, reached the fourth redoubt on Woronzoff Road and then, under fire from French and Turkish artillery, swung left to find squadrons of the Heavy Brigade facing them. Inexplicably, the Russian column stopped about 400 yards away. Sir James Scarlett, commanding the British brigade, slowly and meticulously brought his troopers into proper formation. Satisfied at last, he called out, "Sound the charge!" The cavalry moved forward, as Pemberton notes, as calculatedly as the preparations made for it. At eight miles an hour, two squadrons of the Scot Greys and Inniskilling Dragoons disappeared into the Russian mass. Other squadrons charged from different angles. The Russians broke, first at the rear, then on the flanks, moving back to the relative safety of the captured redoubts. The Russian cavalry, 2,000 strong, were not so much defeated in the usual military sense as stunned by the audacity of the 600 troopers of the Heavy Brigade.

On 5 November, Menschikoff attempted to dislodge the British Light and Second divisions from the Inkerman Heights east of Sebastopol. Fog, hanging amid the rocks and twisted brushwood, blanketed the jagged ground. Units lost their way. Leaders lost their units. So many officers were killed in the intense, vicious, often hand-to-hand fighting that in one Coldstream Guards unit a doctor took over and led a charge. The fighting ended after eight hours. The Russians were thrust back. The British had 2,000 casualties. The French, who came to their aid, lost at least 1,760. The Russians, according to Somerset Calthorpe, may have lost between 10,000 and 15,000. Raglan thought their losses were closer to 20,000. The allied wounded and dead, interspersed with the Russians, were strewn everywhere across the battlefield. The hospitals were jammed to capacity.

On 14 November, as a herald of things to come, a hurricane slammed into the Crimean coast. Seven British supply ships went down. Campsites were torn apart. The men had to move in small groups, holding hands, or be blown across the ground. Then the hail came. Then snow. Winter closed in on the peninsula, entrapping the armies.

Gloom descended on the British and French. St. Arnaud, desperately ill, was replaced by General Francois Canrobert. He let it be known that he did not want any more costly battles and certainly not an outright attack on Sebastopol. Raglan saw only that his army verged on extinction. Battles had claimed their share of casualties, to be sure, but those men infected with cholera and a host of intestinal maladies fell in far greater numbers. After the Battle of Inkerman, only 16,000 British soldiers were fit for duty. By January 1855, the Grenadier Guards regiment could muster only 128 men out of an original 1,000. By February, the entire Guards Brigade could field only 300 men, a tenth their original number. The situation was exacerbated by an inept administrative system that Raglan was unwilling or unable to bend to his will.

Yet, some good was accomplished by the two battles at Balaclava and the Inkerman. Menschikoff's flanking actions were muted, giving the allies opportunity to establish siege positions around Sebastopol. And the Russians within Sebastopol used that same time to strengthen the city's defenses.

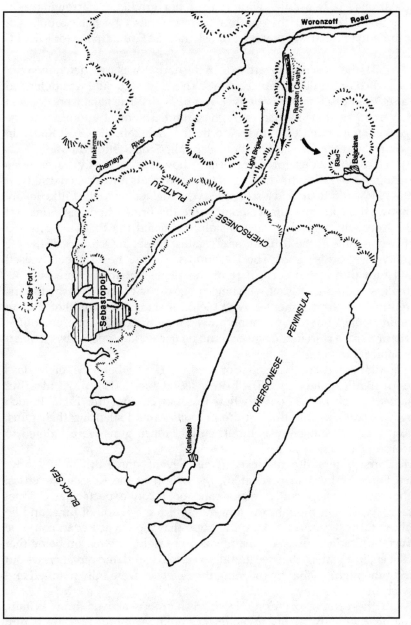

Map 7 Sebastopol Region

THE SIEGE OF SEBASTOPOL

Sebastopol harbor, home to the Black Sea Fleet, is a four-mile-long slot. The entrance is two miles wide, the harbor gradually narrowing as it penetrates inland. On the south side, surrounded by Sebastopol, is a two-mile-long tongue of water, variously named Southern Bay or Man-of-War Harbor.

By 1854, the west or seaward side of the harbor was well defended with forts and coast artillery emplacements. The landward side was defended by a series of disconnected but overlapping walls. The gaps were covered by six main bastions located on high ground. The most important to the siege were the Little Redan to the north, the Malakoff, the Great Redan in the center, and the Flagstaff Bastion, also called the Bastion du Mât.

Allied preparations for siege began, however modestly, as early as September 1854, with the digging of entrenchments. The French dug west of the Woronzoff Road and also between the Malakoff and the Little Redan. In between, facing the Great Redan, were the British trenches. Somerset Calthorpe, who was on Raglan's staff, estimated the Russians directed eighty-one guns at the British lines. Against these, in October 1854, were seventy-three British guns. The 24-pounder was the most frequently used allied gun during the early part of the siege. But there were also 32-pounders, some 8-inch guns with long-range capacity, and 10-inch mortars. The British also experimented with their new Lancaster gun that shot an oval projectile. The stubby cannon proved inaccurate (only one shot out of thirty fired hit a ship in the harbor), and its use was hampered by frequent mechanical problems.

The first allied bombardment opened on 17 October 1854, eight days after the Battle of Balaclava. The British, alone, fired 21,881 projectiles. But disaster struck at 8:45 A.M., when Russian counter-fire hit a French magazine, causing about a hundred casualties and silencing their guns. Another French battery was hit. Then all French guns were ordered to discontinue firing.

The first bombardment lacked focus. Seventy-three British and fifty-three French guns had fired along the length of the Russian defenses. Although debris flew in all directions and looked quite spectacular, Colonel Charles Windham thought the long-range firing a waste of time, and he chalked up to wishful thinking the hope that the Great Redan could be reduced by cannon fire. Windham was quite right, one reason being that Todleben, in a pattern that became all too familiar, ordered repair crews out during the night so that by morning the defenses were fully manned and serviceable.

With the coming of spring 1855, fresh troops arrived from Britain, bringing the army to just over 48,000 men. Anthony Sterling, Colin Campbell's brigade major, wanted men in their mid-twenties or older who possessed the strength to withstand the rigors of campaigning. What the

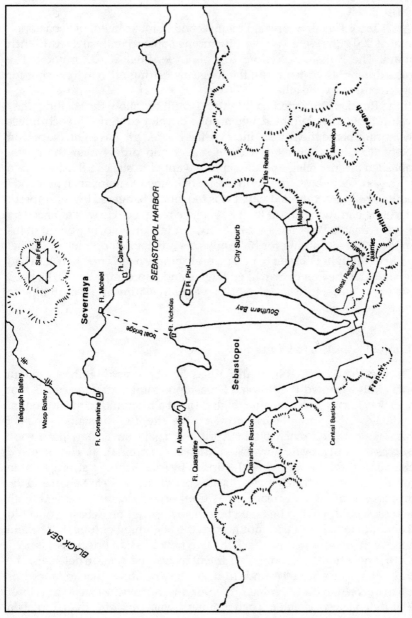

Map 8 Sebastopol

British received, according to Sterling, were pale and weak boys in their
teens who were barely trained. But the Turkish contingent grew by several
thousand, and a hardy Sardinian unit arrived. The French army swelled to
90,000.

April 1855: The allies opened their second bombardment of Sebastopol.
A total of 520 guns were involved, including some recently arrived 13-inch
mortars. The British, according to Calthorpe, fired 30,633 rounds. The
bombardment lasted ten days, the Russians getting off only one shot for
every five fired by the allies.

If the Russians expected an infantry assault to follow the shelling, they
were undoubtedly delighted when none developed. Since French forces
now outnumbered the British, their wishes carried great weight. Napoleon
III kept flooding Canrobert with messages and orders over the newly
established electric telegraph. Bonaparte wanted to starve Sebastopol into
submission. Canrobert, timid and fearful of losing too many men in bloody
assaults, willingly complied. But it was too much. Badgered by his emperor
and feeling a growing strain with Raglan, he resigned. He was replaced by
General Aimable Pélissier, a short, feisty, crude man who, in pursuit of his
own ideas, cared nothing for his emperor's amateurish opinions. Colonel
Windham thought Pélissier to be a prime example of bad manners and bad
language. But the Frenchman liked Raglan and, more importantly, he liked
many of his ideas. Pélissier also had a very large army and was itching to
use it.

Limited Attack, 6 to 9 June 1855

During the March lull in the allied bombardment, Prince Mikhail
Gortchakoff assumed the Russian Sebastopol command. One of his first
orders was to take the Mamelon, high ground a thousand yards in front of
the Malakoff. Mounting thirty guns on the site, the Russians launched
sorties against the French on 18 April and again on 5 May. Both were
unsuccessful, but they demonstrated Russian determination. They showed
the same determination against the British by establishing a strongpoint in
a gravel pit, dubbed the Quarries, located between the Great Redan and the
right flank of the British trenches. As Calthorpe correctly observed, both
positions would have to be taken before any assault on Sebastopol could
be contemplated. Pélissier announced at the beginning of June that he and
Raglan were determined to attack the two new Russian positions.

On 6 June, a tremendous bombardment rocked the Russian defenses. The
British fired nearly 33,000 rounds from artillery positions that advanced, as
Vauban decreed in the seventeenth century, as the trenches were dug closer
to the defensive perimeter. Their gunnery was very effective. Todleben
called it murderous. This time the Russians responded with only one shot
for every thirty from allied guns. Somehow, Todleben's civilian work force
managed to repair most of the damage.

At 6:00 A.M. the French infantry charged, swarming into the Mamelon and the bastion known as the Ouvrages Blanc. The Russians counter-attacked, but the French held at a cost of 3,000 casualties. Seeing the Mamelon in French hands, Raglan ordered his troops to take the Quarries. The Russian counter-attacked six times. The British troops, totalling 1,200 men, half of whom were now casualties, held on to their newly won position.

The Great Redan and the Malakoff loomed before the attackers. They would have to be taken. It was too late to discuss the military necessity of such attacks. Honor had to be served. After suffering so much, having dug so many graves, only a conclusive victory was going to satisfy the allies.

The Assault of 18 June 1855

A final assault was scheduled for 18 June. The plan called for a massive two-hour bombardment to soften the defenses. As diversionary move-ments developed on the flanks, the French—18,000 men in three columns—would attack the Malakoff. A rocket was to signal their advance. Then the British, 8,000 strong, would attack the Great Redan.

The Redan was modeled after the French caponire, having two tiers with casemented guns. It sat atop a 300 foot hill. Both diagonal walls were 15 feet high and 210 feet long. An outer ditch, 20 feet deep and 14 feet wide, girdled the walls. The Russians also constructed an abatis—a tangle of felled trees and thorn bushes—50 yards in front of the Redan.

The British planned to attack the Great Redan in three columns. Each had a hundred riflemen to lead the attack and kill Russian sharpshooters and gunners. There were 10 sappers in each column to help cross the ditch, and 200 men carrying 20 ladders. The main assault groups of 400 men per column, each reinforced by another 800, were to follow the ladder parties. The columns, huddling all night in cold and wet trenches, needed to cross 450 yards of open ground—the killing zone—to reach the Redan.

Promptly at 4:00 A.M., the artillery opened fire, the number of guns, depending on one's source, varying between 600 and 800. The bombard-ment smashed the Sebastopol defenses. Whole sections of parapets disap-peared, and cannon were destroyed outright or dis-mounted. Optimism ran high among the allies that all would go well. But this was the Crimea, and the plan was already unravelling.

First, Pélissier got in an argument with General Pierre Bosquet, com-manding the French assault force, and replaced him with St. Jean d'Angely, who knew neither the troops nor the terrain. Second, d'Angely complained that he could not expect his men to remain safely concealed for two hours until the attack signal. Pélissier unilaterally advanced the assault time and only then told Raglan, who had no option but to agree. Third, to everyone's astonishment, General Mayran's troops on the French right moved into action between the Little Redan and the harbor batteries. Although several of his staff officers assured him he was mistaken, Mayran confused a sparking artillery projectile for the signal rocket to advance. The Russians immediately opened fire with guns withdrawn during the previous night to protect them from the allied shelling. The French withered under the fire. Mayran was hit and carried from the field. Now there was nothing else for it: Pélissier fired the signal rocket. The French army advanced, confused by altered timing and lacking reinforcements that were understandably late getting into proper position. Russian artillery pounded the advancing columns.

Dawn broke, and Raglan could see clearly that the French attack was crumbling. Rather than renew the bombardment to counter the Russian cannonade, Raglan took the advice of Sir George Brown and ordered an immediate British attack.

Everything that could go wrong did. Those British guns that were still firing independently were ordered to cease. The men in the cramped trenches staggered forward. No one bothered to calculate the effects on them of the cold and wet night, much of it without sleep and without food. All order was immediately lost. They were raked by Russian gunfire as they "went over the top." The British sharpshooters went down. The ladder parties were cut to pieces as they eagerly abandoned their loads and sought refuge. Officers, exposing themselves to enemy fire, urged the men on to no avail.

The British assault came to a bloody halt. French casualties were 3,051, and the British lost 1,553. Charles Windham concluded that the plan was haphazard in its inception and that the Russians were not going to surrender just because the British troops gave a hearty cheer just before charging.

Ten days after the attack, Lord Raglan died of cholera.

The September Attack

Despite the eulogies following his death, Raglan became the goat, not the Wellington, of the Crimean expedition. He was the field commander and was responsible for what happened. But during the previous winter and spring, the English press blasted the government, and a parliamentary inquiry called into question the whole conduct of the war. Even though many wrongs were made right by June 1855, the failure of the Redan assault stimulated new critical waves. The press and the public wanted a new commander who had imagination and vision, one with experience and a little dash.

The government, true to its ways and deaf to the outcries, selected Sir James Simpson to lead the army. He was a sixty-three-year-old Guardsman who had last seen action at Waterloo.

All that Simpson and Pélissier had to do was wait for the Russians to run up the white flag. For, even though the allies could not penetrate Sebastopol's defenses, the Russian army suffered severe and debilitating casualties. On 16 August, the Russians attacked French and Sardinian positions along the Chernaya River that feeds into Sebastopol harbor. The Russians left 8,000 dead on the battlefield. Beginning the next day, the allies again subjected Sebastopol to a prolonged bombardment, causing a thousand casualties each day. Unwittingly, the allies were bleeding the Russians to death.

Waiting was not what Simpson and Pélissier did best. A fascination with a conclusive victory spurred the commanders. In a mood anticipating the bloody assaults of World War I, they thought that with more troops, a heavier bombardment, and one more try they could master the Sebastopol defenses.

Pélissier took the lead in planning the next attack. Simpson subscribed to it not only because the French army was larger but also because he lacked any ideas of his own. The plan called for a three-day bombardment followed by a two-stage assault. First, the French would attack the Malakoff, the Little Redan, and all intervening positions. The Malakoff secured, a signal rocket would be fired to commence the second assault. French and British troops were to attack from the end of Man-of-War Harbor west to the so-called Barracks Battery. The British primary target was still the Great Redan. Simpson did plan the British phase of the assault, a dangerous recapitulation of the June debacle: 200 riflemen were to lay down covering fire for forty ladder parties; a 200-man work party would bridge the ditch; 1,000 men would follow and attack the Redan. Garnett Wolseley called the plan faulty and puerile because it reeked of all the elements that had guaranteed the June failure. Moreover, officers and men from different regiments were thrown together in the various assault groups. Windham later complained that only one in fifty men recognized him.

On the morning of 5 September, 803 allied guns opened fire. The Russians reeled under the impact. The shelling continued through the next day and the next. By the morning of 8 September, 4,000 Russians lay dead and wounded.

At noon on the eighth, the French rushed forward, throwing ladders across the Malakoff ditch. Within only three minutes they were inside the bastion. A few minutes more and the position was completely theirs. The attack on the Little Redan was repulsed, however, with considerable loss.

At 12:10 P.M., Pélissier signalled Simpson that the Malakoff was in French hands. Simpson raised a flag bearing the cross of St. George to signal the British advance. The Russians fired grapeshot at 200 yards, and British casualties quickly mounted. Despite the intense fire, some men made it to the Great Redan and clambered up ladders and into the bastion. They were promptly killed. Most of the advancing troops, the few that were left, took cover at the base of the Redan. Many men, shocked by the carnage, never left their trenches.

Two thousand four hundred forty seven British troops were killed or wounded.

Windham bitterly noted that the "whole thing was a botch." The London *Examiner* soon expressed a growing consensus that "every blunder that had been committed on the 18th of June appears to have been more fatally repeated on this terrible day." Wolseley's assessment was quite right: the plan was both faulty and puerile.

Just as Pélissier and Simpson were wondering what to do next, a great explosion shook the Malakoff. Then a magazine behind the Little Redan exploded. Fires could be seen blazing across the town. At 4:00 A.M. on 9 September, the Great Redan magazine exploded, followed by those in the Flagstaff Bastion and the Garden Battery. Unknown to the allies, the explosions and fires covered a well-executed evacuation of Sebastopol.

CATEGORIES OF COMBAT

The Malta siege was an example of the beginnings of gunpowder warfare. Muzzle-loading cannon and the arquebus were the technical innovations that heightened the level of slaughter. The Sebastopol siege is an example of mid-nineteenth-century sieges that signalled the end of muzzle-loading gunpowder warfare. It would not be long before breach-loading and rapid-fire weapons were introduced. Yet, ends have a way of turning into beginnings. To understand the pivotal character of the Sebastopol siege we must turn to the categories of combat.

Were the subject not siege warfare, it would be necessary to discuss the confrontations between cavalry formations or those between cavalry and artillery or cavalry and infantry in some detail. Since the subject is sieges, cavalry actions were peripheral to the central issues of battle. Not only peripheral; largely irrelevant. That is not to minimize what the Heavy Brigade accomplished, or minimize the drama of the Light Brigade, or dismiss Campbell's stand with the 93rd Highlanders against Russian cavalry. Rather, these actions did not materially affect the outcome of the siege as such, however much they contributed to keeping the Russians away from allied lines.

Excepting the charge by the Heavy Brigade, the British cavalry was poorly used and handled throughout the campaign. They could have attacked the Russians retreating from the Alma with great effect, but Raglan would not release them. After the Heavy Brigade charged, Cardigan watched the Russian cavalry pass within 500 yards of the Light Brigade and did nothing. This much can be said: Never again did the Russian cavalry, much less their outlying army, pose a threat to the allies. For their part, the British cavalry was reduced to the role of crowd control.

Artillery versus Artillery

Artillery was the obvious weapon of the siege. Whose artillery would dominate was considered crucial to the outcome.

The Russians made clever use of their artillery by repairing destroyed emplacements at night when the British usually stopped firing, withdrawing many guns from harm's way, and disguising batteries. The Russian gunners were effective at long ranges, blowing up three British and French magazines. These explosions created the largest en masse casualties among the allied gunners. Obviously, the Russian artillery remained effective throughout the siege.

What, then, did the allied bombardments accomplish? Great amounts of masonry were blown to bits. Gun positions were destroyed or temporarily put out of action. Great numbers of casualties were inflicted. Yet, the allied infantry attacks suffered consistently high casualty rates. An anomaly lurks here.

One way to resolve the problem is to review the types of targets available to the allied gunners and the types of projectiles they used. Sebastopol had a six-mile perimeter, one-third of which faced the British. The Great Redan, with its massive walls, absorbed a high percentage of British artillery rounds. Three types of projectiles were used: round shot, some of it weighing 200 pounds; explosive shells; and shrapnel. Round shot had a bludgeoning effect but was not always efficient. Round shot could hit a parapet and ruin it or dismantle a gun carriage. It could penetrate some walls, but it might be fired at another wall at point-blank range and inflict little damage. In the end, round shot never did effectively bring down the Sebastopol walls. Explosive shells and shrapnel shells were detonated by timed fuses that needed to be cut just the right length to do the desired damage, a precise task not always achieved. Explosive shells did not necessarily explode on impact or after penetration. Their effect was mostly on the surface of things. That might cause some damage and kill, but the projectile was not able to consistently turn masonry into dust. Shrapnel was used to clear walls of defenders, a job done with considerable efficiency considering Russian losses. But shrapnel could not and did not penetrate encased guns. Consequently, despite long-term damage, the short-term effect of covering fire by allied artillery seeking optimum damage before infantry assaults did not have the desired results. Raglan and Pélissier reluctantly concluded after the June attack that they over-estimated the damage done by their artillery.

Artillery versus Infantry

The effectiveness of artillery on infantry in the open field was grimly demonstrated at the Alma. For example, the Russian Sousdal Regiment, already savaged by the marching fire of the Highland Brigade as they ascended the Kourgane Heights, was raked by two horse artillery batteries that followed the Scots. The Russians were in packed columns. The gunners could not miss. Entire rows of soldiers had their heads blown off. Unable to withstand the tempest of shot and shell, the Russians staggered away.

Attacking the fixed positions at Sebastopol was a different order of experience for both sides. Now the British were exposed to devastating fire, and it was the Russian gunners who held the advantage. They held that advantage because, despite the heavy and protracted bombardments, they were still able to man their stations. Calthorpe wrote of the "dreadful slaughter" of Mayran's French column during the 18 June attack. Already out of synchronization with the main assault, he marched his division directly into two artillery batteries that responded to his advance with explosive shells and grapeshot. The first attack on the Malakoff was equally disastrous, as the Russians tilted their gun muzzles downward and literally showered the attackers with grapeshot.

But the second attack on the Malakoff was successful because the French dug their approach trenches to within several yards of the wall. Thus, they shortened the killing zone. The shorter distance did not give the Russian gunners time to react. Additionally, Russian casualties from the preliminary bombardment were high and the wall tops were severely damaged. Smoke and fire obscured vision, and the stress caused by their constant exposure to allied fire was certainly considerable. Any efficiency the Russians enjoyed in the first attack was taken away because the second attack developed so quickly.

The British attack on the Great Redan was a different story. Doubtless, the Russians stationed there were severely punished by the September bombardment, but the Redan was a caponier. Although the gun emplacements on the upper level were damaged, those on the lower level were still very much operational. Furthermore, the British troops had to cover 450 yards of open ground. The Russian gunners therefore enjoyed firing at a distance, breaking up the British formations in the wide and lengthy killing zone. Those who made it to the wall were too few in number to take the bastion. Thus, the wider and longer the killing zone, the less likely an attack can succeed.

Infantry versus Infantry

The problem faced by the British and French infantry at Sebastopol was not really any different than that faced by the Turks at Malta or the Crusaders at Jerusalem. They were required to cross the killing zone between their trenches and the bastions and then climb the defensive walls in order to engage and overcome the Russian infantry.

In both the June and September attacks, the British plans were formulas for disaster because, as Colin Campbell and Duncan Cameron, who commanded the Black Watch concluded, only forty British soldiers would ever get to the wall top at one time, assuming nothing went wrong (a situation analogous to the attack by the Janissaries against Fort St. Elmo on Malta). But everything did go wrong. The riflemen who were supposed to clear the parapets were cut down. The ladder parties were shot to pieces. A high ratio of officers were killed or wounded, and those who survived were not often recognized by the men they commanded. The attacks collapsed into disorganization as the troops scrambled for cover and refused to move forward. The British infantry never got close to the Russian infantry, leaving the contest in control of the Russian artillery.

The French, as we know, quickly and successfully attacked the Malakoff in September. Their men pushed across the rapidly bridged ditch and into the bastion. The defenders were overwhelmed. By its very construction, a wall is not a defense in depth; thus, the wall that screened the Malakoff could not contain the numbers of infantry needed to push back the French once they crossed the ditch. The taking of the Malakoff was pivotal to the offense. Because of its position in the defensive perimeter, its conquest exposed other bastions to French fire from the flanks and rear. The loss of the Malakoff doubtlessly encouraged Gortchakoff to blow up the remaining bastions and evacuate Sebastopol.

A fair conclusion is suggested at this point: Except for the battles at the Alma and the Inkerman, opposing infantry formations did not engage. Instead, as in World War I to follow, the infantry bore the brunt of casualties, but at long range. Artillery, not rifle fire, was the persistent killer.

Prisoners and the Wounded

Few prisoners were taken by either side until Sebastopol was actually occupied by the allies. The Russians taken at the Alma were abandoned wounded. At the Inkerman, allied troops found 1,100 Russian wounded left on the field. Conversely, the Russians captured some troopers at the Charge of the Light Brigade and also captured Turks in the redoubts along Woronzoff Road. Charges were made after the Inkerman that the Russians bayoneted French and British wounded. An angry note was sent to the Russians, who replied that the allied generals were misinformed about such incidents.

British casualties during the Crimean War averaged over 2,000 men per battle. The differences between killed and wounded were reasonably constant. At the Alma, 362 were killed and 1,621 wounded. In the first assault on the Redan, 266 were killed and 1,287 wounded. The second attack left 385 dead and 1,886 wounded. These numbers seem minuscule in comparison to twentieth-century battles, but it must be remembered that the effective British force at the Alma was around 24,000 and that the army seldom swelled above 40,000. Equally, the shock of these casualty figures among the British public reflected the fact that their army did not fight a major engagement between Waterloo and the Crimea.

Wounds were mostly from rifle and musket balls and artillery shells of various types. Many men of both sides also suffered bayonet wounds from such closely fought battles as the Inkerman and the Malakoff.

Artillery wounds were related to the projectile used. Round shot either shattered a body or severed a limb. During the June assault, a signalman was hit in the chest by a round shot that, as Calthorpe observed, "literally knocked him to pieces." Nearby, Captain Brown of the 88th Regiment was hit by a shot that cleanly severed his arm. At the Alma, a sergeant's arm was severed. He picked it up and calmly walked to the rear. Grapeshot could shred an entire rank of men if the cluster kept a closed pattern. But Sir Harry James was leaning out of a parapet, talking to Raglan, when a single errant piece of grape only grazed his head.

Most Russian units still used smooth-bore muskets; most of the British and French used the new Minié rifle. Muskets were notoriously inaccurate after a hundred yards, but a sharpshooter from the Rifle Brigade, using a Minié, allegedly knocked a cossack officer out of his saddle at a reported 1,300 yards.

A major problem during the war was retrieval of the wounded from the battlefields. Even if a truce was called for that purpose, as when the French took the Mamelon, wounded were often difficult to find. At the Alma, wounded were still being brought into the regimental surgeries two days after the battle. The problem was worse at the Inkerman because of the rugged terrain. Moreover, the men were often in wretched shape, their wounds exacerbated by thirst, weakness, diseases already contracted, and infection from ground contact. The regimental surgeons did the best they could.

If the wounded survived the regimental surgery, they were shipped to a miserable excuse for a hospital in Balaclava, there to await shipment to Scutari in Turkey. Overcrowded and disease-ridden, the Scutari hospitals were an utter and inhuman disgrace. The chances of survival early in the war were poor to slim. Only after the reforms of Florence Nightingale did the situation improve.

The numbers of wounded were greater than could be attended. Were that situation not tragic enough, the medical facilities and staffs were completely overwhelmed by the sick. Various diseases killed 15,724 British troops, cholera being the most prevalent cause.

The Will to Combat

Such words as *resolute, brave, determined*, and *steadfast* are commonly used to describe the Sebastopol defenders. All are worthy but they are also rather vague. There were, in fact, some quite specific factors related to the willingness of the defenders to live and die under the conditions of a siege, considering that the Sebastopol hospitals were, if anything, worse than the British. The port city was meant to be defended, the possibility of siege a reality to anyone living there. The numbers of forts and bastions probably encouraged a reasonable expectation that the garrison could withstand a siege. Given their immediate access to the Black Sea, the presence of the fleet, and their proximity to such bases as Odessa, there was the added expectation that, should they be subjected to a siege, relief was nearby.

But the unity of the civilian population was as important as all the military preparations. Sebastopol was not a city that just happened to develop on the Crimean coast. It was a city meant to be a military base, a city consumed by its military installations. Practically the entire population was either related to or economically dependent on the garrison. That population was one, ethnically, religiously, and linguistically. There was no minority population hovering in the shadows. There were no strangers to cast out.

When those factors were woven together under the general strain of war and the immediate stress of siege, the result was a sense of common danger, common loss, and common destiny. Vice Admiral Vladimir Korniloff was the driving force in making the population consciously realize that commonality. Todleben may have recruited the civilian population to labor on the defenses, but Korniloff co-opted their souls. Much as in the First Crusade, he had holy relics paraded around the walls, prayers and chants offered. And the priests blessed all. The great and righteous efforts of the population, mirrored some ninety years later by their descendants against a Nazi siege, took on the character of a holy war. God was surely on their side.

But what sustained the British army in the field, given the atrocious conditions they experienced early in the campaign and the losses incurred attacking the Great Redan? The answer is deceptively simple. They sustained themselves. They were a volunteer professional army. Some of the regiments, such as the Guards, had not been out of Britain or experienced combat since Waterloo. But others were battle tested, enduring the rigors of garrison duty in strange lands and fighting in the many Victorian "little wars." They were long service men, in for twenty years, and they knew what soldiering was about. Whether from the middle class or the rookeries of Britain's industrial cities or from Ireland's bleak rural districts, they shared common bonds of tradition and experience within their regiments. Under the conditions of war and the immediate stress of siege operations, they came to depend on one another, even including the recent recruits. They were brothers in common suffering, whether from the dangers of shot and shell in the killing zones before the Redan, or from heat and cold, or from disease. They might die where they stood but they would die together. Thus, when Colin Campbell told his "thin red line" there would be no retreat, that they must die where they stood, Private John Scott called back to him, "Ay, ay, Sir Colin, and needs be we'll do just that." There was no religious crusade among these men. Instead, there was a professional, prideful imperative to do their duty. If that meant dying together, so be it; if that meant not getting out of the trenches before the Redan, then so be it. For the first duty of the good soldier is to survive. No one was shot for disobeying orders. The attack plan was ultimately too stupid for that.

The men hung on. Some even got home.

AFTERMATH

The Russians did not collapse into disintegration. Gortchakoff planned and executed an orderly withdrawal from Sebastopol by marching 35,000 to 40,000 troops and civilians across a floating bridge near the harbor entrance. They found refuge in Severnaya and its protective forts. Dutifully, the allies brought forward their artillery and bombarded them, but there was no urge to attack. The governments, exhausted and bored by the whole affair, agreed to hold a peace conference in February 1856. An accord was signed at the end of March.

Simpson resigned as commander of the British expeditionary force and was replaced by William Codrington, a Guardsman. The young and inexperienced British reinforcements underwent intense training and were turned into first-rate soldiers. Their food, housing, medical, and recreational facilities were much improved, making Crimean duty quite acceptable.

Most of the generals disappeared from the limelight. Most, but not all. Lords Lucan and Cardigan were dragged through the newspapers, as blame for the disastrous Charge of the Light Brigade was debated. The Duke of Cambridge, who distinguished himself at the Inkerman, became commander-in-chief at the Horse Guards. Colin Campbell went on to command the British army in India during the Great Mutiny of 1857 to 1859. Many junior officers, such as Wolseley and Windham, would have long careers—some more distinguished than others.

Spurred by the ineptitudes displayed in the war, the British army underwent a series of reforms. The regimental system was given new life as the old numbers were replaced by names that reflected royal patronage or the regional placement of new permanent depots. For example, the 93rd Highlanders ultimately became the Argyll and Sutherland Highlanders. Enlistments were shortened to twelve years, and a reserve system was inaugurated. Significantly, the purchase system of obtaining commissions and promotions was abolished in favor of professional training at the Royal Military College in Sandhurst.

The French army, a model of efficiency at the beginning of the war, dwindled from neglect. More French soldiers died of disease following the fall of Sebastopol then ever before. Supplies diminished. Morale dropped. They became a forgotten army, shoved into the background by an emperor searching for new glories.

What, then, did Sebastopol mean? I shall let the general historians argue its political importance. From a strictly military viewpoint, to lean on a literary conceit, the taking of Sebastopol was "a lame and impotent conclusion" to the war. True, the fortifications were destroyed and the city was abandoned for years. The Black Sea Fleet was rendered ineffective. But the Russian army was not defeated.

Yet, there was a long-range importance to the siege of Sebastopol, so often dismissed in modern literature as a minor event. For the siege, much like the Malta siege before it and the American Civil War sieges to follow, was a battle of attrition. Artillery did not open gaping holes in the defenses, nor did it stop the allied assaults against them; artillery did make both forces bleed. But weaponry, as noted earlier, soon changed. What did not change was the tactical stagnation that insisted frontal assaults were the proper approach to siege warfare. The consequences of that differential development between technology on the one side and tactics on the other were played out in World War I.

Illustration 1: The Capture of Jerusalem. This miniature illuminates a thirteenth-century version of William of Tyre's *History of the Crusades*. The First Crusaders are seen using catapults, ladders, and a siege tower. Above, in gothic frames, like stained glass windows, are scenes from the Passion of Christ. (By permission of the Bibliothèque Nationale, Paris. MS Fr. 352, fol. 52v.)

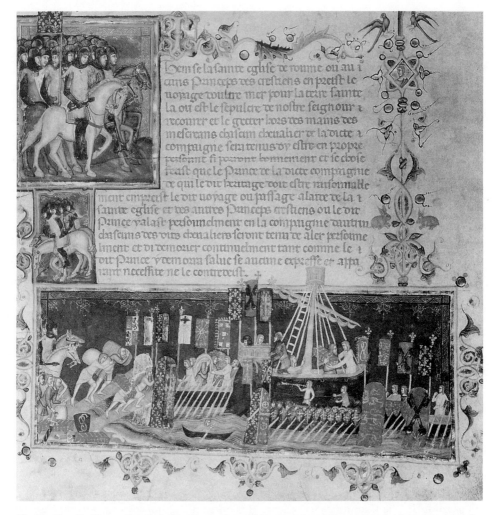

Illustration 2: Departing for the Crusades. This miniature illuminates a late fourteenth-century Statutes of the Order of St. Esprit. Taking ships from Marseilles and Venice gave later Crusaders a mobility not enjoyed in the First Crusade. (By permission of the Bibliothèque Nationale, Paris. MS Fr. 4274, fol. 6r.)

Illustration 3: An Artist's Interpretation of the Fall of Sebastopol, 8 September 1855. From a lithograph by and after Thomas Packer. The Great Redan is left of center, and the Little Redan is to the far right. The three vertical explosions are Russian demolitions. (By permission of the Parker Gallery, London.)

Illustration 4: Three Gurkhas in a Trench at Kut-al-Amara. One of them is using a periscope to observe the Turkish trenches. (By permission of the Imperial War Museum, London.)

Illustration 5: British Home-made Weapons at Kut-al-Amara. These include a remote control sniper rifle, bombs, and a mortar made from aircraft parts. (By permission of the Imperial War Museum, London.)

Illustration 6: Smoke Rising Above Singapore. The Japanese bombed Singapore with near impunity. The smoke from oil storage tanks blanketed the city. (By permission of the Imperial War Museum, London.)

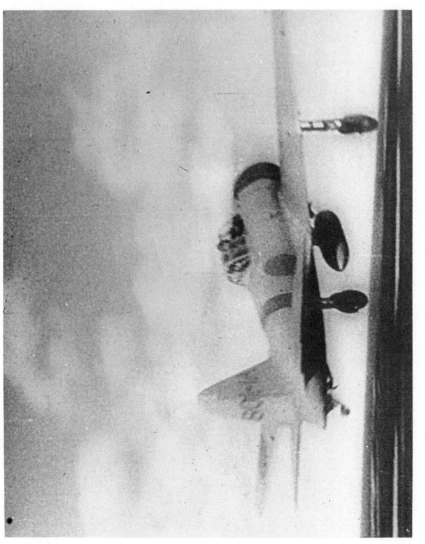

Illustration 7: A Japanese Zero Fighter. This carrier plane is similar to the type that helped create offensive domination over the defenders of Singapore. (Courtesy of the National Archives.)

Illustration 8: U.S. Sherman Tank. This was the principal Allied battle tank of World War II. With good speed, range, and a 75mm gun, the Shermans dominated the German Pz Mark IV tanks, but not the later Tigers. (Courtesy of the National Archives.)

Illustration 9: German Tiger Tank. This one was captured by U.S. forces. An 88mm gun and 100mm armor made it a formidable weapon. It was developed too late for the sieges at Leningrad and Stalingrad, but on the Western Front, where it became largely a defensive weapon, it took five Shermans to knock out one Tiger. (Courtesy of the National Archives.)

Illustration 10: Two U.S. Abrams M1A1 Tanks in the Kuwait Desert. These tanks, part of the Marine Corps battle group, participated in Operation Desert Storm. The Abrams out-maneuvered and out-fought Soviet-built Iraqi tanks and easily penetrated their defensive lines. (Courtesy U.S. Department of Defense.)

Illustration 11: U.S. F-117A Stealth Fighter. This plane, its distinctive silhouette seen from beneath, was part of the 37th Tactical Fighter Wing about to be deployed to Saudi Arabia. The F-117A played a key role in escalating Iraqi defenses. (Courtesy U.S. Department of Defense.)

Chapter 5

Kut-al-Amara, December 1915 to April 1916

In late 1915, British Major General Charles Townshend, unable to push his Anglo-Indian division to Baghdad, retreated down the Tigris River to Kut-al-Amara. The Turks immediately surrounded the force, their siege and Townshend's response to it becoming passive through the early months of 1916. All efforts to relieve Kut failed, at great cost to the British. But the siege opened an unanticipated theatre of war.

Mesopotamia, land of the Tigris and Euphrates rivers, birthplace of ancient civilizations, was dirt poor in 1914. The Turkish rulers of the region had crippled it by neglect. The canal system that had fed rich farmlands was broken down. The Tigris was filled with silt and ran shallow in the beastly hot summers and overflowed its banks with winter rains and spring floods, turning the surrounding countryside into bogs. There were too few roads and little rail. The flat land was unrelieved except for scattered villages and a couple of cities, Baghdad and Basra, that offered few amenities.

Yet, in 1914, the British army marched into that unforgiving environment short of men, short of artillery, without reliable maps, lacking sufficient transport and medical facilities, opening a theater of war that would consume men and materiel at a rate that threatened operations on the Western Front in France.

No one expected a major campaign in Mesopotamia when World War I started. But the campaign developed, anyway, all topsy-turvy. The answer as to why that happened centers around the nearly forgotten and unplanned siege of British and Indian troops in Kut-al-Amara, an insignificant and grubby little town located on a U-shaped bend of the Tigris River.

CONFUSED GOALS

5 November 1914: The British declared war on Turkey to reverse increasing German influence in Mesopotamia signalled by the Berlin-to-Baghdad railroad. German aspirations made it clear they might push through Mesopotamia and threaten Egypt and the Suez Canal and, more immediately, endanger oil facilities in lower Mesopotamia (now part of Iraq) and in Persia (now Iran).

Anticipating a declaration of war, Indian Expeditionary Force D sailed from Bombay in mid-October 1914. It consisted of elements of the 6th (Poona) Division. On 3 November, they landed on the left bank of the Shatt-al-Arab to protect the oil facilities at Abadan. The division then moved north against limited Turkish resistance and, on 21 November, took Basra.

General Sir Arthur Barrett, the commander, understandably wanted a buffer zone between Basra and the Turkish army that had obligingly retreated. His orders allowed him to advance as far north as he thought necessary to protect Basra. Qurna, where the Tigris and Euphrates join to form the Shatt-al-Arab, seemed logical. On 3 December, Barrett moved against Qurna. The garrison surrendered on the nineteenth. The north rim of the Persian Gulf was secured. London was satisfied.

Enter General Sir John Nixon.

Nixon was given command of the newly constituted 2nd Indian Army Corps, a force that included the Poona Division, the 12th Indian Division under Major General George Gorringe, the 6th Cavalry Brigade, and various support troops. Nixon was instructed by Sir Beauchamp Duff, commander-in-chief in India, to prepare a plan for an advance to Baghdad. This idea was not approved either by Lord Charles Hardinge, India's viceroy, or by the London War Cabinet. A copy of the instruction in fact was mailed to London, but it did not arrive until May 1916. London believed with some justification that, considering the military commitments being made, the Indian government would assume full responsibility for Mesopotamia. However, no sooner was Nixon in office than he requested more troops to counter what he believed to be an impending Turkish counter-offensive. London let it be known that it would not sanction any operations beyond the established defensive perimeters. This communication was forwarded to Nixon by the Indian government with its notation that he should use his own discretion in protecting the oil facilities.

That addendum opened the door for Nixon's own wishes to take Baghdad. As Lieutenant Colonel A. Kearsey notes in his analysis of the campaign, Nixon believed that his orders constituted a policy change from defense to offense. Accordingly, operations commenced against the Turks still in the Basra area, then against Ahwaz, thus securing a northeast perimeter. Action against Nasiriyeh was undertaken in July 1915, securing the west flank of Qurna. Meantime, in May, Nixon decided to advance against Amara, 60 miles above Qurna on the Tigris River. Major General Charles Townshend, now commanding the Poona Division, was given the mission. The Turks, under the command of Nur-ud-Din, withdrew 153 miles further upriver to Kut-al-Amara. The temptations were too great: If the Turks retreated every time a British soldier took the field, then a march against Baghdad was not only possible but inevitable.

To understand how a limited campaign escalated into an unwanted and wasteful siege, we must first grasp the nature of the British leaders in the region and their perceptions of the resources available to them.

BRITISH LEADERSHIP IN MESOPOTAMIA

Both the London war cabinet and the Indian government were willing to accept advice from their field commander based on the rationale that those on the spot knew best. The problem was that neither authority really understood General Nixon, and they failed to fully appreciate the well-known vagaries of General Townshend's character.

Sir John Nixon, age fifty-eight, was born in India in 1857, the year the Great Indian Mutiny erupted. His father was an officer in the Bombay Infantry. Not surprisingly, John was sent to the Royal Military College at Sandhurst and graduated at age eighteen. Returning to India, he saw action along the Northwest Frontier. Beginning in 1881, he spent fifteen years doing staff work and was brevetted a lieutenant colonel in 1896. He subsequently commanded a cavalry column in the Boer War and was made Companion of the Bath in 1901. Back in India, he received a series of promotions to general in 1914.

Nixon's career was solid but not spectacular. His big chance, indeed, his last chance, to make his mark came with his appointment to Mesopotamia. Barrett's early success against the Turks filled Nixon with optimism. The march against Baghdad was a realistic goal, for he inherited from Beauchamp-Duff a mental trap in which each move up the Tigris necessitated a further move upriver that needed to be secured by yet another move upriver.

What Nixon—and others who should have known better—did not realize was that the early successes were an illusion. Yes, the British and Indian troops did defeat Turks. But which ones? The Turks were faced with a triple threat: The British were marching up the Tigris, other British and Australian troops had landed in the Dardanelles, and the Russians were a potential problem on their northeast frontier. Of the three, the Dardanelles seemed the greatest threat. So it was into the cauldron of Gallipoli that the Turks sent their best troops.

Unknown to Nixon, that commitment meant that all the Turks could offer the British in lower Mesopotamia were poorly trained Arab levies, whose reliability was always open to question, and second-rate Turkish troops fit only for garrison duty. When Nixon was informed later in the campaign that 15,000 Turkish troops were at Ctesiphon, he did not believe the report. Nor did he believe later information from London that another 30,000 Turks were marching to reinforce Baghdad and that the German General von der Goltz was taking overall command in Mesopotamia and that a clever Turk named Khalil Pasha was to be the frontline commander. It was as if Nixon resented any facts that intruded on his growing fantasy.

Not only did Nixon refuse to believe reliable intelligence reports, he also consistently over-estimated the condition of his men, the capacity of their weapons, and their ability to survive, much less fight, in a hostile physical environment where the only source of water was the muck-filled Tigris. He under-estimated the capacities of his medical staff to do their job faced with a shortage of facilities and supplies that rivalled the Crimean War scandals, and consistently under-estimated the number of wounded that any given battle would produce. He over-estimated the capacities of the primitive docking facilities at Basra to handle the needs of a major campaign. Worst of all, his mind was bound by the gallop-and-dash tactics of the Northwest Frontier. He was incapable of foreseeing that Mesopotamia would breed the kinds of battles being fought on the Western Front. Therefore, Nixon offered his superiors an uninformed, naive optimism, his plans rooted in ignorance, half-truths, deceptions, and outright lies.

One reason for Nixon's fraudulent behavior is that he shared one characteristic with his colleagues in France. He was a château general, commanding from Basra or Amara, nearing the front lines only a few times, invisible to his troops, never really interested in the visual proof of his folly as the wounded poured downriver. He was surrounded by a staff too willing to agree with his every assessment and plan.

But there was also a second reason for Nixon's behavior: Major General Charles Vere Ferrers Townshend.

Townshend is at best a study in contrasts. His father was a minor railway official of no special gifts or pretensions—except one. He was presumptive heir to the marquessate of Townshend. He never came close to the title himself but Charles, as grandson of the marquess, yearned for it, and the circumstances of life brought him very close to assuming it.

Townshend was commissioned in 1881 and posted to the Royal Marine Light Infantry. His first action was with the relief column sent to Khartoum, Egypt. He was good enough to be mentioned in dispatches. In 1886, he was transferred to the Indian army and there hopped from one regiment to another, seeking career advantages. He campaigned along the Northwest Frontier where, for forty-six days, he and his men withstood siege by tribesmen at Chitral, an action for which he was awarded a C.B. In Egypt again in 1898, he earned a Distinguished Service Order for actions at Atabara and Khartoum and was brevetted a lieutenant colonel.

He returned to India in 1899, but the Boer War proved a greater attraction. Off he went but no sooner did he arrive than he left for England, having found "the atmosphere in South Africa uncongenial," meaning

nt or his superiors were put off by his

nd's liking. As Kearsey states, his excel-
military historian were unfortunately
ted to being a professional houseguest,
mboyant for his superiors, Townshend
d him a brigadier general in Rawilpindi.
s sent to Mesopotamia and given com-
reputation preceded him and he was
er officers who found him to be quite
ss and regaled them with stories.
saw in Townshend's visits a means by
hen who had to carry out his orders.
neral needed an audience. Townshend
eption of the army, meant promotion.
when he earlier shifted between units.
eneral and he wanted to be Marquess
arch on Baghdad, not to subdue the
nor of that ancient city. What a mar-
...that would be.

To achieve his personal ambitions, Townshend alternately exaggerated and minimized his division's capacities. He did much the same with his estimation of his Turkish opposition. In short, Major General Townshend was quite capable of lying.

Consequently, the Mesopotamian campaign lurched forward into a swamp of mendacity, misconceptions, faulty assumptions, faulty intelligence, and cross-purposes.

THE BRITISH ARMY IN MESOPOTAMIA

As early as July 1914, Lord Hardinge informed planners in London that only two Indian divisions, perhaps three, and a cavalry brigade would be available to serve in Europe should war break out. Any demands beyond that would endanger India's internal safety. But the opening of the Mesopotamian front was seen by all as a modest affair both in its goals and troop demands. What nobody seemed to realize was that the Indian army was ill prepared to fight any campaign beyond its borders.

When hostilities began in Europe in August 1914, British officers and non-commissioned officers of any experience serving in India were sent back to England to train Lord Kitchener's New Army. The Indian army had to make do with the young, the inexperienced, or the over-aged. India was short of artillery and rifle ammunition and did not have the means to make any. The available artillery pieces were fewer than a modern division required, and there was a critical shortage of heavy artillery. As Kearsey notes, the Indian army possessed only four aircraft, lacked radio equip-

ment, and lacked essential medical services and supplies. The reserve force
was small and most of the men had less than eight months of training.
British regiments could only draw replacements from depots in Britain,
very difficult once the Western Front developed an insatiable need for men
and yet more men.

The 6th (Poona) Division was at the heart of the siege at Kut-al-Amara.
Although units were constantly shifted about, the structure of the 6th
followed that of other Indian divisions, except that there was one additional
brigade. Townshend commanded four infantry brigades of four battalions
each. One battalion was British and three were Indian. For instance, the 16th
Brigade of Major General W. J. Delamain contained the 2nd Dorsetshires,
the 66th Punjabis, the 104th Rifles, and the 117th Mahrattas. The division
also included a pioneer unit, engineers, signallers, supply and transport
units. Attached was an artillery brigade of about thirty-five guns, mostly
18-pounders.

Substantial problems limited the division's capabilities. A standard
division in 1914 was armed with fifty-six 18-pounders plus several howitzers. Neither the Poona Division nor any other in Mesopotamia was supplied that number. Although the 18-pounder was a solid weapon, the
division needed heavier artillery, more howitzers, and a large number of
mortars—but they did not discover any of this until it was too late and,
even then, there was nothing they could have done. The problems that
plagued corps-level service contingents also plagued the Poona Division.
They did not have any transport, they were short on medical services, and
their communications system was poor. Were all this not enough, the British
battalions within the division were soon pared down to about half strength,
the men diverted to other, usually non-combat, duties.

But Nixon and Townshend shared the thought that the Turks were no
match for their plucky troops. Just as on the Northwest Frontier, a bit of
dash, some quick maneuvering, and rows of British steel would send the
beggars packing. What these two leaders did not remember was that such
assumptions were often dashed in the rocky wastelands of the Northwest
Frontier by more than one band of raggedy tribesmen.

THE CAMPAIGN

In late May 1915, Joseph Austin Chamberlain became secretary of state
for India. Hardinge, the viceroy, now fully caught in the Baghdad plan,
wired him in London that an advance against Kut-al-Amara was essential;
Nixon also cabled Chamberlain, telling him that taking Kut was necessary
to the security of the oil facilities. The new secretary, probably befuddled,
sanctioned the advance on 20 August. The chain of involvement up the
Tigris River was getting longer, and authorities in India and London lacked
the fortitude to cut it.

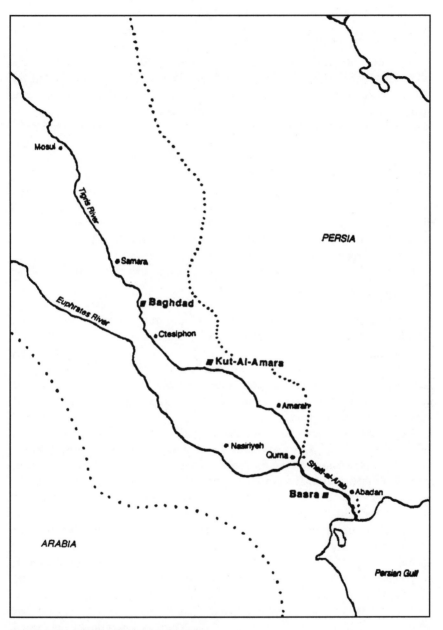

Map 9 Lower Mesopotamia

On to Ctesiphon

The northward advance began 1 September, when Townshend's division went upriver to Ali Gharbi. This modest movement was not without a dispute. Townshend, quite rightly as things turned out, wanted supplies and ammunition for six months' campaigning positioned at Amara. Nixon adamantly refused, declaring that only six weeks' reserve was allotted the whole of the Mesopotamian command. Townshend must tailor his plans to that reality. But Townshend was convinced that, considering current supply and transport limitations, he could not sustain a protracted campaign.

The next phase of the march was in heat that soared to 120° F. Some men were transported upriver by boat, but most slogged across the parched, featureless ground. Their goal was the Turkish defense line a few miles below Kut, where trenches extended to the Suwada marsh. The Turks built three redoubts north of the marsh, extending to the Ataba marsh. Southward, on the opposite side of the river was the so-called Es Sinn Line, a heavily entrenched position three miles long. By 27 September, Townshend's troops were ready to attack. Nixon, in a rare moment, joined Townshend at his command post.

The attack plan was clever. A direct assault on the Es Sinn Line would convince the Turks that was the point of the main attack. The redoubts would also be attacked. Meantime, a reinforced brigade was to march north beyond the last redoubt and flank the Turkish line. But the plan was poorly coordinated and executed. The flanking brigade got lost, and troops working along the Tigris River bank met unexpectedly stiff resistance. In the end, however, Nur-ud-Din had enough and withdrew his troops northward, abandoning Kut-al-Amara.

Buy 5 October one of Townshend's brigades was at Aziziyeh, sixty miles above Kut. On 24 October, over Lord Kitchener's objections, London renewed permission to take Baghdad. Nixon was optimistic. He had been promised additional divisions—as soon as possible. He pronounced the number of river craft at his disposal to be sufficient. And he was confident that Townshend's division would suffer no more than 400 casualties in what was looming as an inevitable battle at Ctesiphon. But the situation was becoming too strung-out for Townshend. He did not mind the idea of going to Baghdad, but he did mind being the only division committed to any fighting, especially since he just received information and 20,000 Turks were at Ctesiphon.

Ctesiphon was another bleak town on the Tigris River except for two features that set it apart. The first were the ruins of the palace of Shapur I, dated from circa 250, a great Sassanian Persian structure featuring a 100-foot-high brick barrel vault. Second, Ctesiphon was the reputed burial site of Suleiman Pak, a disciple and servant of Mohammed.

Ctesiphon was protected by a formidable defensive network. A six-mile-long trench line, reinforced by fifteen redoubts, extended northeast from the riverbank. Two strong redoubts, designated VP, faced the British right. Further along was an L-shaped mound, dubbed High Wall, each arm 500 yards long, 250 feet wide at the base, and 50 feet high. Another large redoubt was positioned behind a wide and deep ditch. Parallel to the first trench line and two miles to the rear was the second defensive line. This ran along a string of low hills. A third line was further to the rear. Nixon doubted that 20,000 Turks were in these positions. Unfortunately for the Poona Division, Nixon was quite wrong. Nur-ud-Din commanded 18,000 infantry, 400 cavalry, a swarm of Arab irregulars organized into a camel corps, and 50 pieces of artillery.

Townshend's battle plan was similar to that used at Es Sinn. He divided his division into four columns. The 17th Brigade was to attack the enemy center as a ruse. Then another brigade was to attack on the right and swing around to the Turkish rear areas, a distance of about five miles over open ground. A flying column commanded by Sir Charles Melliss, V.C., was to sweep further right and attack the second Turkish line and their camps at Qusaiba. When all these attacks were under way, Major General W. J. Delamain's 16th Brigade, reinforced by other infantry, was to attack the most important redoubts on the right. With British artillery pounding the VP, a full advance would be made all along the front. Gunboats would give added support from the river.

The battle opened with gunboat fire and artillery pounding the Turk's center positions. The British infantry on the right moved forward. The Turks responded with artillery and machine gun fire that stalled the advances as much as a thousand yards from their objectives. Delamain's men persisted, broke through the Turkish wire, and routed the defenders in the VP position. The Turkish first defensive line collapsed by 1:30 P.M. The 17th Brigade moved to support Delamain's advance at the VP, but the movement took them directly across the front of some well-entrenched Turks who hit them with rifle and machine gun fire. The brigade was decimated. By later that afternoon, Townshend realized that nothing more could be done and called for all action to be broken off. Twelve thousand British and Indian troops entered the battle, of whom 4,200 were killed or wounded. Townshend lost a third of his British officers, nearly half his Indian officers, and a third of his division.

The Turks lost 9,500 killed and wounded, and another 1,230 were captured.

Townshend sent a message to Nixon, stating that his men were exhausted and that another engagement "would probably meet with disaster." He announced his decision to march downriver to Lajj because "every sound military reason points to the necessity of retirement."

The Retreat to Kut-al-Amara

Nixon ordered Townshend to stay at Ctesiphon, thinking a retreat would give the Turks time to recover and attack; moreover, such a move might encourage a full-scale Arab uprising. But Townshend was already in Lajj when he received the message. He sent a reply to Nixon, telling him that considering the losses his division sustained—claiming that every brigade was no little more than battalion strength—it would have been "madness to remain at Ctesiphon a moment longer. Nothing will alter my opinion. I have acted for the best."

The wounded from Ctesiphon, nearly 3,000 of them—almost 700 percent more than Nixon estimated—were sent downriver on boats and barges. They were already suffering from exposure, near-drowning in flooded ditches, too few orderlies, too few doctors, too few medical supplies, and from the nearly inhuman transport that brought them from the battlefield to the river. Packed together in slow-moving craft, with no further medical care and no protection from the sun, they wallowed in their own filth, their wounds maggot-infested, their bodies covered with sores. Those who survived reached Basra on 17 December.

Nixon cabled his superiors in India that the medical arrangements were working "splendidly."

Townshend decided on 27 November to abandon Lajj, concluding the enemy could easily surround his force. He moved downriver to Aziziya, then on to Um-at-Tubal. By 2 December, the Turks were only two miles away in vigorous pursuit. Townshend ordered a rapid retreat. He pushed his men relentlessly, getting from them a forty-four-mile march in thirty-six hours across the flat desert. They had little water, little food, and practically no sleep; they sweated all day and froze all night. Men that fell out of the swiftly moving column were set upon by roving Arabs who either cut their throats or stuffed their mouths with sand to suffocate them. Later, carts were sent back to pick up the stragglers, but most were already dead.

The Poona Division finally reached Kut-al-Amara. Townshend thought it a fine place to receive reinforcements.

THE SIEGE OF KUT-AL-AMARA

In 1915, Kut had a population of 6,000 packed onto a peninsula a half-mile long and a quarter-mile wide. It was a mud town; it was a dung town. The houses were mud. The streets were mud. Walls were mud. Sewage, even from houses with cesspools, flowed freely into the streets. Animal dung was everywhere. Flies were everywhere. A senior British military officer complained that Kut was the most unsanitary town occupied by the British in the whole of Mesopotamia.

Kut's principal existing defense was an old polygonal fort only 150 yards square near the neck of the peninsula. Townshend enlarged the fort with

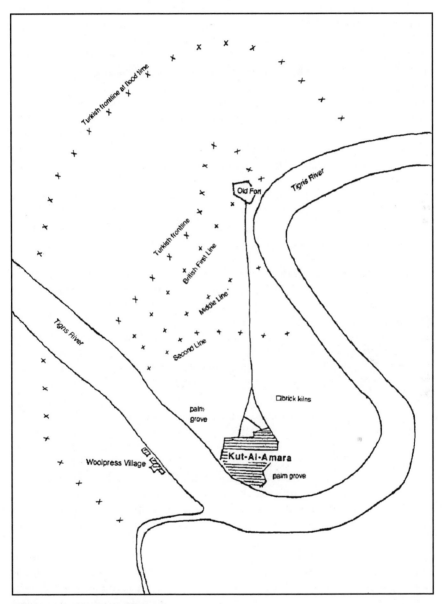

Map 10 Kut-al-Amara

earthworks and outer trenches and loopholed the walls for riflemen. Some blockhouses near the fort were torn down lest they be used as range-finders by Turkish gunners. He replaced them with a barbed wire screen and trenches supported by four redoubts. A second line was constructed some 150 yards back toward the town. Soon after, a so-called middle line was built in between. Two field guns and four howitzers were placed around brick kilns about 300 yards northeast of the town. A palm grove upstream screened another battery, and still another battery was placed behind the middle line. Two more guns were placed in the old fort and two more behind the northwest trench line. A small group of buildings that the British called Woolpress Village were directly across the river from Kut. Townshend evacuated the Arabs, and two Indian regiments moved in. When finished, the Kut defensive perimeter extended 2,700 yards, most of it riverbank.

Townshend wanted to expel the Arab civilian population from Kut but Sir Percy Cox, political attaché in Mesopotamia, objected. So, the Arabs stayed, some cooperating, some sniping at the British soldiers, some stealing everything that was not nailed down, and all draining valuable supplies.

Nixon sent Townshend yet another cable, this one putting forth three dubious assumptions. First, Nixon believed that the occupation of Kut would stop Turkish movement southward. Second, retreat from Kut was an option of last resort. Third, Nixon estimated that a relief force would reach Kut in two months. But Townshend, the student of military history, knew his division was encased in a difficult situation. He had moved from a mobile offense to a static defense, and there was no room to maneuver. And he could be starved into submission. With those realities in mind, his decision to remain in Kut is perplexing, especially since his reason for leaving Lajj was that the Turks could have surrounded him. What did he think was going to happen at Kut?

True, he claimed his troops were exhausted, that morale was low, and that the division had been savaged at Ctesiphon. Although the last point was correct, the other two remain doubtful. Delamain later stated that his brigade could have continued the southward march beyond Kut. Also, during the march to Kut, the division's rear guard fought some sharp actions against the Turks, showing a remarkable capacity to fight effectively.

Lurking among all those perplexities was Townshend's own desires. Perhaps he saw not the realities that faced him but some romantic image of holding out against great odds, of being rescued, of being showered with acclaim and promoted to lieutenant general. In any case, Townshend cabled Nixon on 3 December, "I mean to defend Kut as I did Chitral."

The siege of Kut can be divided into three phases: Phase I, December 1915, was characterized by a strengthening of Kut's defenses and by Turkish attacks; Phase II, mid-January 1916 to mid-March, was a period of rain and floods and a general settling in by both sides; Phase III, mid-March to 27 April, was the period of collapse and surrender. Throughout the second and third phases, there were continuous efforts to rescue the Kut garrison.

Phase I: December 1915

The Turks surrounded Kut, sealing the peninsula neck with a complex trench system and artillery positions. More trenches and gun emplacements were dug around the river loop. Once in place, the artillery started an intermittent shelling.

The shelling intensified during the late afternoon of 10 December, causing explosions in the old fort, the middle line, and the town. The Turkish infantry rose from their trenches near the old fort and charged the British defenses. The British and Indian troops waited until the Turks were very close and fired a massive rifle volley. The front row of attackers went down. Another volley and another. Each time the ranks of attacking troops thinned. British artillery sprayed the Turks with shrapnel. The assault troops were butchered. The survivors slowly withdrew to their trenches.

The attacks continued through 13 December, but the Turks could not get close to the British lines, leaving behind at least 800 dead and numerous wounded. The frontal assaults temporarily over, they harassed the British with sporadic artillery shots and sniper fire. And they kept digging. By 16 December, they had six trench lines facing the old fort's northeast corner. Once these were in place, the Turks extended saps toward the British lines, getting closer each night. They also shelled the British barbed wire until it was nearly gone.

Fearing an attack or mining of their positions, two anti-sapper parties, each numbering about a hundred men, were sent into the Turkish trenches on the night of 17 December. They completely surprised the Turks in the saps, killing forty of them and capturing their tools.

The Turkish 52nd Division attacked the old fort on Christmas Eve, penetrating one bastion where artillery fire destroyed the walls. Even though the two British cannon in the fort were wrecked, the defense stabilized. The 103rd Mahrattas and the Oxfordshire-Buckinghamshire Light Infantry clambered into the rubble and, using controlled rapid rifle fire and hurling grenades from only thirty feet away, forced the Turks to retreat, leaving behind 2,000 casualties. Another attack that night was also repulsed. The dead and wounded who fell outside the perimeter were difficult to recover because of sniper fire. After two more days, a truce was called and many wounded were brought into Kut's hospital. By then it was too late for the many left in the killing zone who bled or froze to death.

Nur-ud-Din decided to attack no more. He marched his army south to dig defenses at Sheikh Sa'ad and block British relief efforts, leaving enough troops around Kut to man thirty miles of trenches.

Nixon's assumption that the Poona Division could stop the Turks from moving further south was a figment of his imagination. Townshend's little force was trapped, and there was no way out.

Phase II: Mid-January to Mid-March 1916

Townshend, by his own admission, reminisced about his heroics at Chitral, holding out against great odds, enduring hardships—why, he mused, he might hold out longer than the Turks did in the five-month siege at Plevna in 1877. Indeed, he even cabled Nixon that he was going to make Kut into a second Plevna, a point he was certain the Turks would not overlook. And like the Turks at Plevna, Townshend meant to sit tight and wait for rescue.

Food rations determined how long the Poona Division could last. On 3 December, Townshend told Nixon he had one month's rations. A few days later the estimate grew to two months, at least according to a cable sent in the morning. That afternoon, Townshend was certain he possessed twenty-seven days' rations. On 24 January, he said rations would last fifty-six days. The twenty-sixth was the day he cabled that he could make Kut into another Plevna, for great quantities of grain were found in Woolpress Village, and there were 3,000 animals that could be slaughtered, enough for eighty-four days.

As winter closed in on lower Mesopotamia, the rain-swollen Tigris overflowed its banks, turning the adjacent land into muck and flooding the low-lying trenches at Kut. Sleet pelted the troops and cold invaded their bones. Gloom descended on the garrison, not only because of the weather but, as well, the expectation of imminent relief gave way to the realization that they would not get out of Kut. The Turks were not attacking but, as insolent reminders of their presence, they sent artillery shells into Kut each morning and evening. Also, each day at dusk, a German plane flew over and dropped a few bombs. On the whole, Kut became a quiet front, isolated and static.

The principal fighting by January 1916 was in the British relief force's efforts to bludgeon their way through to Kut. Known as the Tigris Corps, it was commanded by Lieutenant General Fenton Aylmer, V.C., who earlier distinguished himself in India. In 1891, whilst serving as a captain along the Northwest Frontier, he received his Victoria Cross for exceptional valor during an attack on a native fort. As a major, he led the relief force to Chitral and rescued Townshend.

Despite long experience and proven ability, Aylmer was beaten in Mesopotamia before he started. Troops and supplies arrived at Basra in sufficient quantity, but the inadequate port facilities were still creating havoc and, once landed, everything and everyone moved to the front in a trickle. Troops were sent upriver without any coherent plan, so that the Tigris Corps was less the result of clear planning than a haphazard bringing together of those units that could find transport. Sir George Buchanan, an expert on port facilities, was brought from India, but the changes he inaugurated did not have appreciable effect until late May, too late for the Kut garrison.

The name "Tigris Corps" was really too grand. In December 1915, Aylmer could field the 7th Division under Major General Sir George Younghusband, plus two infantry brigades, the 6th Cavalry Brigade, and only forty-six artillery pieces, together with the usual support and service personnel, a total of about 19,000 men. This may seem a formidable force, but most of the units never before served together and their field officers did not know one another. Many of the men were a moment beyond being raw recruits, few had ever been in battle, and even fewer knew what they were doing in Mesopotamia. The shortages of transportation and medical facilities, supplies, and artillery persisted. Aylmer had a couple of aircraft, but they were inadequate even by 1916 standards and were often grounded because of weather conditions or needed repairs.

Prepared or not, on 4 January 1916, Aylmer marched the Tigris Corps toward Sheikh Sa'ad, where Townshend reported two Turkish divisions, supported by cavalry and artillery, were headed. This was confirmed by a scout plane that finally got off the ground, but the pilot reported seeing 10,000 Turkish troops in strong entrenchments around the village, a figure higher than Townshend estimated. Younghusband's division moved forward to block further enemy movement and to bridge the river. Nixon then ordered Gorrigne's 12th Division, with cavalry and artillery, to move upriver from Nasiriyeh as a diversion. That was sound thinking, but Younghusband's idea of a blocking movement was to directly attack the Turks, launching his men simultaneously along both riverbanks. Major General G. V. Kemball's 28th Brigade, reinforced by the 92nd Punjab Infantry, the 6th Cavalry Brigade, and artillery, attacked along the south bank. The north side positions were attacked by the 19th, 21st, and 38th brigades supported by the recently arrived 16th Cavalry Brigade.

Fog shrouded the ground as the British cavalry moved along the south bank. When they broke through the fog, they saw the Turkish positions two miles ahead. But the enemy line extended further south than supposed and, as the British moved to flank, they found themselves further and further from the riverbank, leaving considerable gaps in their advancing line. Turkish artillery, machine guns, and rifles fired on them. Many British troops were still 500 yards from the Turkish lines when the attack bogged down.

Brigadier G.B.H. Rice's 38th Brigade moved along the north bank without being able to see the Turkish lines. The featureless land, fog, and mirages made sighting almost impossible. The attack stalled. The only completed part of the plan was the building of a bridge.

The British attacked again the next day. The 28th Brigade captured the Turkish front trenches and took 600 prisoners. The 38th Brigade was to hold its position on the north bank, as it were a hinge, as the 19th and 21st brigades swung around to flank the Turks. The attack began at noon, 7 January, but within two hours the two brigades were disoriented. Some battalions found themselves uncomfortably close to the Turkish lines and attacked them without artillery support. A composite battalion of the Black Watch, the Seaforth Highlanders, and the 6th Jats charged across open ground only to be cut down by concentrate rifle and machine gun fire. The Turks counter-attacked, trying to turn the British north flank, but were driven back by the 19th and 21st and by artillery fire that finally was effective because the targets were mobile and more easily observed.

The British stopped their attack that night. Exhausted, wet and shivering, hungry and thirsty, the men settled into their positions, awaiting the next day's slaughter. On 9 January, Nur-ud-Din, his troops just as miserable as the British, having suffered terrible casualties, withdrew from Sheikh Sa'ad.

Nixon and his staff had anticipated only 250 casualties; in reality there were 4,262. Once again, the men suffered and died from wounds, exposure, poor planning, and an understaffed medical service. The doctors and orderlies did the best they could, but the situation was hopeless. The wounded who managed to survive the trip downriver to Amara were stuffed into an overcrowded hospital.

The first battle to relieve Kut was over. It was not the last. On 13 January an engagement was fought at the Wadi-Nakhailat defile, resulting in 1,600 British casualties. The First Battle of Hanna was fought eight days later: 2,741 casualties. On 8 March, an engagement took place at Dujaila, resulting in 3,500 casualties. The Second Battle of Hanna was 5 April, with 1,885 casualties. The fight at Sannaiyat on 8 April resulted in 1,807 casualties. On the seventeenth, at Bail Isa, there were another 1,600 casualties. At Sannaiyat again on 22 April 1,300 fell. Thus, in a five-month rescue effort, the relief force lost 24,000 men killed and wounded, representing 60 percent of all the men involved and a little more than twice the number they were trying to get out of Kut.

Any hope of relieving Kut was abandoned after 22 April. But, if the truth be known, the relief effort was over in principle in early March at Dujaila where, enduring heavy losses, the British could not penetrate the Turkish defenses. Nothing would change in the following weeks. All the British could do was lose an army, and that was accomplished with frightening efficiency.

Phase III: Kut, Mid-March to 27 April

Although Townshend reported in late January that he had eighty-four days' rations, the situation by mid-March was getting desperate. Basic rations were supplemented by slaughtering the bullocks, mules and, last of all, the officers' horses. Many Indian troops, because of religious prohibitions, refused the meat ration. Special dispensation was granted by religious leaders in India, but there was still resistance. The meat ration caused all sorts of intestinal disorders, especially colic and dysentery. Scurvy, beriberi, and jaundice were also quite common. By 16 April, the flour allowance was cut to four ounces a day.

The relief force made attempts to reduce the food crisis with aerial drops. A few flimsy aircraft made 140 runs, dumping 125-pound packages from the planes at altitudes over 5,000 feet to avoid anti-aircraft fire. Many bundles fell within Kut, but a lot fell in the river and some even in the Turkish lines. The *Julnar*, an old paddle-wheeled steamer, was loaded with 270 tons of supplies and, on the evening of 24 April, sailed upriver. The boat immediately came under Turkish fire and then, only eight miles from Kut, fouled its rudder on cables stretched across the river. Most of the crew were killed in the ensuing fire-fight, the few survivors taken prisoner. Lieutenant Commander Cowley, the navigator, was executed on the spot.

General Nixon faded along with the Kut garrison. He was vilified in Britain when the deplorable medical situation became public knowledge. And his own health collapsed. On 9 January, he was replaced by Sir Percy Lake. Arriving in Basra, Lake ordered a three-months' supply of food and ammunition stockpiled, exacerbating the port situation. But he did move to alleviate the medical problems and improve communications.

When all relief efforts ground to a halt at Sunnaiyat on 22 April, it became apparent to Townshend that there was nothing left but surrender, so he suggested that Lake open negotiations toward that end. Townshend imagined that an honorable surrender was possible and looked forward to leading his men back to India under parole. Khalil Pasha now commanded the Turkish army in Mesopotamia, taking over from Nur-ud-Din in January. He contacted Townshend almost immediately, saying that Townshend had heroically done his duty, and politely offered to accept his surrender. But Townshend refused, allowing the moment to pass when honor and his garrison could have been saved. For, in April, Khalil no longer offered to negotiate but demanded unconditional surrender. Townshend wrote Khalil that he would surrender all his artillery and give him a million pounds sterling in return for parole.

Enver Pasha, the Turkish war minister to whom all offers were referred, rejected Townshend's proposal. The fall of Kut was important to Enver beyond any military value. Together with the British defeat at Gallipoli, utter humiliation of the Kut garrison would demonstrate to the Arab world the extent of Turkish power. Therefore, Khalil made it clear to Townshend that there would be no deals.

On 29 April, Townshend sent a cable to Lake: "I have hoisted the white flag over Kut."

Townshend may have thought this simple act of capitulation was the end of his troops' suffering. It was only the beginning.

CATEGORIES OF COMBAT

The various categories of combat applicable to the Kut siege cannot be fully understood without begging obvious conclusions. The British army was ill prepared to fight an extensive campaign in Mesopotamia. The original limited goals of protecting the southern oil fields and Basra were easily achieved and could have been easily consolidated. But no limits were set for the defensive perimeters. That allowed personal ambition to redefine the goal: Baghdad. The ensuing march north was based on a stupid miscalculation by Nixon and his staff of the logistical support necessary for the march, a gross miscalculation of Turkish resolve, and irresponsibility at the highest levels of British and Indian government decision-making.

Furthermore, lacking sound intelligence, confused by the terrain, and lacking mobility, the British were constantly forced to fight battles when and where the Turks decided. They mounted frontal assaults against disguised Turkish positions, the troops of the relief column advancing over ground that offered no cover. The consequence was a series of battles that, despite their smaller size, mirrored those on the Western Front.

Artillery versus Infantry

The most glaring British inadequacy was artillery support. At the beginning of World War I, a British division had seventy-five artillery pieces— field guns and howitzers. The divisions in Mesopotamia fell far short of that number. Moreover, the guns they had were often the wrong type, firing the wrong ammunition.

It is correct that Townshend's artillery severely punished the Turks who dogged his retreat from Ctesiphon and were helpful in repelling the December infantry attacks against Kut. When those attacks stopped and the Turks dug in, Townshend bitterly complained that most of his guns were useless and should be consigned to a scrap heap. Turkish targets were too far away to be hit accurately, and the field pieces had a flat trajectory that made it impossible to hit any target located behind a defensive work.

That same problem plagued the relief force. At Dujaila, for instance, British artillery regularly hit targets located on earth mounds but the trenches below were untouched. Mortars and howitzers would have made a significant impact.

Any effective fire was compromised by lack of proper munitions. The British infantry discovered time and again that their artillery bombardment failed to cut the Turks' barbed wire. Shrapnel shells failed, as they did on the Western Front, and there were no high explosive shells available. At the First Battle of Hanna, the British preliminary bombardment hoped to silence the Turkish artillery, cut their wire, and cause either the destruction or evacuation of the frontline trenches. The Black Watch and the 6th Jats attacked but were soon mired in mud up to their chests. The Turks, who were not dislodged and whose trenches remained intact, opened fire. Only seventeen Scots and Indians survived.

Although the Turks enjoyed artillery superiority throughout the Kut siege, they also were plagued by problems. Their artillery could not dislodge the British infantry from Kut's old fort. They did cut the British wire, but the infantry could not sustain their subsequent attack. When the Turks sealed Kut and bombarded it, they used a big Krup howitzer to lob shells into the British perimeter. These exploded with an enormous bang but did little damage.

Turkish artillery was more effective against attacking British infantry. At Ctesiphon, the British 17th Brigade was heavily shelled by Turkish guns located behind the great vault, breaking up their advance. At Sheikh Sa'ad their artillery likewise caused heavy casualties in G. V. Kemball's brigade. At Wadi-Nakhailat, Rice's brigade was raked by shrapnel. The Turks did all this firing with relative impunity because the British could not mount effective counter-battery fire. How successful the Turks were is measured by the distance between the blunted attacks and the Turkish lines. Thus, the British were stopped at various places 400 yards, 500 yards, and 2,000 yards from the enemy wire. Because of the flat terrain and the distances the infantry had to cover, the killing zone was greatly extended, and the Turks could inflict heavy casualties without much personal engagement.

Infantry versus Rifles and Machine Guns

Although the Turks enjoyed artillery superiority, it was a slim advantage. The consistent damage to British infantry was done by rifle and machine gun fire. This was especially the situation for the relief force.

At Sheikh Sa'ad the composite Highland Battalion (2nd Black Watch and Seaforths) moved toward Turkish lines about a mile to their front. The Turkish artillery opened fire, but it was at 350 yards that their infantry responded with massed rifle and machine gun fire. Nearly a thousand men were lost. At First Hanna, the Black Watch was again cut to pieces, its surviving strength 150 out of some 800 men. In the same battle two Dogra battalions were reduced to 25 men. At Sannaiyat the 7th Division advanced toward unseen Turkish lines. The Turks opened fire at 800 yards. Most of the division's 1,200 casualties fell in the first twenty-five minutes. At Second Hanna, the 13th Division walked across open ground into enfilading machine gun fire. When Gorringe saw the battlefield, he asked why a line of British soldiers he saw ahead were not dug in. The answer was "Because they are dead." The 13th lost 1,885 men.

What is sometimes forgotten is that the British gave as good as they received, with resulting high Turkish casualty rates. The first Turkish attack against Kut's old fort left 800 dead. Or, at Bait Isa, Khalil gathered 10,000 men for a counter-attack against recently lost trenches. The British 8th Brigade bore the brunt of the attack. When it was over, there were over 4,000

Turks strewn about the field in great heaps. The riflemen of the 8th each fired an average of 400 rounds. They used the Lee Enfield Mark III, arguably the fastest working bolt action rifle available. A soldier could fire between eighteen and twenty-five shots during what the troops called "the mad minute," creating a lethal and near-impenetrable barrier.

Thus, when the British were on the defensive, their weapons were as effective as were those of the Turks.

Infantry versus Infantry

Certainly it could be argued that long-range firing was a contest between infantry formations. The operative feature was the range. Infantry versus infantry traditionally involved formations closing on one another, resulting in hand-to-hand combat. There were occasions when the British and Turks entered such confrontations. Such fighting was accounted for in any battle plan but just who the specific soldiers would be was a chance factor related to who could get across the killing zone, push through the wire, over the parapets, and into the enemy trenches. Generals might be told that the Black Watch made it into a Turkish trench, but twenty-five survivors do not constitute a battalion. Not a single officer or sergeant may have survived. If enough men survived to guarantee a fight, what took place was more like a melee than a controlled engagement.

The weapon most used when the two sides collided was the hand grenade. These were thrown back and forth in great number, either to break up the attack wave or to kill the defenders. Once in the trenches, bayonets, clubs, pistols, knives, mess kits, shovels, literally anything at hand, were viable weapons.

The Turks at Kut, showering grenades on the defenders, took the outer defenses of the old fort. A counter-attack, preceded by a grenade barrage, rooted the Turks from their hard-won positions. At Sannaiyat, the British were forced from captured trenches by a grenade attack. At Bait Isa, the British 7th and 9th brigades made it to a line of Turkish trenches with few casualties. They bounded over the parapets, thinking the Turks had evacuated. In fact, they were still there, packed into warrens and dugouts, seeking refuge from British artillery. Using clubs and bayonets, the Gurkhas wielding their curved knives, the Turks were either killed or taken prisoner. Khalil restored stability with a counter-attack that brought the British to an abrupt halt.

Once again, we see shadows of the larger conflicts on the Western Front in these encounters. The gallantry and dash of Northwest Frontier campaigns was transformed in Mesopotamia into grotesque battles of attrition.

The Will to Combat

The Turks assuredly had the greater will to combat. Constantly under-estimated by the British staff, they proved a tenacious foe who pressed their attacks with great courage and vigor. Faith drove them. Confidence washing in from Gallipoli drove them. Iron discipline drove them. They fought with conviction and imagination.

The British leaders, mired in incompetence, had little to recommend them. No one bothered to tell the men why they were fighting in Mesopotamia. The fledgling soldiers looked about the barren landscape and wondered if all the hardships and death were worth it. Those men brought as reinforcements from France felt insulted by being relegated to a second-class theatre of war.

Despite these feelings, the willingness to fight was never an issue in the British army. The men in Mesopotamia, as in the Crimean War, overcame or at least set aside their doubts and resentments and fought as best they could under the circumstances. As in the Crimea, they had no place else to go. Certainly discipline kept them at their duties, and so too did a sense of pride. The question remained how long those elements of cohesion could be sustained under the influence of disaster.

Part of the answer is found in a debilitating structural ineffectiveness present in the British army in Mesopotamia. First, the army was an amalgamation of troops that never before worked together, whose officers were often new to their men, and who, many of them, were under-trained. Any sense of unity within the constantly shifting organizational parameters was impossible. An army fielded without such unity under conditions of great stress, physical hardship, and lacking purpose, cannot be effective. Second, units arriving in Basra were sent forward in dribbles and thrown into the fighting. The 2nd Black Watch was wrenched from France, dropped into Mesopotamia, and shot to pieces. Everything around them—the landscape, the enemy, even their comrades—was strange. Third, generalship was poor. The troops bore witness to the inept logistics and poorly executed battle plans. The continued emphasis on frontal attacks without proper artillery support revealed a lack of imagination and a crying need for new tactics. Thus, to draw on John Baynes's conclusions from his book *Morale*, when troops suffer from lack of water and food, when they are marched to exhaustion, when they suffer from lack of equipment, when heavy casualties are repeatedly experienced, and when the wounded are poorly treated, then the staff suffers from incompetence.

The above conclusions apply mostly to the conduct of the relief force. Inside Kut, the situation was different. Even though Townshend put them in a lamentable situation, even though they would get sick, starve, and lapse into lethargy, and even though Townshend would hand them into a humiliating and inhuman captivity, most soldiers remained intensely loyal. But, as the promise of being relieved dimmed, many units withdrew into themselves, only superficially doing their duty. No one was attacking them. They certainly were not attacking anyone, for Townshend's strategy was total pacificism. If they found techniques of survival, if they could somehow become less visible by further inactivity and self-isolation, they might yet get out of the hell-hole. This was opting-out, a form of internal desertion in which they waited, and waited. Maybe if they pulled into their holes far enough, the bloody war might pass them by.

Wounded and Prisoners

Perhaps no more need be said of the British wounded. Men died waiting for evacuation from battlefields, died on the downriver barges, and died in the overcrowded, understaffed hospitals. The misery invoked by Nixon would not diminish until a change of command following the Kut siege.

When Townshend raised the white flag, the Poona Division was herded together and marched nine miles upriver to Shumran. The men and officers were separated, the latter going by boat to Baghdad, the men made to walk. Given only a few biscuits, a handful of dates, and little water, the already sick and undernourished soldiers were in no condition for such a march. Hundreds fell by the wayside and were clubbed to death by the Kurdish guards or murdered by hovering Arabs and then stripped of anything of value.

The remnants reached Baghdad on 17 May. Most were shipped to Samara and on to Anatolia. Major Generals Delamain and Melliss constantly protested the brutal treatment of the men. These officers and the American council in Baghdad worked to change those conditions, even using their own money. Finally, the critically ill and wounded were repatriated. Some cooks and medical orderlies were assigned to those that remained. By 3 June, however, fully a third of the captives died or were murdered by their guards.

By the end of the war, 1,755 British enlisted men died in captivity. Only 837 made it home, many by their own devices. Of the 10,486 Indian enlisted men captured at Kut, 7,423 survived, the imbalance with the British prisoners attributed to a slightly more benign captivity than the slavery to which the British were frequently subjected and also to the ways in which the Indian troops immediately fell to caring for one another.

Townshend, in stark contrast, spent his captivity living in a handsome villa near Constantinople. He indicated no interest in his men's welfare. Rather, he ingratiated himself to the Turks, fancifully carving out a role for himself as a key negotiator between the Turks and British at war's end. Although he was released to carry out his dream, the British snubbed him.

AFTERMATH

Major General Stanley Maude replaced Percy Lake as Mesopotamian commander on 17 August 1916 and immediately set about turning the area into a first-class war theatre. Two dozen planes were provided, heavy artillery and high explosive shells were supplied, and reinforcements arrived. The number of river boats was increased, and pilots were found who knew the river. A narrow gauge railway was built between Basra and Nasiriyeh, and a vehicle road was built between Basra and Sheikh Sa'ad. Dock facilities at Basra were finally improved, and Amara was turned into a fine supply depot.

By the end of February 1917, Kut was recaptured. On 11 March 1917, British troops entered Baghdad. By the end of April, Samara was in British hands and the campaign was over. Britain now controlled the Tigris and Euphrates and all the oil deposits.

The Kut siege nevertheless remains a contradiction. It was both unintentional and unnecessary and became a tragic defeat for British arms. As an outgrowth from it, Maude's campaign, more an act of redemption, placed Britain in a strategically advantageous position in the post-war deliberations. Yet, for all this, Kut has received only scant attention, overwhelmed by a fascination with the Western Front.

For all that, this presentation of the Kut siege reinforces the conclusion drawn from Malta and Sebastopol that frontal assaults against well-entrenched troops are foolish and suicidal. Furthermore, the sacrifice of 24,000 to save 12,000 was poor mathematics. Certainly the vision of Baghdad that drove so many minds to despair over Kut could have been avoided, should have been avoided. Townshend could have kept on marching south. He did not. But once enclosed in Kut, a cold logic should have been applied by the Indian government, and surely by London. The relief efforts, under-manned, under-supplied, and under-gunned, could not succeed. The effort was a waste of resources that could have been used elsewhere—unfortunately without a guarantee of any more wisdom in their use than shown in Mesopotamia.

But that was a lesson of military history which, like the lessons of Malta and Sebastopol, was not learned and would be repeated a quarter-century later half a world away at the other end of the Asian land mass.

Chapter 6

Singapore, 7 December 1941 to 15 February 1942

On 7 December 1941, the Japanese landed on the northern Malay Peninsula, beginning a march south to the British naval base on Singapore Island. The British, who considered such a campaign improbable if not impossible, were unprepared and gave up one position after another along the peninsula. That created overwhelming morale and organizational problems. They surrendered in February. The Japanese victory signalled the end to European dominance over Asia.

7 December 1941: The Day of Infamy. Planes of the Imperial Japanese Navy attacked Pearl Harbor, severely damaging the American Pacific Fleet.

7 December 1941: Two Japanese convoys approached the Malayan coast. One steamed toward Singora in Thailand. The other headed for Kota Bharu, about 150 miles south in the British Federated Malay States. Their ultimate objective was Singapore. To reach Singapore the Japanese army would have to march through 400 miles of jungle, pelted by tropical rains, ford 25 rivers, wade through swamps, and endure crushing heat and humidity. The prize was worth the sacrifice because Singapore, the Gibraltar of the Far East, would open the door to further conquests.

To the British, such a campaign bordered on the impossible. The rigors of a march down the Malayan Peninsula notwithstanding, any force impudent enough to attack Singapore would learn the meaning of impregnable. Great shore batteries defended the coast, R.A.F. planes zoomed overhead. Then, if necessary, the Royal Navy would steam to the rescue, as if it were a waterborne cavalry. Practically everyone believed in Singapore's military strength. Nearly everyone said the Japanese were inept. Reality proved another order of experience.

There were three Singapores in December 1941: The island, the city, and the naval base.

The island is twenty-seven miles wide, east to west, and fourteen miles long. The coastline totals some seventy-two miles. In 1941, most settlement was in the southeast around Singapore City and Keppell Harbor. Military installations, factories, and plantations occupied the island's eastern precincts. The west side, cut by streams and swamps, contained a few plantations but was mostly jungle.

Singapore City was an ethnic mosaic. Britons, Australians, various Europeans, Malays, Sikhs, Hindus, Moslems, and a large Chinese population comprised its half-million population. Wealth poured into the city from shipping, tin mining, rubber plantations, banking and commerce. Life was relaxed, outdoors, and comfortable. Old European class lines and ethnic origins blurred in the common quest for profit, making it unimportant in this Eastern stew pot what one had been or where one came from.

In 1921, the Committee for Imperial Defense, against the advice of Admiral Sir John Jellicoe, selected Singapore as the location of a key naval base in the Far East. Money was appropriated, a site on the Johore Strait selected, and work begun. A controversy soon emerged about how best to defend the base. Air Marshall Sir Hugh Trenchard argued for air power. The Admiralty stuck by the virtues of big guns on big ships. The Admiralty won. Construction contained at an eventual cost of £60,000,000.

The sprawling base, really a self-contained community, was protected by massive concrete bunkers and emplacements with 15-inch guns. Several batteries of smaller calibre were scattered about the island. The theory was that any seaward assault would be repulsed by the coast artillery. If, by some flight of imagination, an attack did come down the peninsula, the army and the R.A.F. would keep the enemy stalled. Until what? For how long? No matter what the direction or source of attack, the answer was the same. Singapore was to hold out at least seventy days, by which time the fleet would arrive and put everything right. That judgment was made in 1921. It stuck.

On 3 December 1941, just four days before the Japanese landings, Sir Robert Brooke-Popham, the British commander-in-chief, Far East, announced that the Japanese were not going to attack Malaya, much less Singapore. He believed that the strongest defense was the "illusion of impregnability" that Singapore held among the Japanese. Brooke-Popham was dead wrong. The illusion did not ensnare the Japanese, but it did wrap around the minds of British decision-makers like a cocoon, distorting their perceptions of themselves and their future enemy.

The illusion, the myth, of impregnability and British indomitability was an act of self-proclamation, strengthened by ill-founded assumptions and disdain of the Japanese. They could not attack because they were incapable of such a campaign. Japanese planes, made of wood, easily disintegrated, and their pilots were so near-sighted that they could not see their targets. Their capital ships, with pagoda-like superstructures, were top-heavy. The average soldier was a peasant incapable of independent action and was easily disoriented by surprise. They were led by incompetent officers only a step away from feudalism.

No, Japan was not a threat to Singapore. Who then? The comfortable conclusion was that there were no serious enemies in the Far East. Even when the Japanese took over French Indo-China following the fall of France in June 1940, no one in authority saw the implications for Singapore.

DEFENDING SINGAPORE

The Chiefs-of-staff in London generally agreed that the primary function of the Singapore garrison was the defense of the naval base, not the island, not the city, and certainly not the Malay Peninsula. However, Major General W.G.S. Dobie, Malayan commander in the late 1930s, questioned that function, warning that an attack down the peninsula was the greatest danger. With considerable prescience, he thought landings were possible at Singora and Jota Bharu. He wanted defenses built on Singapore Island's north shore and in Johore. £60,000 was dedicated and some work started. Eventually, a few airfields were spotted along the peninsula, but without regard to their own defensibility. Entrenchments and pillboxes were built at Kota Bharu, and the so-called Jitra Line was established in the northern peninsula to protect the airbase at Alor Star and the roads leading south from the Thai border. Brooke-Popham added to these measures by inventing a plan code-named "Operation Matador" by which British troops, marching north from the Jitra Line, were to cross the Thai border should the Japanese land at Singora.

Dobie's insistence that a land attack was the main threat introduced an unanticipated ambiguity into Singapore's defensive scheme. If the naval base was the defensive priority, but installations were built along the north shore and in Johore, then that implied a defense of the island. The positions built in the northern peninsula considerably expanded the defensive perimeter to include the peninsula. What was the defensive priority after all? There was no clear answer, and that created administrative and tactical bewilderment.

Nonetheless, in December 1941, Singapore seemed smugly secure—at least on paper.

Despite the size of the naval base, there was no naval squadron permanently based in Singapore. That void was filled on 4 December 1941 when HMS *Prince of Wales* and HMS *Repulse* arrived, accompanied by four destroyers. Prime Minister Winston Churchill, sharing the conventional wisdom that a land attack was unlikely, believed that in the event of war the Japanese would raid with fast battleships just as the Germans did in the Atlantic. The two British capital ships, *Prince of Wales* fresh from chasing the *Bismarck*, would persuade the Japanese to stay home.

The British and Commonwealth forces seemed large enough, numbering about 88,500 men. The largest contingent was 37,000 Indian troops. There were 19,600 British and 15,200 Australians. There would also be a Volunteer Defense Force of 16,500 men. These troops represented thirty-one battalions organized into three divisions of two brigades each. They were supported by about 100 artillery pieces. The army also had some 250 Bren Gun Carriers and other armored cars. There were no tanks.

Brooke-Popham requested over and over that more aircraft be sent. The chiefs-of-staff had long promised 336 first-class machines, but on 7 December only 156 planes of all types were on station. These included two bomber squadrons flying Blenheim Is and IVs, a reconnaissance squadron using American Lockheed Hudsons, five fighter squadrons using the American Brewster Buffalo, and two torpedo squadrons flying the bi-wing Wildebeeste. The general defensive plan, assuming the naval base held out the magic seventy days, was for the fleet to arrive and sink any enemy ships missed by the coast artillery. The army would sweep the beaches of any troops that managed to get ashore. The R.A.F., meantime, was to maintain air superiority.

However adequate these forces looked on paper, their actual fighting capabilities were limited.

Prince of Wales and *Repulse*, without carrier support and with only a weak promise of land-based air support, were vulnerable to air attack, but the Admiralty dismissed the possibility that planes could sink their big ships. There was a more fundamental problem. Whether Singapore held out seventy days or a year made little difference. By the end of 1941, the British navy had already endured Dunkirk, German bombing raids on their home ports, losses in the Atlantic convoys, the threat of German surface raiders, and a savage war in the Mediterranean that included losses in Greece, Malta, and Crete. There was no fleet to send. The two great warships were more symbols than real power. Anyone looking at the small and decrepit destroyer escort must have realized that. No matter. Within five days after their arrival both ships were sunk.

The ground forces were of unequal quality. Some top line units, such as the 2nd Battalion, Argyll and Sutherland Highlanders, were in place, but they were about the only troops with extensive jungle training. The 22nd Australian Brigade, in Singapore eleven months, was thought trained and acclimated. But the 27th Australian Brigade arrived only in September 1941. Most of the Australian and Indian units were filled with fresh recruits—some had never fired a rifle. Worse, most of the experienced officers and non-commissioned officers were siphoned away to the Near East or back to Britain to train the new army. The British units wondered whether they might not be more useful at home since Hitler's forces were just across the English Channel and were bombing Britain. The Australians, likewise, would rather have been at home or at least with their comrades in the Western Desert. These sentiments anticipated a profound morale problem.

The big shore batteries were the soul of the defenses. The 15-inch guns were positioned around Changi at the east entrance to the Johore Strait. They were supported by 9.2-inch batteries. Six-inch batteries were located at the west entrance to the strait and, with some added 9.2-inch guns, at Keppell Harbor in the south. Many of these guns, legend aside, could fire onto the peninsula, but they were supplied with armor-piercing ammunition, appropriate for naval warfare but quite ineffective for land war.

The R.A.F. also suffered deficiencies. Brooke-Popham, in October 1941, pronounced the Buffalo fighter adequate for Malaya. He erred on two important points: He under-estimated the quality of Japanese aircraft, led by the famous Zero Mark II fighter, and he over-estimated the Buffalo. Looking like a barrel with wings, the Buffalo cruised at 180 mph, about the same speed as Japanese bombers. It took nearly twenty minutes for the plane to reach 20,000. Originally designed for the United States Navy, it was declared obsolete in 1940. The British Blenheim bombers could carry only a 1,000-pound bomb load, and they were vulnerable to fighter attack. The Wildebeeste chugged along at 100 mph and could carry only an 18-inch torpedo that needed to be released a few perilous feet above water. Eventually fifty Hawker Hurricanes arrived, but the Japanese had already established air superiority. Given the aircraft requirements in Britain and in the Western Desert, there were no more planes to send.

As badly flawed as the Singapore defenses were, the young and inexperienced troops would have to face the Japanese as best they could.

LEADERSHIP

General Archibald Wavell cabled Winston Churchill on 16 January 1942 that little or nothing had been done to fortify Singapore Island along the Johore Strait and that the naval batteries were ineffective against Japanese ground forces.

Churchill recoiled: "I cannot understand why I did not know all this," he wrote in *Hinge of Fate*.

The answer, incredible as it seems, is that no one bothered to tell him.

That significant communication gap was built into both the organization and quality of Singapore's leadership. Singapore had two commanders, one military and one civilian. The military officer commanding Malaya reported to the London war office. The governor general, who could make his commander role as functional as he wished, reported to the colonial office. There was an air officer, commanding, Far East, who reported to the air ministry, and a naval commander who reported to the Admiralty but was subordinate to the commander for China. Over all was the commander-in-chief in London and, ultimately, to the prime minister. This organization, with a lack of focus reminiscent of the Crimean War, emerged less from rational planning than from the dictates of time and circumstance.

Shifts in key personnel further muddled leadership. In April 1941, C.W.H. Pulford was named R.A.F. commandant, Far East. In May, Arthur Percival was named commander for Malaya. Brooke-Popham, commander-in-chief, Far East, was relieved on 25 December by Sir Henry Pownall. His tenure lasted about two weeks, after which time Wavell took command to preside helplessly over the final act. Ordinarily all that shifting could be thought routine, but times were not ordinary. During the most crucial months of 1941, the Singapore leadership was most fluid. No one really took hold of the situation. Wavell, coming from the Western Desert, tried but it was too late.

Ponderous organization was made dysfunctional by the personalities involved. Three men stand out from a lengthy cast.

Lieutenant General Sir Arthur Percival was in command of all ground troops. He was considered remote by some, unimaginative by others. A graduate of Rugby, he started life as a London clerk, then enlisted in the army in 1914. He was commissioned within a month, as were many public school graduates in Lord Herbert Kitchener's New Army. Three years later, Percival was a lieutenant colonel commanding a line regiment on the Western Front. He earned the Military Cross, the Distinguished Service Order, with bar, and the French Croix de Guerre. With war's end, he stayed in the army and distinguished himself at various staff colleges. Assigned to Singapore, he supported Brooke-Popham's Matador Plan and requested reinforcements to bring his force up to forty-eight battalions and two tank regiments. But for all Percival's awareness of the need to be stronger, his actions once the Japanese landed left much wanting. Thus, it was not until 23 December that he selected defensive sites on Singapore's north shore, and it was not until 7 January that some work was actually started. Percival blamed the civilian government for the delays. A more assertive commander would have overcome such an impediment. As London *Times* correspondent Ian Morrison wrote, Percival was a man without convictions, colorless, and negative. James Leasor concluded that Percival lacked the conviction, energy, and imagination necessary to carry his subordinates' confidence.

Sir Shenton Thomas was the governor general. He came to Malaya in 1934 after a long career in Africa. As the other commander in Malaya, Thomas strongly resisted expansion of the Volunteer Force, claiming it would take men from the plantations, factories, and mines that he believed were Singapore's real contribution to the war effort. He was also suspicious of arming any Chinese lest they be communists. Colonel John Dalley and Major Frederick Spencer Chapman tried to convince Thomas that a defensive guerrilla force was needed to stay behind Japanese positions to sabotage and collect information. Thomas refused. He believed that no European could live in the jungle behind Japanese lines (Spencer Chapman would last three years), and that, should such operations become known, they would undermine the confidence of the civilian population. Thus, the very person who could have organized a coordinated defense and garner the energy of the civilians became an obstructionist. Morrison concluded with characteristic anger that Thomas was not only short, fat, and red-faced but unperturbable, unimaginative, complacent, and indecisive.

Sir Robert Brooke-Popham, commander-in-chief, Far East, at least until 25 December, is a study in contrasts. He learned to fly in 1911 but by 1914 was considered too old for combat. As a wing commander, however, he directed his fighter squadrons through the battle of Neuve Chapelle in 1915, receiving the DSO. He was brevetted a brigadier general in 1916. He resigned from the R.A.F. in 1937 but quickly re-joined in 1939 and was sent to Singapore in September 1941. He argued vigorously for more aircraft and urged that more airfields be built along the peninsula. He was told by his masters in London that such activity might provoke the Japanese. Brooke-Popham's response was the Matador Plan, by which British troops operating out of the northern peninsula would move against Japanese landings at Singora.

Despite the urgency of his requests and the innovative character of Matador, Brooke-Popham was the same man who declared the Buffalo fighter adequate for Malaya. Perhaps he was bowing to military reality, but it was an error in judgment, nonetheless. Worse, on 8 December, the morning after the first Japanese air raid on Singapore City, he issued an order of the day that he co-authored some months before. "We are ready," the order boasted. "We have plenty of warning and our preparations are made and tested." None of the statement was true. When the Japanese bombers flew over the city, not a single fighter rose to challenge them, the anti-aircraft fire was ragged and uncoordinated, and no air raid sirens sounded. The British *Official History* concluded that the order was "out of touch with reality." Brooke-Popham was another heir to the myth of Singapore's invincibility.

In sum, as James Leasor writes, Singapore's leaders "were aging men cast in molds too large for them," and lacked aggressiveness and new ideas. The problems confronting them simply overran their inherited solutions.

THE JAPANESE CAMPAIGN

A new myth was born when the Japanese struck Malaya: The campaign was originally planned in the early 1920s, and their divisions were trained for jungle warfare. None of it was true. The Japanese discussed the possibility of attacking Malaya in the early 1930s, but only in general terms. Detailed planning did not begin until September 1941 and Tomoyuki Yamashita was not given command of the 25th Army, the invading force, until November. As Lieutenant Colonel Masonobu Tsuji, the invasion's director of military operations pointed out, even Yamashita's staff was a "scratch team" put together just before operations began. Two divisions of the 25th Army, the 5th and 18th, gained combat experience in China but the third, the Imperial Guards, was a ceremonial unit much in need of war training. That work was resisted by the Guards officers, whom Tsuji found truculent and disobedient. Supporting these three divisions were 200 assorted artillery pieces, a tank brigade, 459 army planes, and another 158 from the navy. The navy also assigned a cruiser, 10 destroyers, and about 5 submarines to the operation.

None of the ground troops were specifically trained for jungle duty. Instead, a research unit on Hainan Island, to which Tsuji was assigned, gathered all existing information about jungle warfare and survival. Some exercises were run, but with troops of the 23rd Army. All the information was finally distributed to the invasion troops in a pamphlet entitled *Read This Alone—And the War Can Be Won*. Among the topics discussed were water purification, meals, disease and insect bites, weapons care, and proper clothing. Spencer Chapman, returning from a reconnaissance patrol, reported seeing the Japanese dressed in sneakers, football shirts, and a variety of hats. Many were riding bicycles that he thought were taken from civilians. Actually, 6,000 bicycles had been issued to each division. He concluded the Japanese showed great determination but were basically second-class troops. He did add that they travelled much lighter than British soldiers, who were so weighed down with equipment that "they could hardly walk, much less fight."

The Japanese landed at Singora at 2:00 A.M., 8 December 1941, on tempestuous seas that literally tossed many soldiers from their boats onto the beaches. Perfunctory Thai resistance ended about noon. What of Matador, the plan that was supposed to counter the Japanese landing? On 5 December, Brooke-Popham received permission from London to employ the plan if the Japanese showed any intentions of landing. Although the Japanese convoy was sighted the next day, only a first-stage alert was called. At 8:00 A.M, 8 December, London wired Brooke-Popham that he could do as he saw fit. That was six hours after the Japanese landed at Singora and another hour and a half before he was even notified of the landing. It was too late for Matador.

The Japanese also landed at Kota Bharu. The British defenders, firing from pillboxes and from behind barbed wire entrenchments, forced the assault wave to dig in on the beach. British bombers finally arrived and set two transports afire. Gradually, the invaders inched their way forward, digging paths with their hands and helmets. They charged and took the first defensive line. Re-grouping, they charged again and took the second defensive line. The defenders fell back. Kota Bharu was taken the next day and two airfields were captured on 13 December. Kuala Kuli was taken six days later, together with seven British planes, 157 autos and trucks, and large supplies of gasoline, ammunition, and bombs.

The main column at Singora swung south to attack the Jitra Line. Their advance was temporarily halted when, near Changlun, about twenty miles south of the Thai border, they found a bridge demolished. British artillery

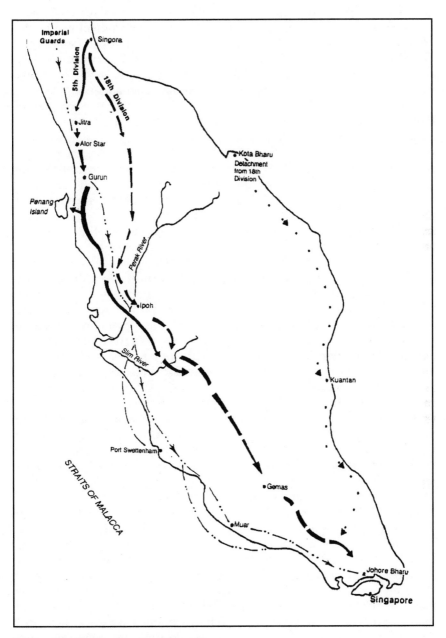

Imperial
Guards

Singora

5th Division

18th Division

Jitra

Alor Star

Kota Bharu
Detachment
from 18th
Division

Gurun

Penang
Island

Perak River

Ipoh

Slim River

Kuantan

Port Swettenham

STRAITS OF MALACCA

Gemas

Muar

Johore Bharu

Singapore

Map 11 Malayan Peninsula

opened fire, causing many casualties. Despite the intense shelling, the Japanese repaired the bridge, and ten medium tanks moved forward under cover of a heavy rain. Lieutenant Colonel Tsuji followed them in an auto. Four miles down the road they found ten un-manned British field pieces. The artillerymen had sought cover from the rain under nearby trees. Tsuji estimated that as many as 3,000 defenders similarly left their positions. Now virtually unopposed, the Japanese resumed their advance.

The Jitra Line was established just before the war as a complex of trenches, pillboxes, concrete bunkers, wire entanglements, and minefields. Some British officers estimated they could hold out for at least three months. Events dictated otherwise. The 11th Indian Division was exhausted by a march to the Thai border and back to the Jitra Line, where they found their old positions badly flooded. But, as the primary defenders, they did have the support of field artillery, mountain gun batteries, and most of an anti-tank regiment.

On the night of 12 December, the Japanese cracked the Jitra Line with 500 men and some tanks. Only hours later, and reinforced by two infantry battalions, the Japanese routed the weary and despondent defenders. Three thousand British and Indian troops surrendered. The road south was open.

The British, officers and men alike, were not only exhausted but bewildered. The army was forced into a defensive posture for which it was not prepared. The navy was supposed to be the principal defensive weapon. Where were they? *Prince of Wales* and *Repulse*, on 8 December, left Singapore with their destroyer escort to disrupt Japanese landings at Singora. At first Pulford, the R.A.F. commander, said air cover could be provided. But the fields at Kota Bharu were captured and, after only twenty-four hours of fighting, there were just 55 of 110 planes still operational in the northern peninsula. Those aircraft were about to be recalled to Singapore. Air cover for an operation to Singora was now impossible, so the task force sailed to a point off the east coast near Kuantan, believing they would find new targets in the area. Japanese planes attacked the ships on 10 December. *Prince of Wales* and *Repulse* were sunk in two hours. Neither ship had fired their big guns in the defense of Singapore.

With naval support destroyed, with air support going fast, the army in the north was very much on its own. Percival decided on a series of hold-and-withdraw maneuvers. Driven from one position, the troops retreated to the next and held until penetrated or out-flanked. Then they withdrew to the next position. The idea was to make the Japanese pay for every mile—and with luck, find a defensive line that could be held. The plan was self-defeating. Nothing seemed worth defending—who wanted to die for a position that was going to be abandoned anyway? Implicitly, without any direct orders, the defensive posture along the peninsula changed from stopping or at least stalling the Japanese to one of sheer survival. Interestingly, on 22 December, *Life* magazine, an American photojournalism weekly, told its readers the jungle was Singapore's greatest protective shield. To the British and Indian troops it was a constant, suffocating enemy.

In the meantime, on 19 December, the unopposed Japanese took Penang Island, off the west coast. The British and European populations were evacuated surreptitiously the night before, leaving the Asiatics behind. That devious movement undermined the confidence of the Asians in Singapore. By New Year's Day, the Japanese were at Kuantan and Kampar. They broke the line at the Slim River. They leapfrogged by sea to Port Swettenham. They pushed through Kajang, the Muar River line, Gemas, and Batu Pahat. At last, on 31 January 1942, after fifty-five days, they stood at Johore Bharu. Across the Johore Strait, just over two miles away, was Singapore Island.

THE SIEGE OF SINGAPORE ISLAND

The Japanese Plan

The Japanese made certain assumptions about taking Singapore: First, because of the large civilian population, the British would not fight to the last man; second, Japanese artillery batteries could neutralize British guns protecting the naval base; third, Bukit Timah Heights, just north of Singapore City, would be the final line of British resistance.

The Japanese assault was quite simple. With air superiority over the island, domination of the enemy defenses was already achieved. The tactical problem was how best to cross the Johore Strait, as it were, the castle moat. The opening maneuver was an artillery bombardment by forty-eight 15cm howitzers and sixteen guns of other calibres. They hit the airfields and entrenchments east of the Kranji River. Artillery of the Guards Division and the 5th Division fired on other airfields and oil storage tanks. Remaining batteries ranged their fire along the island's north shore.

The Imperial Guards moved about in a visible manner from the causeway to the east mouth of the Johore Strait. That was a ruse to attract the defenders to obvious landing areas. But the 5th and 18th divisions were hidden in jungles to the west. At the appointed hour, they crossed the strait in collapsible boats, landed, and advanced through the jungles and swamps of the island's west side. The Guards Division subsequently crossed near the causeway and, further east, took Ubin Island in the strait.

The Japanese had 30,000 men and 440 guns (including captured British weapons), but they were running low on ammunition, gasoline, and other supplies. The quartermaster was so concerned about shortages of artillery ammunition that he advised delaying the attack. Yamashita, never in awe of British capabilities—in November he reduced his army from five to three divisions—knew they were exhausted and demoralized. He had to maintain momentum. The attack would go forward.

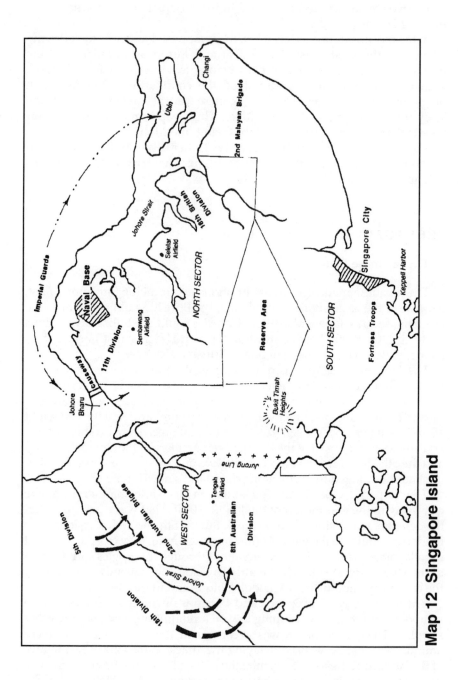

Map 12 Singapore Island

The British Response

British forces numbered 85,000 men on Singapore, of whom 15,000 were non-combatants. Several fighting units were under-manned and in need of new equipment. Reinforcements did arrive in mid-January. These included two brigades of the 18th British Division and various Australian units. Many of these men were fresh recruits, many with only a few weeks' training.

Churchill told Wavell on 20 January that there should be no thought of surrender until after fighting in the "ruins of Singapore City." But Churchill did not know of the civilian horde that retreated to the island with the troops. Furthermore, Shenton Thomas, according to Percival, blocked the army's defense construction because he was afraid it would panic the population. Yet, on 12 January, *Life* correspondent Cecil Brown reported that the population was visibly bewildered because the realities of the constant bombings conflicted with the too few and overly optimistic public communiqués issued by Thomas and Percival. There was also a prevailing civilian attitude that, war or no, life would go on as usual. When troopers wanted to fell some trees on a golf green, club members objected because the course would be spoiled. When Lieutenant Colonel Steedman went to an army supply depot for barbed wire, he found the depot staff on half-day vacation.

Percival wisely decided that he could not defend the whole island perimeter, so he divided the island into three sectors. The North Sector, extending from the causeway east to Changi, was defended by III Corps, comprising the 11th Indian and 18th British divisions. Most artillery was placed with these units. The South Sector, from Changi southwest to the Jurong River, was defended by two Malayan brigades and various fortress troops. The 8th Australian Division and the 44th Indian Brigade guarded the West Sector from the Jurong Line back to the causeway. They were supported by three artillery regiments and three anti-tank batteries. The Jurong Line was the key to the western defense. It extended along a three-mile ridge, its purpose to block an attack from the west toward Bukit Timah Heights and Singapore City. As a final defense, engineers blew a seventy-foot gap in the causeway.

The Attack on Singapore Island

After several days of pin-point artillery preparations, the Japanese 5th and 18th divisions launched 13,000 men toward the north shore at 10:30 P.M., 8 February. Another 10,000 followed at dawn. Most were in rubber boats or on rafts. Many soldiers simply waded across the Johore Strait when they discovered that the water was only four feet deep at low tide. Although British forward posts sighted the assault craft, no searchlights were turned on because the staff was afraid they would be shot out. Worse, the artillery did not open fire. A four-gun battery at Timgah airfield had 4,000 rounds of high explosive shells. No firing orders were given, nor did the gunners see any signal rockets. Telephone communications were disrupted by artillery fire and bombing, but no one thought to use the radios, which may or may not have worked. When some guns did commence firing, the results were indifferent because there was no reliable artillery spotting. That left the 22nd Australian Brigade in the West Sector without support.

On 9 February, the 22nd withdrew under incessant Japanese attacks. It was not orderly. Men were lost in the jungles and swamps, and units lost contact with each other. The brigade streamed to the rear. The panic-stricken among them were clad only in shorts and some had no boots, having thrown away everything that might hold them back.

In contrast, the Japanese landings on the Kranji Peninsula near the causeway met stiff resistance from the 27th Australian Brigade. By midnight, their attack was stalled. Earlier, Brigadier D. S. Maxwell, commanding the 27th, requested he be allowed to withdraw for fear of being outflanked. General Heath denied the request. Yamashita then advanced the Imperial Guards to break the stalemate. Reluctantly at first, the Guards crossed the strait and attacked. Maxwell's anxieties apparently increased. At about 4:30 A.M., he unilaterally withdrew his men. The *Official History* stated that he was eventually given permission to do so—but whether that was ex post facto remains unclear, for it was not until 5:10 A.M. that West Sector headquarters knew of the movement. The result of Maxwell's withdrawal was catastrophic. A gap opened in the defenses, clearing the way south to Bukit Timah Road and exposing the rear of the Jurong Line. Brigadier H. B. Taylor, holding the center of the line with remnants of the 22nd Australians, added to the confusion by mis-reading a secret withdrawal plan sent by Percival. Rather than seeing the plan as a contingency, Taylor read it as an order and immediately withdrew to new positions. Major General H. G. Bennett, commanding the West Sector, was furious but let the withdrawal stand. The Jurong Line now had a gaping hole in its center. Rather than being plugged, the entire line was abandoned. The way to Singapore City was open, and only collapse could follow. The Japanese were but a few moments away from victory.

Despite low morale, defections from the ranks, and minimal or non-existent support, many British units kept on fighting. On 11 and 12 February, the remaining men of the 22nd Australians, heavily out-numbered, withstood repeated attacks by two Japanese regiments from the 18th Division. At the same time, units of the British 18th Division blunted an attack along the Bukit Timah Road. These brave actions by the defenders were not decisive but only temporary reprieves from what now seemed inevitable—surrender.

Bombing at will, the Japanese turned Singapore City into an inferno. Devastation was everywhere—crumbling buildings, fires, burst water mains and sewer pipes draining into the streets. Fuel storage tanks ran to waste. There were 2,000 civilian casualties each day. Bodies were in the ruins, the streets, and in the canals. Groups of soldiers, without leadership and without discipline, sullenly gathered about town. Gangs of armed men looted or forced their way onto boats, hoping to escape.

On Sunday afternoon, 15 February 1942, Lieutenant General Percival met General Yamashita in the ruins of the Ford Motor Company plant near Bukit Timah. Under the gaze of the gathered press corps, Percival unconditionally surrendered. Churchill and the military establishment never forgave him. The siege of Singapore had ended and, with it, European domination in the Far East.

CATEGORIES OF COMBAT

Infantry versus Infantry

In truth, the final question was never how long Singapore could hold out but how soon it would fall. Furthermore, the siege did not begin when the Japanese reached the Johore Strait; nor did the attack on the island answer the question of how soon the siege would be over. All that took place in the jungle, along the roads, and at the bridges of the Malayan Peninsula as a contest between infantry formations. That does not discount the importance of artillery nor, especially, the influence of tanks and air power. Rather, it is a realization that infantry conquers or loses territory.

The dour tenor of so many historical studies aside, the British infantry often fought very well, indeed, sometimes staggering the Japanese advance but never often enough and never conclusively. On 15 December, for example, at Gurun, about thirty miles south of the collapsed Jitra Line, the Japanese attacked elements of the 11th Indian Division, penetrating positions held by the 1/8th Punjabis. Brigadier W. O. Lay, commanding the 6th Brigade, personally led a counter-attack. The savagery and determination of the Punjab bayonet charge surprised the Japanese, who fell back. Hours later, however, the 11th Division withdrew. Five days later at the Muar River in Northern Johore the largely under-trained 45th Indian Brigade, just off their troopship, were thrown into battle and were immediately attacked by the Imperial Guards. Two battalions of the 45th, badly mauled, managed a counter-attack. Remnants of the brigade were re-grouped by Lieutenant Colonel C.G.W. Anderson. He gathered what was left of an Australian battalion and tried to escape encirclement. A roadblock stood in their way. Several attacks by the ragtag force failed. Anderson then personally led a bayonet charge and cleared the barrier. Brigadier H. C. Duncan, staying behind with the rear guard, led an attack against a freshly reinforced Japanese column supported by tanks. Duncan was killed, but Anderson brought out 850 men. It was the ferocity of these attacks by the young Indians and Australians and the unquestioned gallantry of their leaders that made the Imperial Guards hesitate when ordered to attack Singapore Island. As Leasor put it, "the Guards had lost some stomach for war."

If some defenders occasionally fought with such determination, why, then, did they fail to fight that way consistently? A litany of standard answers leaps forward: The men were inexperienced and under-trained, they lacked pride in their units which comes from long service, and the policy of hold-and-withdraw was debilitating both physically and emotionally. Also, Percival and his staff were of little help. Removed from the battles, sequestered at headquarters in Singapore, their staff work was often sloppy, and they did not have the means or the inclination to inspire confidence.

Reasons for failure can be multiplied, but fundamental to them all was the gradual disintegration of the army units. Disintegration is not merely the loss of organizational integrity; there is as well a disbelief that the system will work and that the values for which one might die are worth the cost. When the belief and value systems come crashing down, there is nothing for the soldier to do but hang on and try to survive. The expression of that survival might take the form of associating one's fate with smaller and smaller groups, from the battalion down to the squad. However, the final association may be with an informal, extra-military grouping that is a fortuitous banding together of men who, in mutual despair, associate survival with that group's continued existence, a condition present during the last weeks at Kut-al-Amara. The men might overtly desert. They might also stay in place but psychologically disappear, opting-out, internally deserting, choosing to ignore the mandates of duty in favor of conformity to informal group norms. For if the formal, military norms can only guarantee death, then those of the informal group, even though un-tested, might lead to survival. Two examples illustrate this process.

The Japanese scooped up 3,000 prisoners near Changlun, men who had wandered from their posts allegedly looking for shelter from the torrential rains. I suspect many of these men inwardly deserted before the battle. Afraid and inexperienced, their level of confidence in stopping the Japanese foundered before it was tested. They did not run away; they simply stopped being soldiers.

The Japanese later attacked and penetrated the Jitra Line. Major General Murray-Lyon, commanding the Jitra defenses, thought his situation was worse than it actually was and ordered a general withdrawal to Alor Star. This was fifteen miles away, a hard march through jungle, swamps, and heavy rains. Units were separated, officers lost their men, but most made it to Alor Star. Others did not. Dis-spirited at giving up a defensible line, having turned their back on the enemy, knowing full well it would be only a matter of time before Alor Star was abandoned, clusters of men formed their own groups and walked across country to the coast, found boats, and headed south, one group getting to Sumatra. Some groups simply foundered, not knowing quite what to do.

The context of battle was a major contribution to disintegration. Most of the men had never seen a jungle. But neither had the Japanese. The difference, as we shall see, is that the Japanese soldiers knew why they were in Malaya; the British troops did not. That lack of understanding, combined with youth, inexperience, fear, and exhaustion, proved lethal in a jungle environment. One direction looked like another. Trails disappeared into fetid growth. Muffled sounds were magnified by imagination—a broken stick, a falling branch, rustling leaves—animal or enemy? Japanese sometimes were disguised as natives. Who were the enemy? Rain—200 inches in the uplands was not unusual—flooded trenches, obscured vision, and distorted or disguised sounds. When the rain stopped, the humidity soared, sapping energy, wrapping the mind in wet cotton. Compasses went askew, telephone lines shorted or were cut, boots and jackets rotted. Artillery, once in place, resisted movement from the muck. Vehicles stalled. The machinery of war, already abused by bad planning and neglect, came to a coughing halt. The system was not working. Again, the men surrendered, walked away, or opted-out.

The peninsula survivors who finally crossed the causeway to Singapore Island were a tired and beaten lot. However, the last to cross the causeway, their remaining two pipers playing, were the Argyll and Sutherland Highlanders, the proud beneficiaries of traditions formed by actions such as the "thin red line" at Balaclava and the regiment's determined attacks at Lucknow during the Great Indian Mutiny. But there were only 250 men left of the original 900.

The worst was yet to come.

The Artillery Component

The effectiveness of British artillery was uneven. At Jitra, the Japanese were at first concerned by the intensity of British fire, Tsuji indicating he thought they had encountered a powerful defense. The Japanese were in a difficult situation, unable to advance anywhere along their line. Then British fire suddenly moved to a rubber plantation where there were no targets. The Japanese, concluding that the guns were firing without artillery observers, simply moved around the bombardment and continued their attack. At Gurun, British artillery supporting the 28th Brigade initially caused heavy casualties among the Japanese, slowing their advance. But, once again, the firing was in random patterns because it was undirected by observers.

British anti-tank fire was usually quite accurate, if for no other reason than that their targets were visible and closer. Ranges of fifty yards were common. At Jitra the leading Japanese tanks and accompanying armored vehicles were subjected to heavy anti-tank fire. Casualties mounted. However, any hope of successfully spiking the Japanese advance collapsed for lack of support, lack of reliable intelligence, and the ever-present concern about being outflanked. When the order to withdraw arrived, the British abandoned about fifty guns.

The battle for Singapore Island placed the artillery of both sides in a more traditional role than experienced in the highly mobile campaign down the peninsula. The Japanese had 440 guns to place the length of the Johore Strait. But knowing where they would attack, they alternately spread and concentrated their artillery along the shore. The British were blind to the locations of enemy guns because the Japanese made good use of the jungle to disguise their emplacements. In contrast, the Japanese could see the British north shore positions from the height of the Johore Palace towers, enabling them to place their shots with considerable accuracy. British artillery, without eyes, could only put down harassing fire. Also, their guns, especially the 25-pounders, were restricted to 20 rounds per gun per day. The Japanese allotment was 100 rounds per field gun and 50 rounds for heavier pieces. That allotment was for the preliminary bombardment. The allotment for the island assault was 400 rounds per field gun and 125 rounds for the heavier pieces.

When the Japanese launched their attack against the West Sector, most British guns did not fire until after the landing. Thus, once on the island, the Japanese encountered frequent heavy artillery fire, as when the Imperial Guards attacked the fortifications at Changi. Unfortunately for the defenders, a familiar pattern was repeated. Tsuji observed that most of the British shells landed harmlessly in treetops, meaning the gunners were again firing blind. The Japanese scattered their batteries among the trees of the rubber plantations, not only obscuring them but, as well, leading the British to over-estimate the number of guns facing them.

The British artillery defense overall was characterized by undirected and uncoordinated fire, by poor communications that resulted sometimes in not firing at all, and by a constant attrition of equipment and supplies as a consequence of abandonment. This unsteady performance helped feed the growing disaster.

Tanks

The British did not have tanks because the chiefs-of-staff did not believe them appropriate to jungle warfare. But the Japanese had fifty-seven tanks in the invasion force. Broken up into company formations, they were used as close support for the infantry. At Jitra, on 10 December, Punjab units of the 11th Division were attacked by tanks and motorized infantry. "Firing indiscriminately ahead and on to both sides," the British *Official History* noted, "the Japanese tanks broke through." Tsuji thought they looked like "angry cattle running amok."

Obviously the Japanese used tanks to punch holes in the British lines. But I should like to add an observation made by John Keegan, Richard Holmes, and John Gau in their study *Soldiers:* The real effect of tanks may not be as weapons but in their psychological impact. They can lift the morale of the attacking troops, making them feel invincible, a fact attested to by Tsuji, who closely followed the advancing Japanese infantry. Equally, tanks can demoralize an enemy. This was especially so in Malaya, where the use of tanks came as a complete surprise to the British. Even though British anti-tank fire caused severe casualties in some tank units, there were never enough guns at the right places to make a permanent impact. The Japanese just kept coming—demoralizing enough; added to this was the fact that many young soldiers, particularly among the Indian troops, had never seen a tank. Their training and expectations had not prepared them for the onslaught they encountered.

Air Power

The relentless Japanese attack bore remarkable resemblance to the German blitzkrieg in Europe. General Yamashita visited Germany in 1940 and, however unimpressed he was with Adolph Hitler—thinking him as interesting as a minor clerk—he was much impressed with the blitzkrieg idea, involving coordination between infantry, artillery, armor, and air power. Under Yamashita's command and Tsuji's planning, air power became an extension of the ground war, what Keegan would call "flying artillery." Every major objective down the peninsula and on Singapore Island was subjected to intense bombing. In traditional terms, the Japanese air force flew over the British defenses as surely as the First Crusaders vaulted Jerusalem's walls. That gave them unrelinquished offensive domination over the island.

The R.A.F. could not stop the Japanese attacks. British aircraft continued operational, but their pilots ascended to their deaths. The clunky Buffalo fighters could not compete with the agile Zero. The Japanese fighter flew at 331 mph, could stay aloft with added fuel tanks for six to eight hours, and was armed not only with two machine guns but, as well, two 20mm cannons. The plane could also carry a 550-pound bomb. The Japanese twin-engine bombers—Sally 2s, Nells, and Bettys—were as fast as the Buffalo and were well armed against fighter attack. The Sally and Betty carried 2,000-pound bomb loads, twice the capacity of British bombers.

The Japanese bombers flew over Singapore City at 20,000 feet in tight V-formations, dropping their loads wherever they pleased. When they left, dive bombers swooped in to drop shrapnel bombs. Then fighters raced across the city, strafing anything that moved.

Civilian casualties were beyond anyone's estimations, partly because refugees from the peninsula doubled the population, partly because there were no air raid shelters. In 1937, Thomas's civil government decided against shelters because the water table was too high and because their construction in the city might unsettle the population. Instead, camps were constructed outside the city with capacities for 350,000 each. They quickly filled and overflowed.

The air raids, like the tanks on the peninsula, had a visibly negative psychological effect in a city already experiencing fractured confidence. The news that Asians on Penang Island were left behind during the evacuation left Asians in Singapore wondering if they, too, were to be sacrificed by their British masters. The Asians and the British did not establish reciprocal affection in a city where the only common belief was in profit. Now there was only common suffering. The inability of the military to stop the air raids, the deserters roaming the streets, and the clamor to board anything that floated were clear indications that the city was ripe for capitulation.

The Will to Combat

A profound despair gripped the defenders. Exhausted by the trek down the peninsula with all its seemingly useless battles, distracted by news from Britain or Australia or India, bewildered as the naval base facilities were systematically destroyed by their own demolition teams, and wondering what there was left to defend, the British garrison reached the end of their spiritual endurance. If their leaders could inspire a greater sense of purpose, if the troops were better trained, if there were more experienced men in the garrison, if artillery and air support had been effective, if . . .

The Japanese had their own problems. They were low on ammunition and nearly out of gasoline. The men were tired and they had many casualties. But Yamashita realized the British did not know either the strength or condition of his army. He actually considered his attack on Singapore Island a great bluff. Despite their physical and logistical condition, the Japanese kept going with obvious determination. Why? The pamphlet *Read This Alone—And the War Can Be Won*, now appended to Tsuji's book, *Singapore: The Japanese Version*, was distributed to every soldier. Within the lessons on jungle survival was also a statement of purpose. The Japanese soldiers were to liberate the Far East from white colonial domination. Therefore, the war was a clash between races in which no mercy was to be shown the enemy. Killing a European (Germans and Italians excepted) would lighten the heart and dispel the anger felt from years of European oppression. Singapore was a major step in the unification of all Asia within the utopian Japanese Co-Prosperity Sphere. Victory meant not merely the military defeat of the British; it meant their complete humiliation.

Underlying that need to humiliate their enemy was a cultural context extending back to the days of feudal Japan. Honor, loyalty, and a willingness to die for the emperor—the *bushido* code of the samurai class—were old ideals brought forward, as Keeghan and Homes state, and fused into the modern Japanese army. Even the common soldiers were now samurai. Thus, the Japanese troops could relate to historical traditions, even if romanticized and propagandized, and that turned their campaign into a moral imperative.

AFTERMATH

The Japanese certainly did not have a walk-over victory at Singapore. Tsuji indicated that they suffered in the overall campaign 3,507 killed and 6,150 wounded. The British did not know they inflicted such harm. Certainly the frontline troops did not know what they had done. But Percival and his staff, who should have known, were equally oblivious. All they could see was a constant failure to stop the enemy. This was a failure of their intelligence capability and faulty staff evaluation of those reports that were made. In fact, many reports were never evaluated because they were never properly processed, just put on a pile of papers and ignored. There would be delaying actions on Singapore Island, but there would be no stand among the ruins of the city.

What became abundantly clear to the British as they surrendered, and what has been subsequently reinforced by historians, was that humiliation was only partial payment for surrender. Atrocities were the full measure. As an ineluctable consequence of Japanese xenophobic military indoctrination (rooted in the idea of *gaijin*—that non-Japanese are inferior and devils or dirty pigs), of the preening morality of their cause, of viewing British soldiers as dishonorable for not having died in battle rather than surrendering, there were many instances of brutal, inhuman conduct.

When the Japanese broke through the British lines at Parit Sulong, they captured contingents of Australian and Indian troops. They beheaded 110 Australians and 35 Indians. At Ipoh in Kuala Lumpur many Chinese were decapitated and their heads stuck on poles as a warning to the civilians to behave. On Singapore Island the Japanese entered the Alexandra British Military Hospital on 13 February, under the impression that artillery spotters were using the building. Medical personnel were lined up in a hall and bayoneted. A patient on an operating table was run through. Other personnel were roped together and packed into small rooms. Later, some of these groups were taken out and bayoneted. Chinese within the city were herded into stockades where the Japanese secret police made selections for execution. The Japanese took over 130,000 prisoners of war. The *Official History* states that total casualties, including these prisoners, numbered 138,788. If accurate, the British forces suffered fewer battle casualties than did the Japanese. No matter. The Japanese prevailed. What awaited the prisoners was a hellish existence in which they were tortured, beaten, and starved in prison camps such as the one at Changi or worked to death on the roads and railways the Japanese wanted built in Burma.

Tsuji regretted the atrocities, saying they were not planned or approved by the army staff. Yamashita, at his war crimes trial, said he was not responsible for the behavior of troops beyond his immediate control. That defense did not wash, and he was executed. Tsuji, ordered by Tokyo to disappear rather than be taken prisoner, lived and travelled incognito in Asia until, cleared of war crimes, he was able to return to Japan.

In retrospect it is easy to say that Thomas, Percival, and Brooke-Popham might have done more, could have done more, that they might have stopped the Japanese a little longer. To shift all the anger and guilt for the loss on these men and their staffs has been quite easy. None was a compelling personality. None was particularly attractive militarily or even historically. But for all their faults, I cannot escape the conclusion that the fall of Singapore was fore-doomed as early as the initial planning of the base. Despite the great illusion surrounding the place, despite the brave messages demanding a fight in the ruins of the city, Singapore was a poor joke, badly planned from the onset. The assumption that naval power would protect the base was planned obsolescence in an age turning to air power. My assertion is a trifle glib because, in the 1920s, air power had few advocates. However, by 1940, the future of air warfare was being clearly written in the skies over Poland, Holland, Belgium, and France. Of course, there is the added dismal thought that even if the British had provided sufficient planes and had established aerial superiority over Singapore, they would not have known how to take proper advantage of it, given their primitive state of tactical air support in early 1942. It mattered not. Because the fleet was considered its salvation, Singapore was always rated low on the military and fiscal priority lists. The great base because a victim of its own myth.

Once the Japanese landed at Singora and Kota Bharu, the British attempts at reinforcements were as much a bad bargain based on faulty arithmetic as were the attempts to relieve the Kut garrison in 1916. Singapore—whether that included the Malayan Peninsula, the island, the city, or the naval base—never really had a chance.

Chapter 7

Five Sieges: Constants and Variables

Sieges, as the five foregoing examples demonstrate, are a complex battle form. In the broadest sense, sieges express the technological, organizational, and cultural characteristics of the societies that spawned them. Thus, for example, the Crusaders were not merely any army invading the Near East. They were Europeans, mostly French at that, who were nurtured in the bosom of Western feudalism and the values taught by Roman Catholicism. These factors conditioned the perceptions they had of their enemy and the manner in which they fought. More narrowly, within confined physical space and a prolonged duration of time, sieges can also express, or expose, an army's technological and organizational shortcomings and any strain that exists between the army's formal values and the realities imposed by battle. Such was the case in Singapore, the defense of which was muddled from the start, hampered by inadequate equipment, and debilitated by plummeting confidence in the overt values of the military. Sieges can be planned or unintended, a tactical necessity or a strategic maneuver. Their significance can reach beyond the purely military aspects of the conflict and affect, as did the Crusade, the direction of the whole culture. Or a siege, such as Kut, may be doomed to insignificance except to those fated to die in it.

Even a cursory examination of the sieges offered here suggests that they have similarities that link them regardless of time or place. They are also separated by some important differences. What follows at the risk of some redundancy is a sorting out of the similarities and differences, the constants and variables.

SIEGES AS A FORM OF BATTLE

Histories of sieges, as noted earlier, often are narratives of who did what to whom, when and where, or portraits of the evolution of weapons technology and fortress building. These approaches are not misplaced, for they are an essential part of military history. The problem with narration is that it tends to dehumanize the battles by seeing them as movements of large units or utilizes sieges to reveal the personalities of various commanders. The technological approach can also dehumanize by viewing sieges merely as changes in weapons systems and defenses.

But sieges, first and foremost, are human conflicts, the most constant factor of any battle. George Patton went to the heart of the matter when he said in so many words that a battle is a place where a soldier tries to kill the other poor son-of-a-bitch before that soldier can kill him. Humans kill humans. That is the essence of battle. And more: Being human conflicts, sieges are therefore moral conflicts. Defeat entails not merely the triumph of one weapons system over another but, as John Keegan notes in *The Face Of Battle*, the moral disintegration of the opposition, bringing the enemy to the point where it can go no further physically, emotionally, or ideologically.

Another constant shared by sieges with other battle forms is that they are bewildering, filled with noise, unbearable sights, destruction, terror, cruelty, and even tenderness. The difference, the variable, between sieges and other types of battle is that sieges have historically taken those characteristics and confined them spatially to a given place. Battles have grown larger in terms of the space they consume, from Agincourt's narrow field to the 2,000-mile World War II German advance into Russia. True, the 1916 battles in Mesopotamia fought by the relief force ranged over miles, but the Kut front was only yards wide. The Japanese fought their way down the long Malayan Peninsula, but once at the Johore Strait they were confronted by the narrow front of Singapore Island.

Military histories commonly point out the savagery that seems constant in sieges. Terrible things happen in sieges: Decapitated heads and fetid corpses catapulted back and forth, a town's survivors slaughtered, and prisoners launched on death marches. That brutality is related to the spatial restrictions imposed by sieges. The opposing forces face each other in physical proximity along a static front over an extended time period, creating a context for the intensification of their actions and responses. With luck and/or tenacity, the defenders may force the offense to leave, as at Malta. Yet, at the same time, Malta exemplified the savagery of spatially constricted combat in which the cry was "Take no prisoners." When the defense wins, they can pick up the pieces of their lives, until then destroyed by the siege. If the offense wins, they often unleash on the defense's survivors the full fury of pent-up frustrations and hatred born, as at Jerusalem or Kut, not just from ethnic, political, or religious differences, but as a response to the audacity of the defenders to hold out, making the offense battle longer than they thought really necessary.

Battles, as Keegan also notes, require that the two sides agree to fight. Sieges, perhaps more than any other battle form, require that agreement.

The defenders must accept the proposition that a siege is the best solution to whatever military problem they face and that such an action is in their collective best interests. The offense must come to the same conclusion. Sometimes, as at Kut, the decision comes about incidentally. Sometimes, as at Jerusalem, a siege is inevitable. At Malta, however, La Valette enticed Suleiman into the siege. In 1854, the Russians probably thought their little war with the Turks was over when they withdrew behind the Danube frontier. But Sebastopol harbored the Black Sea Fleet, an untouched and threatening power that taunted the British and French. Singapore sat like a fat beetle, waiting to be swallowed by a predator. The Japanese obliged.

Every battle must also have its leaders, those who make the command decisions. But, as with most battles, our five examples represent a considerable but predictable pattern of variations. First, over the broad historical sweep, there was a transition from traditional leaders—such as the lords who led the Crusade—to increasingly bureaucratic leadership—such as the line-staff organizations at Kut and Singapore. Second, with each siege reflecting points in that transition, the leaders became more spatially separated from the forces under their command. Raymond of Toulouse and Bohemund, for instance, led their men at the point of attack. That is where the feudal lords belonged. But Grand Master La Valette commanded mostly from Birgu, however close it was to the fighting. Raglan observed the battles in which his troops engaged. He was always close to the fighting but just behind it, supposedly to direct troop movements. At least that was the theory. In fact, his field generals and regimental officers conducted the battles. But Kut and Singapore had leadership from afar. Nixon was mostly in Basra, making decisions a hundred miles from the fighting front. At Singapore, Percival spent most of his time in his Singapore City headquarters, sifting through reports that sometimes did not reach his desk until any decision was too late for the troops doing the fighting.

The Crusading lords argued and flaunted their egos and postured; yet, being at the front, they could and did, with considerable effectiveness, adjust to changing battle conditions. In contrast, the army at Singapore was encased in Percival's outdated conception of battle and London's planned obsolescence, unable to adjust quickly to new battle conditions and the need for new organization.

The significance of these five sieges has been repeatedly argued, so I shall not reprise those debates here. Whatever interpretation is given them, whatever ironies and ambiguities they possess, one point is clear. Once the decision to offer siege is made and that offer is accepted, however implicitly, the norms, attitudes, values, and beliefs of the troops will be sorely tested in the ensuing conflict. To win or to lose a siege easily becomes a moral imperative, perhaps the most human of the qualities of this type of battle.

THE SIEGE AS DEFENSE: CONSTANTS AND VARIABLES

The Will To Combat: The Variable of Commitment

When a garrison commander offers siege, he must be certain that he can supply his troops and that he has the weapons necessary to hold back the besiegers. His certainty may be an illusion, but it is a certainty he must possess. He must also be sure that his troops and any remaining civilians within his perimeter are equally committed to the siege.

The commitment of troops and civilians was, in many instances, taken for granted. The governor of a town, such as Jerusalem, was also its military commander. He understood conditions because he was intimately a part of them. If, as was common through the seventeenth century, a warring lord took refuge in a town, he could rely on local loyalties because the place was probably in his domain. From among the five sieges compared, only Sebastopol provides an example of such absolute certainty, in which the largely homogeneous population became a major factor in the city's defense. Malta gives us an interesting twist on the theme. The Knights of St. John were imposed on the Maltese, and there was an initial coolness between the two groups. But once the siege was under way, the Maltese unhesitatingly cast their fortunes with the knights and were crucial to the eventual victory.

Commitment is suspect if the population is at all mixed. Thus, Iftikhar, governor of Jerusalem, quickly sent the Christians packing. Townshend found an all-Moslem population in Kut and, likewise, wanted to expel them. The political officer in Basra would not let him. Singapore had the most diverse population of the five examples. The Asians, mostly Chinese, had no particular loyalties to Britain, a situation made worse by the local colonial authorities who were suspicious of them. Nonetheless, those leaders had ample opportunity to harness the cooperation of the Asians against a common enemy. A volunteer force was finally established, but rather late to do much good. Unfortunately, many Asians felt alienated by such stupid acts as the selective evacuation of Penang Island. The Chinese did form guerrilla groups after the defeat that became, following the war, the cadres of an anti-British insurrection.

Even though civilian commitment is essential to withstanding a siege, there is also a military variable that must be considered. Loyalty of the troops cannot always be taken for granted. Any army has its potential deserters and even traitors. That such acts do not occur more frequently is usually the result of indoctrination, training, discipline, fear of punishment, and concern that such acts might harm one's comrades.

More frequent, and more so in sieges because of their static nature, is the phenomenon of internal desertion. Not wanting to get shot for overt desertion and finding the prospect of military prison uninviting, the soldier, as Keegan succinctly puts it, decides to opt-out and be a soldier no more. Alluded to in relation to Kut and Singapore, soldiers felt isolated and alienated from the normative behaviors and expectations of the army. At Kut, many units simply folded in upon themselves, trying to become invisible. In Malaya, many soldiers near Alor Star simply sat down, abandoning their artillery pieces and other positions, hoping they might go unnoticed. Later, other troops filtered into Singapore City, weaponless, without organization and discipline, and sullenly lounged about, waiting for the end to come.

Objective battle conditions have little to do with internal desertion. Heavy casualties, for instance, may dis-spirit some troops but, as Robert McQuie demonstrates (in T. N. Dupuy's work, *Understanding Defeat*), there is no necessary relationship between casualty rates and perceptions of defeat. Thus, John Baynes discovers that the 2nd Scottish Rifles at the battle of Neuve Chapelle in 1915 were still a cohesive fighting unit even after six days of battle and 70 percent casualties. And Dupuy observes that the disciplined German army in 1944 and 1945 carried on despite high casualties.

Internal desertion is a soldier's subjective interpretation of events that leads him to a moral crisis. Ought he to continue his soldier's role, following behavioral norms, believing that such acceptance has purpose and will influence in some small way the battle's outcome; or should he reject military norms and beliefs, finding them increasingly meaningless because of his psychological isolation from them? If he see continuation as purposeless, he will opt-out. What he does depends on the situation but, in all likelihood, he will find others who feel the same. The decision to do something or to do nothing at all—a viable option in a battle—will frequently be a small group decision, replacing institutional military norms with those of the group's making and related to survival.

The Defensive Perimeter

Every besieged place must establish a continuous defensive perimeter. Jerusalem had a curtain wall. Sebastopol's walls were reinforced by great bastions. Kut was surrounded on three sides by the Tigris River and, on the landward side, by a series of entrenched lines.

Fortifications on Malta were not, overall, continuous because the topography of Grand Harbor precluded such building. Instead, the defenses were jammed together around the harbor inlets, making them contiguous rather than continuous. Each fort and bastion covered another, and the fall of one did not lead to the fall of the others. Fort St. Elmo was eventually captured, and Fort St. Michael took a tremendous pounding but stood. The Turks, unable to get footholds on Senglea and Birgu, and unable to penetrate the mutually supportive fortifications, finally withdrew.

Singapore's defensive problems were built into the earliest plans for the naval base. The notion was widely accepted that the base was to be defended by coast artillery and the Royal Navy. Unfortunately, no definition was given the defensive perimeter. Changes in military tactics and technology over the years, rather than challenging the decision-makers, were mostly ignored. No one wanted to believe, not with the force of a conviction, that the naval base was obsolete and could not be defended in isolation from the island and the peninsula. Born of optimism, indeed, boundless faith in sea power and a correlative resistance to air power, harboring misconceptions about the Japanese and their own capacities, unable to accept reality once hostilities commenced, those charged with Singapore's defense bumbled along, not knowing what they were supposed to defend. Consequently, additions to an expanded perimeter were half-hearted at best.

Defense In-depth

Not only must defenders establish a continuous perimeter or a viable substitute, they must also, as another constant, have a defense in-depth. How the five besieged fortresses achieved or failed to achieve that depth represents variations on the theme.

But for Jerusalem's rather exotic setting, the siege might just as easily have taken place in Britain, France, Germany, or Italy because, among other factors, the means of achieving in-depth defense did not differ from European practices. Jerusalem, fortified for a millennium, looked much like a European castle with its perimeter wall and towers. Depth was achieved in three ways. First, an exterior ditch surrounded the walls. Second, the countryside was gleaned of food, and the water wells were poisoned. Third, the physical position of the city, flanked by two valleys and a ravine, helped keep besiegers at a distance.

The defense was also predicated on incorrect assumptions about the Crusaders. Initially, the defenders probably believed, certainly hoped, the Crusaders would never reach the city. Either the Turks or the desert would stop them, the ultimate in-depth defense. But the Crusaders persevered and took Jerusalem, overcoming their deprivations. One problem with the defense was that its depth proved inadequate. What Iftikhar established was not so much an in-depth defensive zone as a dead zone, a void the offense needed to fill.

A completely different in-depth scheme was used on Malta. La Valette realized he could not stop the Turkish landings. Mustapha and Piali had too many men on too many ships, and they could land most anywhere. By concentrating his defense around the Grand Harbor, La Valette massed his artillery across narrow fronts, enjoyed the advantages of rapid reinforcement and re-supply, and responded quickly to changing battle conditions. The multiplicity of fortifications gave the defenders their needed depth. Artillery batteries gave covering fire to other points, exemplified by the battery located beneath Fort St. Angelo that sunk the Turkish flotilla headed for Senglea. But each position was also independent. The ravelin at St. Elmo was lost and then the fort itself. The cavalier above St. Michael was lost. The castile was overwhelmed. These Moslem victories came, however, at the cost of thousands of casualties, losses that not only bled their army but undermined confidence. Each victory was followed by the realization that there was another bastion, another fort, or another breach to assault. In the end, exhausted by their attritional attacks, discouraged by the defenders' tenacity, weakened by disease and running short of supplies, the Turks went home.

The Sebastopol defenses, like other nineteenth-century seaport defenses, were based on coast artillery and the presence of an intimidating fleet. Wisely anticipating that an enemy would not risk a sea-borne attack, the defenders built a series of walls on the landward side reinforced by strong bastions. These were mutually supportive. Additionally, outworks, such as the Mamelon and the Quarries, gave some depth. Further depth was achieved with mobile batteries behind the bastions and from shipboard guns in the harbor.

But the Sebastopol defenses, superficially similar in principle to those on Malta, differed in one important respect. The bastions appeared mutually supportive, but they were not sufficiently independent. Consequently, when the French took the Malakoff, they internally out-flanked the Great Redan and the Little Redan. What was planned as Sebastopol's greatest strength turned out to be its greatest weakness.

At Kut, Townshend sought to establish in-depth defenses by placing his artillery so that it was supportive of almost any area and by establishing three defensive lines across the neck of the little peninsula. After the December attacks, these lines were not seriously contested. Ironically, the Turks at Kut are seen as the besiegers, but in the field against Aylmer's relief column their role because defensive. They consistently drew the British into battle, determining when and where they would fight. Then it was the Turk's turn to establish two or three defensive lines. If they abandoned the first, it was usually to avoid artillery bombardment. In turn, Turkish counter-barrages and concentrated machine gun and rifle fire frequently stopped British advances.

Singapore's initial reliance on a strongly fortified naval base, using coast artillery and the threat of naval retaliation seems suspiciously like the Sebastopol defenses. Indeed, the efficacy of sea power survived the nineteenth century and conditioned the thinking of Singapore's planners. But all the ingredients for in-depth defense were in place. Had the possibility of a Japanese march down the peninsula been taken seriously, a system of well-defended airfields with proper aircraft could have been established. The defenses at Kota Bharu, the Jitra Line, and the Matador Plan were all good ideas, but they were uncoordinated and too late.

Having all but conceded the Malay Peninsula, a stout defense was needed on the island's north shore. Some of Yamashita's officers were reluctant to attack the island right away because of supply shortages and concern for the men. Seeing the defenders with greater clarity than his staff, knowing the shore defenses were thin, and willing to gamble, Yamashita successfully attacked Singapore Island. Percival's division of the island into defensive zones was appropriate. What he did not realize was that his zoned defense was too thin because of the grave condition of many of his troops and because both civilian and military morale were rapidly deteriorating. These factors, coupled with faulty communications, poorly written orders, and muddled staff work, contributed to the breakdown, exemplified by the premature evacuation of the Jurong Line. Thus, none of Singapore's potentialities for in-depth defense were realized.

Defensive Domination

Domination simply means that the defenders seek higher ground than the besiegers. Many medieval castles, if not on high ground, were built with tiered walls, machicolations, and castle keeps to artificially create domination.

The perimeter ditch around Jerusalem's curtain wall was not only an attempt to establish in-depth defense but, as well, to create domination. At the critical point where the offense reached the wall, they stood at their lowest level in relation to the defenders on the parapets. The ditch literally increased the height of the wall. Exactly the same principal was used in the ditches in front of the Great Redan and the Malakoff at Sebastopol. Thus, the Redan's walls were fifteen feet high and the ditch was twenty feet deep. That meant the offense faced a total escalation of thirty-five feet.

Malta represented a complete contradiction to the principle of defensive domination. The cliffs and ridges around Grand Harbor, what in most instances would be regarded as essential and natural defensive positions, were conceded to the Turks. La Valette believed that if the forts, trenches, and strongpoints were placed on the cliffs, their exposure to enemy fire would have made re-supply and reinforcement very difficult. Moreover, the Turks could have isolated each position and taken them with relative ease. Concentrating the forts and their firepower at the harbor level was a calculated risk because they were susceptible to Turkish fire from above. Indeed, the Turkish guns boomed away day after day, creating a lot of rubble. But when their infantry attacked the rubble, they found it alive with defenders. The attacks wilted.

As with the Turkish gunners on Malta, the allied artillerymen at Sebastopol could not make significant breaches in the defensive walls. Nevertheless, infantry attacks were made against what, for the Russians, was near-ideal defensive domination by their gunners. They brought the British advances against the Great Redan to halt, they cut down Mayran's advance, and they caused high casualties among the other French columns that charged directly into their cannon fire in the June attack.

The Kut siege is irrelevant to defensive domination. Topographically, the flat land, below the Tigris flood level, prevented domination. But when the Turks assumed a defensive role against the relief column, they forced the British to attack them across open and flat ground. The Turks seized what high ground there was and, being more familiar with the terrain and its illusions, they dominated the offense in most situations.

Singapore was more complex. The Japanese established air superiority within forty-eight hours of landing and maneuvered at will over the Malay Peninsula and Singapore Island. When the ground troops reached the Johore Strait, they deceived the British with false fronts and feints. Yamashita, on slightly higher ground than the British, was able to see into the defenses. Defensive domination was, therefore, consistently denied the British. They lost most of their aircraft, observation and targeting were poor, and their Johore Strait defenses were directly under the Japanese guns.

THE SIEGE AS OFFENSE: CONSTANTS AND VARIABLES

The Will to Combat: Offensive Commitment

An offensive commander must not only be satisfied that a siege is the best solution to whatever military problems he faces; additionally, he must be convinced that his forces are committed to the enterprise. That commitment sometimes does not have the same dimension for the offense that it does for the defense in that the offense seldom deals directly with a civilian population. Thus, the issue of commitment is more a military matter for the offense. The commander assumes, or needs to assume, that indoctrination, discipline, and training has endowed his men with the will to fight. That assumption was fairly made in all five sieges, but unanticipated variables occasionally modified the degree to which the will to combat was expressed.

The beleaguered Crusaders standing before Jerusalem suffered considerable casualties and defections during their long march. Undeniably their faith, reinforced by sermons and supposed miracles, gave them needed courage and persistence. But, important as their faith was, the Crusaders were also bound by the common experience of the long campaign. They were the survivors of the first adventure of its kind in the European world, and they would not be denied their goal.

The Japanese at Singapore were driven by a similar level of commitment. At one level, the pamphlet *Read This Alone—And the War Can Be Won* preached hate and death which, joined with the bushido code, gave certainty to their cause, something the British defenders sorely lacked. The result was that Yamashita unleashed on the woeful defenders an unremitting aggressiveness with which they could not contend.

The Turks who besieged Kut and fended off the relief column were close to the Japanese in one important respect. Both Enver Pasha and Khalil

Pasha wanted to utterly humiliate the British, demonstrating to the Arab world the invincibility of Turkish arms. The transfer of the troops who had defeated the British from Gallipoli to Mesopotamia was clever. They imparted to their countrymen their confidence and pride of accomplishment.

At Malta, the Turkish leaders miscalculated their will to combat, clearly demonstrating that faith alone cannot sustain an army. The all-Moslem army that invaded Malta had superior numbers, more cannon of larger calibre than those of the defenders, freedom of the seas, run of the island, and offensive domination. Yet, they lost. By surrendering domination, La Valette drew the Turks into the constricted space of the Grand Harbor, making them fight on his terms and thereby reducing in that confined space the impact of superior numbers. All the attacks the Turks made and all the casualties they suffered accomplished very little in a considerable time span. That created a fertile ground for dissension. Mustapha and Piali blatantly disagreed with each other. The one charismatic leader who might have unified them—Dragut—was killed. The two Algerians, Hasseim and Candelissa, smugly tried to show Mustapha how an attack should be made. Mustapha was not unhappy when their attacks failed. When the Christian relief force landed on Malta and marched to Birgu unscathed, the Moslems were humiliated. The campaign that had started with so much optimism was sputtering. The Moslem departure was a certainty.

A crusading spirit, much less a compelling religious motivation, was completely lacking in the troops that marched against Sebastopol. They fought battles, they froze, they hungered, and they sweated because that was their job. And just as Colin Campbell enjoined the 93rd Highlanders at Balaclava, they would even die if necessary. That was part of the bargain they accepted when they were handed their paltry enlistment bonuses. They were professional soldiers. Their leaders may have been bumbling amateurs, but they were also unquestionably brave men who set examples of conduct for their men. When Lord Cardigan led the Charge of the Light Brigade, he had no doubts his men would be right behind him. He led the charge, as one of his most ardent critics said, "like a gentlemen." Consequently, the leaders of the British army could carry into battle one correct assumption: The men would fight. That kind of soldierly will to combat, void of articles of faith or ideology, is perhaps the greatest moral commitment of men in battle.

Penetrating the Defensive Perimeter

John Keegan notes in *The Nature of War* that an offensive constant in sieges is the necessity to penetrate the defensive perimeter. Four methods have been used with considerable consistency. These are breaching, mining, escalation, and ruse or outright treachery. Although these methods are, themselves, constants in siege warfare, their utilization has varied with specific circumstances and available technology.

Breaching is a method by which the offense tries to punch a hole in the defensive perimeter. If there is no wall, they try to cut a pathway through the defensive positions. Traditionally, this was accomplished by artillery battering the wall face. The results were very inconsistent.

At Jerusalem, the Crusaders' battering ram and catapults could not breach the walls. At Malta, the St. Elmo ravelin was breached rather quickly, but the fort, itself, withstood twenty-four days of constant pounding before the 100 survivors were overrun. Neither Fort St. Michael or Fort St. Angelo were successfully breached. A breach was opened in the Senglea perimeter, but that was caused by a magazine explosion rather than Turkish artillery. Sebastopol withstood five bombardments by as many as 800 guns at one time, but masses of wall were never brought down.

Jerusalem, Malta, and Sebastopol shared the same offensive problem. The artillery barrages were too diffuse and/or the projectiles inadequate to the task. Even as late as Sebastopol, high explosive ammunition lacked reliable fusing mechanisms and penetrating power.

At Kut, Turkish artillery severely damaged the old fort, and their infantry penetrated the position but could not hold against determined counter-attacks. But the Turks bombarding Kut shared a problem with their British enemy: They had too few guns firing the right ammunition. That partly explains why the Turks were content with a passive siege.

Japanese artillery succeeded at Singapore because they possessed the right artillery for the job. What really gave the Japanese gunners an ad-vantage was superior artillery spotting; especially in comparison to that of the British, it was impeccable. Consequently, when the Japanese crossed the Johore Strait, they met little resistance from British guns.

Traditional breaching required that the right cannon fired the right ammunition at the right targets and that those guns opened a gap large enough for the infantry to easily exploit. And that required time the offensive commander might not have because of supply and manpower limitations and because of concurrent events elsewhere in the campaign.

Commanders have tried accelerating sieges by mining at the same time the artillery bombarded the perimeter. Raymond of Toulouse tried mining the walls at Antioch, but the process was too dangerous and time-consum-ing. The Turks on Malta considered mining Fort St. Elmo but discarded the idea when they encountered the solid rock foundation on which it was built. They successfully mined the castile above Fort St. Michael, but when Piali's men charged through the opening, they were trapped by a secondary wall and slaughtered. At Kut, the Turks tried mining the old fort's outer defenses but gave up after vigorous British trench raids were made against their parties.

If breaching and mining fail, the offensive commander must resort to escalating the defenses, that is over-topping them. This was done by using ladders and towers and by hurling various projectiles into, rather than against, the fortifications, using mortars, howitzers, and rockets. Modern warfare has seen the emergence of escalation by air power. The five sieges provide examples of various means of escalation and, in the process, outline a virtual history of siege technology.

On their arrival at Jerusalem, the Crusaders attempted a frontal attack without any preparation. They hurled themselves at the walls, hoping to get enough ladders up to top the ramparts. The assault failed. Trapped in the perimeter outer ditch, showered by arrows, stones, and pitch, the Crusaders pulled back. Fortunately, a convoy landed at Jaffa with the supplies necessary to build proper siege machines. Two siege towers were built and moved against the walls. Although Raymond's men could not overcome the defenders, Godfrey's troops overthrew the opposition, took the wall defenses, and out-flanked the defenders facing Raymond. That opened the city to the Crusaders.

Two great siege towers were also built by the Turks on Malta. One was rolled against the castile but, it will be remembered, the defenders dug a hole in the wall, pushed a cannon through, and destroyed the tower. The defenders captured the second tower and used it as a post for sharpshooters. The Turks had their successes, if only momentary. They did take Fort St. Elmo and they did gain the castile's ramparts by a massive infantry attack. But the defenders managed to hold in the long run, leaving the Turks to attack again and again without positive results.

The British and French at Sebastopol used essentially the same tactics as the Turks on Malta. Preliminary bombardments were followed by infantry attacks. The early attacks failed because of poor planning and coordination. The French were confused by wrong signals, and the British plan was foolhardy from the beginning. It required forty ladder parties to get to the Redan walls, and, of course, they did not gain them. Even if they had, and all the troops arrived as anticipated, only forty men could top the walls at one time, a situation much like that which faced the Janissaries on Malta when they attacked St. Elmo and St. Michael. When a few British soldiers did get into the Redan during the September attack, the defenders quickly killed them. The French, however, took the Malakoff in September. The starting point of their attack was much closer to the defenses than was the British assault. They rapidly bridged the ditch before the Russian gunners had time to react.

The Kut defenses were not successfully escalated. There were two reasons for this. First, even though the Turks did penetrate the old fort through gaps made by their artillery, they could not hold the position against British counter-attacks. Second, Turkish artillery failed to do enough damage to the British defenses to at least give the frontal assaults a chance for success. The ensuing passive siege permitted the Turks to re-direct their resources against Aylmer's relief column; thus, Kut was allowed to collapse on its own.

Singapore exemplified the many changes wrought during World War II. The Japanese were constantly on the move, reflecting the influence of the

German blitzkrieg concept on Yamashita. Once at the Johore Strait, the Japanese enjoyed complete offensive domination. That was established by their air power, the ultimate form of escalation. Mostly, Japanese planes were a kind of flying artillery, softening defensive positions, destroying British installations and supply depots, and spreading terror and disbelief across Singapore Island. By controlling the air war, a scenario repeated in other theatres of war, the Japanese controlled the ground war.

Outright treachery was a time-honored way of penetrating defenses but, among our five examples, it was only useful during the Crusaders' campaign at Antioch. Bohemund conspired with a disaffected tower commander who allowed sixty of Bohemund's men to escalate the walls, take two other towers, and open the city gates. On Malta, a Greek defected from the Moslem forces and gave Mustapha's plans for an attack on Senglea to La Valette. But this was more an act of revenge than of outright treachery.

There were certainly turncoats and spies in the other sieges, but their use was very limited. At Sebastopol, the information such individuals provided the British was usually ignored. Such men were considered beneath contempt and thoroughly mistrusted. At Kut, a few Moslem troops serving in Indian regiments went over to the Turks, but mostly for religious reasons. Many Indian troops who surrendered at Singapore joined the Indian Nationalist Army and fought alongside the Japanese in Burma, but that had no influence on the siege itself. Treachery is difficult to exploit. The traitor often feels that he, himself, will be betrayed. Those using traitors feel that the traitor might be leading them into a trap. Treason, in the end, is a very dangerous game.

Ruse is another matter. The Japanese used it more successfully than did the offenses in the other four sieges. For example, at the Johore Strait, the Japanese placed the Imperial Guards Division on their left flank and moved them about so that the British would see them and think the coming attack was concentrated there. But the actual assault force was at the opposite end of their line, skillfully hidden in the jungle. Artillery batteries were also moved around to disguise the point of attack. Once on the island, the Japanese again disguised their artillery batteries during the attack on Changi to make the British think they had more artillery than they really did.

SOME CONCLUSIONS

The safe conclusion from this discussion is that sieges impose on the forces involved a near-formalistic kind of battle. Time and place change, ideologies of various sorts may be imposed, and technologies change; however, the essence of sieges has remained very much the same—either the defense outlasts the offense, or the offense finds a way to overpower the defense by methods that are astonishingly standard.

My function thus far has been to elaborate within a self-consciously comparative framework certain characteristics of sieges, some of which were first outlined by John Keegan in *The Nature of War*. There is more, however. The five sieges yield several generalizations that can only be provided through a comparative study. I should like simply to list them, more for their heuristic value than as a set of definitive conclusions.

1. The more integrated and elastic the defense, the greater the possibility of withstanding a siege. The more mobile the offense, the better the chance of besting the defenses.

2. The defense must disrupt attacking forces in the killing zone. The greater its length, the better this can be accomplished. This was realized on Malta, before the Great Redan at Sebastopol, and in Mesopotamia against the British relief force.

3. The defense must narrow the width of the killing zone, enabling them to concentrate their firepower. This was done on Malta, occasionally at Sebastopol, but not at Singapore. Not knowing where the Japanese would attack, the island's north shore defenses were spread out, reducing their effectiveness.

4. Infantry crossing the killing zone is the Queen's Move of siege warfare, the point at which the offense is most vulnerable and, equally, the point at which the defense must stop the attackers if it is to remain viable. The attacking infantry must reduce the length of the killing zone, as the French did at Sebastopol in their final assault on the Malakoff, if they are to avoid attritional losses and best the defense.

5. Erwin Rommel said it somewhere: Position warfare (read *Siege*) is about destroying men, in contrast to mobile warfare, in which the emphasis is on destroying equipment. Therefore, casualty rates escalate during sieges.

6. The use of artillery, of whatever description, for the penetration of defenses has been ineffective. Artillery alone did not successfully penetrate defenses with a reliable consistency in the first four sieges. At Singapore, the introduction of air power as a kind of flying artillery led not so much to a penetration of the defenses as to their escalation. Artillery, generally, was a more effective weapon against attacking infantry and against other artillery. Furthermore, the most effective weapon against tanks trying to penetrate the defensive perimeter is not other tanks but artillery (in all its modern equivalents). The effectiveness of artillery is proportional to targeting ability and fire coordination, the lack of which was demonstrated by the British at Singapore.

7. A small garrison with a high level will to combat and imaginative leadership can frustrate and even defeat a much larger attacking force. Malta, again, provides us with a winning example. Conversely, a large garrison with unimaginative leadership and a low will to combat, such as at Singapore, will lose.

8. An army's diverse composition, as among the Crusaders and on Malta, is less important in a siege than the belief system and/or clarity of goals that brings the diverse elements together in the first place. Likewise, any advantages produced by homogeneity are reduced if the troops are inexperienced, if there

is a confusion of goals, and if leadership is unimaginative. The British army at Sebastopol exemplifies the last two of these propositions.

9. When the defense is denied mobility—internal troop movements, equipment repositioning, and resupply—the offense will win. The Kut siege is the classic example of a defense brought to complete stagnation.

10. The defense that loses or concedes domination, Malta being a brilliant exception, will lose if the offense is able to assume the dominant position. In their battles against the Crusaders, the Turks consistently lost defensive domination by one means or another and relinquished it to their opponents. At the other end of the continuum, the British on Singapore never had defensive domination. The Japanese established aerial superiority in the first two days of the campaign and were never seriously threatened by British counter-measures.

11. The commander who defines or re-defines, that is, who shapes the battlefield to his purposes, forcing the enemy to fight in a manner of his choosing, will win. That was accomplished by La Valette on Malta when he purposely relinquished domination, drawing the Turks into the narrow confines of the Grand Harbor. Yamashita at Singapore confounded the experts by launching the impossible campaign down the Malay Peninsula. Sebastopol was nearly a standoff because neither side was able to significantly out-maneuver the other. Uniquely among the five sieges, Townshend killed his own army at Kut by marching it onto a tight little peninsula that restricted all movement and was easily enveloped by the Turks.

12. Sieges, because of their traditionally limited spatial dimensions, amplify the interaction between the opposing forces. If the siege lasts long enough, if the fighting is both frequent and bloody, self-generated parameters of behavior will emerge that eschew traditional norms of military conduct. Certainly this happened at Jerusalem, in Malta, and in Singapore.

13. All other principles and theories of siege warfare notwithstanding, starving an opponent into submission can be, as the ancient Greeks discovered, the most effective offensive weapon. Starvation consumes time, but it also conserves men and materiel. Yet, from among the five examples discussed, only the siege at Kut-al-Amara exemplifies this weapon. More than 400 years earlier, Suleiman's army and navy doubtlessly could have starved the defenders into submission; and, in 1855, the British and French could have forced Sebastopol to surrender without costly assaults. But other factors intervened in both sieges. Suleiman wanted to destroy the Order of St. John, not force their surrender. At Sebastopol, political pressures precluded a passive approach. The allies attacked.

But could the Crusaders have starved Jerusalem into submission? Earlier at Antioch they nearly succeeded in doing just that to the Turkish garrison and, then, they in turn nearly succumbed to starvation when under siege by the Turkish relief force. At Jerusalem, however, the Crusaders were short of provisions and their patience was exhausted. They attacked. At Singapore, the Japanese never considered a passive siege. They demanded the total military defeat and humiliation of the British.

Thus, starvation is an attractive military option, but it is prey to the irrational and unexpected dictates of battle.

All that has been written so far is past tense. Neither a solid historical background nor much imagination is required to realize that the siege of Singapore, the most contemporary of the examples, is a half-century in the past and that the battle appears primitive by contemporary standards. But Singapore was only a prelude. Already by December 1941, the great siege of Leningrad was underway, foreshadowing the struggle at Stalingrad, where men and their weapons were sucked into a bottomless pit. Blatant, wholesale destruction on an unprecedented scale became the norm as World War II unleashed weapons that no one dreamed of a generation before, on a scale that dwarfed all previous wars.

World War II ended with the dropping of the atomic bomb on Japan. The world was finally left balanced between two great super-powers, the United States and the Soviet Union. Would these all-powerful former allies meet in the ultimate battle, hurling nuclear ballistic missiles at each other? The terror and complete destruction such a battle promised seemed to cancel the possibility. More to the point, the availability of such weapons made siege warfare not only an unlikely type of battle but one rendered obsolete.

Chapter 8

The Ongoing Story

RELEASE FROM ARMAGEDDON

The political and ideological conflicts between the United States and the Soviet Union following World War II resulted in the formation of military alliances by each side—the North Atlantic Treaty Organization, representing the United States and its Western European allies; the Warsaw Pact, representing the Soviet Union and its Eastern European allies. The two super-powers pawed each other, connived, negotiated, manipulated, and even battled each other in surrogate wars across what became known as the Third World. For World War II loosened the pre-war imperial network. Areas in Southeast Asia, for instance, that were occupied by the Japanese re-surfaced as post-war power voids in which the native peoples did not always welcome the return of those European nations defeated by the Japanese. Many colonies wanted complete independence or at least more home rule than their European masters were willing to grant. Other colonies, not necessarily involved directly in the war, or marginally so, quickly seized the idea of independence, opening stressful relations with the European ruling nations. Overt hostilities often developed.

In Kenya, the Mau Mau fought against continued British rule for four years. The East Indies revolted against Dutch rule. Arab nationalism swept through Egypt, Iraq, and Algeria, upsetting the old balance of power achieved in the region following World War I. The litany of troubled areas seemed endless: Aden, the Congo, Angola, Rhodesia (now Zimbabwe), Afghanistan, North Borneo, to name only some.

Many insurgent leaders immediately realized that, despite military aid flowing to them from industrial nations, their largely peasant armies could not fight standard European World War II–type battles against their ruling nations. Many of the nations that fought that war, regardless of post-war reductions and discounting nuclear weapons, still possessed enormous destructive capacity. As demonstrated during the Korean War, 1950 to 1953, China and the United States were capable of inflicting considerable damage with conventional weapons.

The insurgent armies typically responded to that firepower by defusing it. They resorted to guerrilla warfare.

Guerrilla warfare is usually fought by small units but, if the war lasts long enough, if outside military aid is received, and if a unifying ideology surfaces, then larger units up to divisional strength are possible. Avoiding large-scale battles, guerrillas emphasize mobility, hit-and-run raids, sabotage, and terrorism. Guerrillas try to live off the land, hiding in forests, jungles, and mountains, co-opting the native population in the name of The People. Where the locals resist, the guerrillas impose themselves by occupying a town or village and resorting to terrorism and intimidation to secure cooperation. In turn, guerrillas are often co-opted by the two superpowers.

Because most colonial insurgency after World War II occurred in areas ruled by Western European nations, the co-opting powers were usually either the Communist Chinese or the former Soviet Union, neither of whom were in positions to acquire colonies early in their own histories. The guerrilla armies often established wider spheres of influence for one or the other patron state.

The British, faced with post-war austerity, gradually withdrew from empire, sometimes peacefully, sometimes reluctantly, and sometimes at the point of a gun. That the British fought several subsequent guerrilla wars with considerable success was attributable partially to their Victorian tradition of fighting small wars in faraway places but even more attributable to their post-war army's willingness to adapt weapons and organization to the situations presented them. That change in attitude was, I think, related to the successes experienced by the British in small unit actions during the war, exemplified by long-range patrols in the Western Desert and commando actions against occupied Europe. Thus, after World War II, the Communist Chinese guerrillas who had fought the Japanese in Malaya re-organized as the Malayan People's Anti-British Army. A twelve-year war ensued. Lieutenant General Sir Frank Kitson observes in his introduction to Michael Dewar's book *Brush Fire Wars* that general staffs are often preoccupied with fielding the largest, most powerful army they can against an enemy presumed to possess weapons similar to their own. But Kitson also notes that presumption is usually wrong in the instance of guerrilla warfare. An army with great firepower will not defeat an insurgent army unless they adopt the tactics of guerrilla warfare. As early as 1952, the British fighting in Malaya discovered that their great firepower was ineffective in a jungle setting where the enemy could not be seen and maneuvered at will. Consequently, the British forces were broken up into small units and went into the jungle after the insurgents. The war, as Dewar himself so clearly states, was won by the rifle and the machine gun and by harnessing native loyalty. Indeed, the British did learn something from the Singapore debacle.

A completely different war was fought in Indo-China. The French returned to the area, expecting to restore their colonial rule, but they ran into a strong nationalist movement led by Ho Chi Minh. In May 1945, he formed his own government and in September declared Viet Nam independent. A negotiated settlement was in process when the French, responding to anti-French incidents, attacked the Vietnamese settlements in Haiphong in December 1946. A full-scale war started, Ho's forces supplied by the Communist Chinese, the French supported by the United States.

The French flirted with the idea of training men for guerrilla warfare, but their main strategy was to draw out the Viet Minh, as the insurgents were known, getting them committed to a formal battle, and then crushing them with the weight of French firepower.

Fortified or entrenched camps, known as "hedgehogs," were a method of combatting the guerrillas that met with some success. These camps bristled with weapons and were surrounded by barbed wire and minefields. They taunted the Viet Minh: "Come and get us if you can." One such camp was established in northern Viet Nam at Na San. The Viet Minh commander Vo Nguyen Giap ordered an attack, only to see his troops cut to pieces by the French. Massive firepower seemed to have prevailed, just as predicted. Other examples could be explored, but no battle in Viet Nam, French or American, quite captures the essence of a siege in guerrilla wars nor gives such a clear picture of the persistency after World War II of the siege methods already reviewed as does Dien Bien Phu.

THE PERSISTENCY OF SIEGES

The Siege of Dien Bien Phu

In May 1953, General Henry Navarre took over the Indo-China command. He was age fifty-five. Trained as a cavalryman, he spent much of his subsequent career as a staff and intelligence officer. Navarre knew his Viet Nam assignment was an unenviable task because there was an emerging sentiment in France to end the war at any price; indeed, several of his colleagues in the army considered the war unwinnable. What Navarre did not know was that he had not been fully briefed. General Raoul Salan, his predecessor, did not show Navarre a government directive dated 24 April 1953, instructing the commander-in-chief, Indo-China, to accept territorial losses rather than risk the security of the French expeditionary force. Nor did Salan nor anyone in government appraise Navarre of the grave doubts circulating about hedgehog operations. For both the government and the military, believing by 1953 that Viet Nam was a lost cause, concluded that

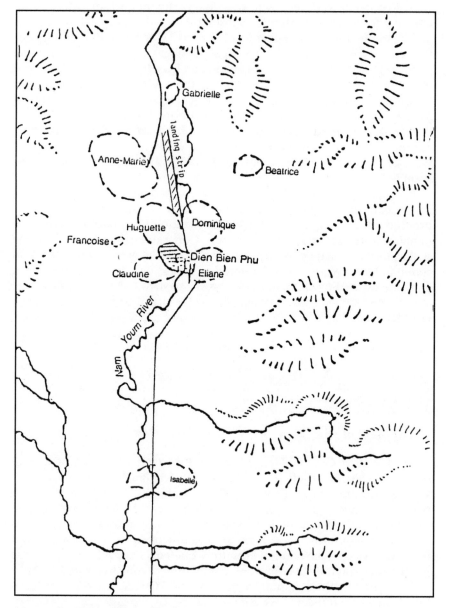

Map 13 Dien Bien Phu

the army should not commit any more men and weapons to an ill-conceived offensive campaign, even if it was stationary.

Yet it was another hedgehog that Navarre planned. Salan did not disabuse him of the scheme. However inconceivable it now seems, given the wording of the 24 April directive, the French government made the contradictory decision to defend Laos, particularly the capitol at Luang Prabang and Vientiane, lest their loss signal the collapse of the French Indo-China Union. Dien Bien Phu was considered by Navarre to be in a good blocking position to prevent Viet Minh incursions into Laos. There was already an airfield located at the edge of the town from which French aircraft could range across enemy territory and, together with ground forces, prevent the region's rich rice crops from falling into Viet Minh hands. But Major General René Cogny, brought from the Mekong Delta to command in Tonkin province, vacillated. At first, he supported the project. Then he opposed it because he believed, given needs in the Delta, there would not be enough troops available for Dien Bien Phu. He knew that European tactics did not work in Viet Nam and that a camp at Dien Bien Phu would not keep the Viets out of Laos. He also knew that the insurgents did not rely on the rice crop of the northern Tonkin region. Moreover, he thought intelligence reports were correct that at least two Viet Minh divisions would be in the region by January 1954. Cogny was joined in his criticism by Colonel Jean Nicot, commanding air transport, who informed Navarre on 11 November 1953 that, considering the number of cargo planes available, he could not guarantee a steady flow of supplies into Dien Bien Phu. Then, on 20 November, Navarre received instructions from the Committee for National Defense in Paris that he was to limit any operations to the means currently at his disposal. In short, there would be no reinforcements and no more equipment expended in Viet Nam. He read the warning, then locked it in his safe, not opening it again until 4 December, almost three weeks after operations began, feigning ignorance of its contents and dismay at its intent.

Navarre, assuming personal responsibility, plunged ahead, his notions about what he could and could not accomplish based on the incomplete briefing by Salan and the assessments of American military advisers. The advisers believed that Giap could not maintain in the field for more than a week or two what was now thought to be a force of four divisions. They assumed the Viet Minh could not maintain a supply line 350 miles long, given French air superiority. They believed the Viets could not get artillery over the mountains and so would have to fire from reverse slopes at considerable distances. They also believed French air strikes would destroy any artillery emplacements the Viets established. Consequently, the Dien Bien Phu airfield was considered usable for landings and supply drops with only minimal losses. Navarre concluded from these assessments that Giap would not attack, having learned his lessons at Na San. But Navarre really hoped that Giap would try again.

French operations began at 10:00 A.M., 20 November 1953, when six parachute battalions descended on Dien Bien Phu. Quickly, the remaining garrison, eventually numbering 13,500 men together with some tanks and supporting artillery, was airlifted to the site.

They found themselves in a valley about twelve miles long and between four and five miles wide. The Nam Youm River twists along the valley floor, fed by smaller streams flowing from the surrounding hills. The hills vary in elevations from 700 feet to around 1,400 feet and are covered with dense jungle. Dien Bien Phu was the largest settlement in the valley, with 112 houses.

On 29 November, Colonel Christian de Castries, another former cavalry officer, took command of Dien Bien Phu. He was later criticized for losing the battle, but he assumed command under a significant handicap. No military operation can succeed if its goals are ambiguous or contradictory. Navarre told de Castries the base was established for offensive operations so that his men could sally forth, roaming the highlands and destroying the Viet Minh, just the job for a cavalryman. Yet, it was clear by this time that Navarre conceived Dien Bien Phu as a defensive position, so much bait to bring the Viet Minh to the valley floor and destroy them.

Dien Bien Phu was the centerpiece of the hedgehog and was protected by parachute units. Within the town were the command post, the main hospital, and mortar emplacements. Ringing this center were various strongpoints—bunkers, dugouts, trenches, machine gun and mortar emplacements, each surrounded by barbed wire and minefields. These strongpoints were code-named, on the west side, Claudine, Francoise, and Huguette and, on the east side, Eliane and Dominique. The airfield angled northwest from the center. Strongpoint Anne-Marie, almost a mile from the center, protected the field's west flank, and strongpoint Beatrice, quite isolated and about another mile from the center, covered the field's east flank. Gabrielle, like a cork in a bottle, was over two miles north of the center. Isabelle was located about two miles south of the center. The various peaks and high ground within each strongpoint were numbered; for instance, there were Dominique 1, 2, and 3, and Claudine 1 through 5.

The French had twenty-four 105mm guns, four 155mm guns, and sixteen heavy mortars. Colonel Charles Piroth, commanding the artillery, was offered more cannon but refused, saying he had enough. The artillery was placed in an open fire center. The traverse given by the open—and un-protected—placement gave Piroth confidence that his guns could silence any Viet Minh artillery firing from any place in the valley. Besides, he believed the Viets could not handle artillery very efficiently. Nowhere in the entire defense complex was there a concrete bunker. Everything was dirt and logs.

By 5 December, four Viet divisions were marching toward Dien Bien Phu. By 31 December, the position was surrounded. Giap kept pouring men and supplies into the zone, eventually assembling twenty-seven infantry battalions supported by twenty 105mm guns, eighteen 75mm guns, eighty 37mm guns, one hundred 12.7mm anti-aircraft machine guns, and mortars varying in size up to 120mm. The Viet Minh brought in supplies on bicycles, each man pushing loads up to 500 pounds. Trucks moved only at night. The French air force saw nothing.

The Viet Minh contradicted all the French assumptions, most important- ly the notion that the Viets could not get their artillery over the mountains and close enough to the French entrenchments to be of any real effect. The Viets dismantled their artillery and carried the pieces into prepared posi- tions that were concealed by jungle. That left the French air force and Piroth's guns hopelessly looking for artillery that was firing into Dien Bien Phu with considerable effectiveness.

By early March, Dien Bien Phu was under steady bombardment. Any aircraft attempting to land was subjected to heavy anti-aircraft fire along the predictable approach line. Colonel Nicot had been correct. The narrow valley left no room for maneuvering, and most planes made straight-in landings. Also, rain and fog made resupply by air difficult and sporadic and hampered French bombing sorties.

By 13 April, the Viet Minh were receiving seventy tons of supplies each day, but the French had not destroyed a single Viet artillery position. That same day, three C-47 Dakota transport planes were destroyed on the runway, and a napalm storage site was detonated by Viet artillery. Still that same day, strongpoint Beatrice came under heavy bombardment, killing a battalion commander and his staff when their dugout received a direct hit.

Dreaded news arrived in the central command post: Beatrice was being attacked by six Viet Minh battalions from all directions. They dug their approach trenches by night, cut the perimeter wire, and cleared paths through the minefields. Bangalore torpedoes were shoved under the remaining wire and exploded as the infantry rose to attack. There was little time to react because the Viet assault started only 200 yards from the inner defenses. One by one the French emplacements collapsed and, one by one, each point of high ground within Beatrice was overwhelmed.

The French fired 6,000 rounds of 105mm projectiles to stop the attacks— to no avail. At dawn on the fifteenth, the French counter-attacked to recover Beatrice with two battalions, but they came under immediate and heavy Viet artillery fire and could not advance. And still Piroth's gunners could not find the enemy artillery.

As the fight for Beatrice was taking place, Gabrielle was attacked by Viet infantry supported by heavy mortar and 75mm gunfire. The first attack carried the summit of Gabrielle, and a second attack on the fifteenth took the local command post. A French counter-attack supported by six tanks, but without artillery cover, tried to cross three miles of open ground and defensive barbed wire. The attack failed, and Gabrielle remained in Viet control.

Colonel Piroth committed suicide, distraught over the failure of his gunners to locate Viet artillery emplacements and by his mistake in leaving his own guns unprotected. De Castries concealed Piroth's death, afraid it might lower morale.

Strongpoint Dominique was surrounded by 15 March. The Viets dug saps out from Beatrice and Gabrielle. They dug past Eliane, around Isabelle, and surrounded Huguette and Claudine. All that took only four days.

Meantime, Colonel Nicot's attempts to supply Dien Bien Phu were becoming more difficult, if not impossible. French fighters and transports were regularly hit by ground fire. The attempts to drop supplies by parachute were only mildly successful because anti-aircraft fire pushed drop elevations from 4,000 feet to 6,000 feet, causing many loads to land in the Viet Minh lines. Furthermore, the landing field was pockmarked with shell holes, and the control tower was in shambles. Only one safe drop zone remained by the end of March.

The principal Viet Minh offensive came on 30 March. Eliane, Huguette, and Dominique were scenes of violent struggles as artillery crashed into the strongpoints and as infantry waves surged forward, were stopped, and counter-attacked. The fighting ebbed and flowed until the strongpoints, pounded by artillery and drenched by rain, were transformed into formless muck. The dead hung on the wire or were hastily buried in the trenches, only to be uncovered by gunfire and rain. By 12 April, as Jules Roy notes, Dien Bien Phu was a charnel house. The opponents were often less than thirty yards apart. Some of the defenders opted-out, internally deserting, picking what they needed for survival from the battlefield and finding risky sanctuary along the Nam Youm River. A battalion of Thai soldiers simply rose from their defensive positions, walked through the Viet lines and down the road toward home. Yet, other soldiers charged into certain death, less to capture some stinking ooze than to show "them" that they could fight. The "them" for the soldiers were journalists, those in government whom the soldiers believed had deserted them, and France in general, where a tide of pessimism was moving public opinion even further away from support for the war.

So small were the spatial dimensions of battle and so dominated by small unit action was the fighting that the siege took on a life of its own, quite apart from French national concerns and even from Navarre's plans. The men fought and suffered because, first, there was no place else to go and, second, fighting and dying is what soldiers are expected to do. Being so isolated, Dien Bien Phu became a kind of pure battlefield in which the moral fibre of the defense and the tenacity of the offense were tested to the last shot fired. The opponents achieved an epiphany of battle.

By 23 April, most of Huguette was lost to the Viets. They overran the airfield on the 25th. On 4 May, all of Huguette was in Viet hands. Dominique, Claudine, and Eliane also collapsed. With nothing to defend but the command center, any hope of holding out much longer vanished. Three days later, 7 May 1954, de Castries, just promoted to brigadier general, surrendered the defenders of Dien Bien Phu.

Political considerations aside, the siege reveals what can happen when the reasons for battle are rooted in deception, ambiguity, and self-illusion. Navarre was not told the things he needed to know. One gets the feeling that Salan, whom he replaced, wanted him to fail. Those in government could have been more forthcoming but were not. Navarre himself knew he would have limited resources but concealed that knowledge. Cogny changed his mind about the operation not once but twice; yet, once the plan was ordered, he did get behind it. At the same time he tried to get Navarre to see military reality but was rebuffed. Navarre knew he was mistaken as early as January 1954. He could have withdrawn from the valley but did not. Ego, ambition, pride, honor, stubbornness, a distorted sense of duty, and an unwillingness to admit the mistake created a battle that need not have been fought.

Dien Bien Phu was the worse possible position for a siege. The narrow valley left no maneuvering room, the Viet artillery fire was deadly accurate, vaunted French air superiority was neutralized, and the various strongpoints were too spatially separated to be mutually supportive. Gabrielle, Beatrice, and Isabelle were particularly isolated and, once taken, provided starting points for the Viet envelopment of the others. Even though the Viet Minh tactics were, as Bernard Fall states, right out of the eighteenth century, the French were unable to stop them because their premise of superior firepower proved false. French gunners and aerial bombers could not find targets in the dense jungle. The concession of high ground and, therefore, domination to the Viets was a major error. Consequently, the Viet Minh, without any aircraft, using manpower rather than machines, defying all odds, dominated, penetrated, and vanquished the French, utilizing standard siege techniques. Theirs was a victory of human will.

Dien Bien Phu hastened the French departure from Indo-China. Peace negotiations ended with Viet Nam partitioned north and south. When the war between these two political entities erupted, the United States, although colonially uninvolved in the region, invested in a ten-year war ostensibly to contain communist aggression in Southeast Asia. American experts were convinced that the Viet Cong, as the Viet Minh were now know, could not field large units, that American military might—a half-million troops, a large naval presence, and the best aircraft in the world—would win. Indeed, the United States won every major battle fought in Viet Nam, including the siege at Khe Sanh, yet lost the war. Despite the lessons to be learned from British actions in post-war Malaya, they refused to fight a guerrilla war by making a major commitment to guerrilla tactics, and they could not co-opt the native population to American goals.

That would seem to end the story of sieges, but further changes in world politics created a new and fertile ground for siege warfare in Kuwait and, in the process, overturned some conventions of this ancient battle form.

The Siege of Kuwait

In 1980, Iraq invaded Iran, inaugurating a bitter eight-year war that bore great similarity to World War I. Waves of soldiers charged across open ground only to be cut down by machine gun fire and churned under by artillery. The United States and some European nations—France, Germany, and Britain among them—helped Iraq with domestic and military aid, fearing that an Iranian victory would spread Islamic fundamentalism across the Near East, endangering oil supplies and otherwise destabilizing the region.

The war ended in a stalemate, an unsatisfactory end for Iraq's leader Saddam Hussein, who hoped a clear victory would establish his credibility as an international force and a key player in Near Eastern politics.

What was definite was that Iraq finished the war with the fourth largest army in the world. Saddam had a million men under arms, another half-million in reserve, 5,500 tanks, 3,500 artillery pieces, and 665 combat aircraft. Additionally, Iraq used chemical warfare against the Iranians and even against the Kurds in northern Iraq. Saddam also inaugurated nuclear weapons and biological warfare research. He purchased more armaments whilst looking for another place where he might flex his military might and be rewarded with the world-class reputation he thought he deserved.

On 2 August 1990, about 100,000 Iraqi troops, including units of Saddam's elite Republican Guard, invaded neighboring Kuwait, reviving a long-standing claim to the territory.

Following World War I, the old Turkish empire was broken into several smaller states, among which were Iraq and Kuwait. Almost immediately, Iraq claimed sovereignty over Kuwait. But since Britain held mandate over Iraq and as Kuwait conducted its foreign affairs through Britain, the claim was turned aside. In 1958, a revolution led by Abdul Karim Qassim overturned the government of Iraq, and King Faisal II was assassinated. The British withdrew permanently from Iraq in 1959. Qassim, through his ruling Baath party, renewed claim to Kuwait. It seemed armed conflict was inevitable, but Britain intervened on Kuwait's behalf, and war was averted. In 1963, Qassim was assassinated by members of his own Baath party. Saddam Hussein elbowed his way to power in 1979.

Thus, the 1990 invasion was an extension of long-standing Iraqi interests in Kuwait. But there were more immediate and practical reasons for the invasion. Kuwait had loaned Iraq billions of dollars to fight the Iran war and wanted re-payment. That nettled Saddam, who considered the Kuwaitis a greedy and self-serving lot. That view was reinforced by accusations that the Kuwaitis engaged in slant drilling, siphoning away Iraqi oil and profits. Saddam also accused them of over-producing oil, driving down oil prices and therefore depriving Iraq of deserved profits.

The United Nations quickly imposed sanctions on all trade with Iraq except for humanitarian goods, an act cheered on by President George Bush of the United States. Then, on 25 August, the U.N. authorized the use of limited naval force to check compliance with the sanctions. Saddam remained intransigent. Urged on by President Bush, who now claimed the sanctions would never work, the U.N., on 29 November, authorized its members to use whatever means were necessary against Iraq if Saddam did not withdraw all his forces from Kuwait by 15 January 1991.

The bravado exhibited by Saddam was based on considerable miscalculation and ambiguity. Western powers and the Soviet Union helped re-arm Iraq after the war with Iran, despite its treatment of the Kurds and known intentions toward Kuwait; yet, nothing indicating a clear disapproval by those powers of Iraqi actions and intentions was forthcoming. Indeed, the Iraqi Foreign Ministry published its version of a meeting between Saddam and April Glaspie, the United States ambassador to Iraq, in which she said that the United States had no opinion about intra-Arab border disputes. Glaspie later told a U.S. Senate committee that the Foreign Ministry edited out her comment that the United States would support its friends and trusted that all disputes would be settled without war. Perhaps Saddam heard what he wanted to hear or ordered Glaspie's comments edited to conform to his own truths. But that he thought the United States would not respond to the invasion was a mistake. The oil interests of the United States and much of Europe were being threatened, and such a destabilization would not be tolerated.

Saddam misjudged, as well, the Soviet Union. Rather than being the long-trusted ally of old, rushing into the U.N. Security Council to veto anti-Iraq resolutions, the Soviets supported the U.N. and tried to arbitrate the dispute. That the Soviets took such a benign position was not surprising, for they were having their own problems. Eastern European hegemony was breaking apart, and the Soviet Union was, itself, on the brink of changes that would lead to its demise. In short, the Soviets needed friends in Europe and in the United States more than they needed Iraq.

Iraq could not find allies among the Arab nations, except for Jordan. Syria, Egypt, Saudi Arabia (fearing imminent invasion from Iraq), the United Arab Emirates, and Morocco joined forces with the United States and Europe to thwart Saddam's ambitions. Altogether, twenty-nine nations contributed to the coalition forces that were to face Saddam Hussein's army.

At first, the coalition forces focused on guarding Saudi Arabia against Iraqi invasion in what was called Operation Desert Shield. By the end of August 1990, 72,000 troops were in the area of the Persian Gulf. By January 1991, 172 coalition ships were supplying the combined forces, and cargo planes landed in Saudi Arabia at a rate of 125 each day. There were now 700,000 men, 1,700 combat aircraft, and 174 naval ships in the region.

In response to the coalition buildup, the Iraqis shifted from an offensive to a defensive posture. They constructed a linear fortress that stretched from the Persian Gulf west along the Kuwaiti-Saudi border. Rows of barbed wire and razor wire, a half-million land mines, sand berms forty feet high, ditches into which oil could be flooded and ignited comprised the "wall." In and around the line was a shallow defense created by artillery and mortar emplacements, tanks dug in to the height of their hulls, and strongpoints. These last were triangular works surrounded by sand berms. In each apex there was an infantry company with artillery and heavy weapons support. Heavy artillery, mostly 152mm and 122mm guns, gave added support. Early reports put the Iraqi forces at between 500,000 and 700,000. After the war, the research office of the U.S. House of Representatives Armed Services Committee lowered the estimate to 187,000. Whatever number was accurate—and the debate continues—Saddam's "wall" had a respectable history. The Iranian army was broken by a similar defensive system. In 1973, during the Yom Kippur War, the Egyptians dug in their tanks and anti-tank missile launchers and destroyed 1,500 Israeli tanks in two weeks. The ultimate source of the system goes back to Soviet defenses, such as Leningrad, during World War II. Saddam, well-pleased, boasted that the coming conflict would be the "mother of all battles."

The 15 January deadline passed without Iraqi compliance to the U.N. resolutions. War was seen as the only solution to the deadlock.

The coalition unleashed ferocious air attacks against Iraqi installations. United States naval ships in the Gulf launched an initial fifty-two Tomahawk cruise missiles against targets deep inside Iraq. Flying only a few hundred feet off the ground, using a guidance system that gave them a three-dimensional topographical reading, most of the missiles hit most of their targets. They were followed by 700 coalition aircraft that struck a variety of targets. British Tornado GR-1 low level fighter-bombers hit key airfields, each plane capable of putting sixty craters in a runway and scattering over 400 mines to impede repairs. Forty-two F-117A Stealth fighters from the United States Air Force, armed with 2,000-pound GBU-27 laser-guided bombs, attacked Baghdad's communications centers and targets in deep bunkers. AH-64 Apache helicopters struck radar and other facilities, but some missed their targets; consequently, Iraqi anti-aircraft fire around Baghdad remained intense, however uncoordinated. But little was seen of the Iraqi air force. For most of the campaign, most Iraqi aircraft either stayed on the ground, where many were destroyed, or joined a stream of planes seeking refuge in Iran. Those few that did seek combat were readily shot down.

The air campaign churned away day and night for weeks, gradually shifting to tactical targets. Roads and bridges were cut. Supply depots and troop concentrations, especially those of the Republican Guard, were targeted. Tactical support aircraft, such as the A-10—dubbed Warthog—bombed and strafed artillery and tank emplacements. These continuous air attacks were made possible because coalition air superiority was established within the first forty-eight hours of the war.

The efficiency of these bombings came under criticism later. Some targets, already destroyed, were inexplicably hit several times. Some so-called smart bombs were not so smart after all, but that was apparently less a consequence of bomb defects than from their being fed incorrect targeting information. The amount of collateral damage (a euphemism for damage done when targets are missed) was certainly to be regretted; nonetheless, when compared to bombing accuracy in World War II, Korea, and Viet Nam, that in the Gulf was the most precise every achieved. Whatever may be decided eventually about the air war, in the end it accomplished its primary mission. Saddam Hussein's command and control apparatus was destroyed. He could not hear, he could not see—the coalition deployed its troops in relative ease and safety.

By mid-February, the air attacks against the Iraqi defensive line increased in frequency and fury. B-52 bombers, flying from Britain, Spain, and Diego Garcia Island in the Indian Ocean, blanketed the area with nineteen-ton bomb loads. Fighter-bombers dropped 15,000-pound compression bombs that collapsed bunkers and dugouts, and U.S. Air Force F-111Fs destroyed 1,500 Iraqi armored vehicles. Fuel-air bombs sprayed mists above the ground which, when exploded, had a terrible compressive effect. Troops were killed, installations collapsed or went up in flames, and minefields detonated. Cluster bombs—like a more sophisticated version of shrapnel—were also used. So devastating were the attacks that up to 50 percent of some Iraqi units were annihilated. The Iraqi leaders sent in disciplinary troops to keep the soldiers at their posts.

Were the air attacks not enough, United States Army and Marine Corps artillery moved up to the wall during the night to shell targets along the front. Using special night vision observation and sighting equipment, they were able to target their guns, fire an allotted number of rounds, pack up, and be gone before the Iraqis could respond.

The coalition forces now had undisputed escalation and offensive domination over the battle zone. The task before them was to penetrate the defenses.

The coalition forces, under the overall command of American General Norman Schwarzkopf, shaped the battlefield by restricting the Iraqi army to a specific front along the Kuwaiti border with Saudi Arabia. Saddam and his generals were convinced that would be the direction of attack. What they overlooked in their optimism was that everything outside that thin line belonged to the coalition. The Iraqi army was rendered immobile by the air war: If they moved, they were hit. The coalition could maneuver at will. Saddam played into Schwarzkopf's hands.

Saddam's assumption about the point of attack was encouraged by concentrating coalition troops along the Kuwait-Iraq border. These included XVIII Corps and VII Corps of the U.S. Army (reinforced by French

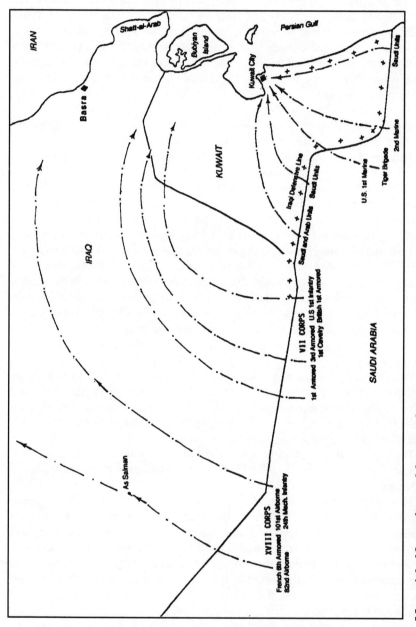

Map 14 Kuwait and Lower Iraq

and British divisions), two Pan-Arab battle groups, and the 1st Marine Expeditionary Force (1st and 2nd Marine divisions reinforced by the U.S. Army armored Tiger Brigade). Special Forces and U.S. Marine units also made incursions across the border. Additionally, 17,000 U.S. Marines practiced amphibious landings in an obvious manner. What the Iraqi leaders could neither see nor hear was the sudden and rapid deployment to the west along the Iraqi-Saudi border of 250,000 coalition troops together with enough supplies for a sixty-day campaign. XVIII Corps, supported by the French 6th Armored Division, was shifted to the desert 200 miles west. VII Corps, supported by the British 1st Armored Division (including the 7th Armored Brigade, the "Desert Rats" made famous fighting Rommel in World War II) took position between XVIII Corps and those units left facing the Kuwaiti border.

At 4:00 A.M., 24 February, the U.S. Marines, the Tiger Brigade, and the Arab battle groups penetrated the Kuwaiti line. The "mother of all battles" was under way. They struck toward Al Jabr Airport and Kuwait City. Using armored vehicles equipped with bulldozer blades, they cut through the sand berms, covered the oil-filled trenches, and ploughed across dugouts and bunkers. The stunned Iraqi soldiers surrendered in droves—those that survived the onslaught.

At the same time, XVIII Corps and the French armored division charged across the Iraqi border, heading ninety-four miles to As Salman, where they destroyed the 10,000 troops of the Iraqi 45th Infantry Division that garrisoned the position. XVIII Corps had 300 Abrams M1A1 battle tanks that raced across the sands at 45 mph and, as they moved, traversed and fired their 120mm guns with devastating accuracy. The armor of the Abrams tank, constructed with depleted uranium, made them practically impervious to anything the Iraqis could shoot at them. The movement by XVIII Corps was a screening maneuver, ultimately directed toward the Euphrates River Valley, to protect the flank of troops moving further to the east. One of the eastern movements they protected was the airlift of some 2,000 men of the U.S. 101st Airborne Division, together with their vehicles and artillery, into the Iraqi desert to establish a base for further operations. For, from that point, another 1,000 men were lifted by helicopter into the lower Euphrates Valley.

VII Corps—the U.S. 1st and 3rd Armored Divisions, the 1st U.S. Infantry Division, reinforced by the 1st British Armored—also sliced through the defensive barrier. The 1st Infantry bombarded Iraqi positions with 6,000 artillery rounds, destroying Iraqi artillery and dug-in tanks, then cut sixteen corridors through the berms and exploded protecting minefields. Their ground attack destroyed the 26th Iraqi Division, most of whose officers abandoned their men. That penetration, spread over a two-mile front, enabled the armored units to make wide arcs to the east, moving toward Kuwait's northwest border with Iraq. British Challenger and Warrior tanks sped through the gap and overwhelmed the Iraqi armored units facing them. In Kuwait, as the Marines and some Arab forces pushed toward Kuwait City, overrunning a thoroughly demoralized defense, other Arab forces took a blocking position to the east. Iraqi troops poured out of Kuwait City, trying to escape to the northwest. The air raids and the positioning of coalition units forced them into a narrow twenty-five mile corridor, where they were relentlessly attacked from the air and on the ground by American and British armored units. In another action, units of the 24th Mechanized Infantry attacked a truck column that was hauling away tanks, destroying seventy-two of them. The desert expanses were one vast killing zone. But it was a killing zone shaped by the offense, not the defense.

Where was the Iraqi resistance? The Marine and Arab units closing on Al Jabr Airport were finally challenged by Iraqi T-62 tanks. This was a Soviet-built machine, mounting a 115mm gun that lacked long-range accuracy. The tank, itself, was protected by 200mm armor plating that was considered marginal by 1991 standards. The Marines' principal battle tank was the M60 A3 with a 105mm gun, but its armor was 250mm thick and was reinforced by reactive armor blocks (layers of aluminum, ceramic, and epoxy to resist heat). The Marines also used some Abrams tanks. The Iraqi counter-attack began at 8:00 A.M., and two hours later about thirty of their tanks had been destroyed by the Marine tanks, missiles, and artillery fire. Tactical air support was received from the Marine air group and naval aircraft from carriers off-shore. Meanwhile, XVIII and VII corps met little resistance as they moved northeast, shifting toward confrontations with the Republican Guard. Most Iraqi units met along the way either surrendered or were annihilated during the miles-long run-and-shoot battle. Iraqi artillery, so effective in the Iran war, was silenced because, in addition to the impact of the air attacks, the mobility and computerized fire coordination of coalition artillery allowed many batteries to be simultaneously aimed at any Iraqi guns that might reveal themselves. The result was saturation counter-fire by the coalition artillerymen that destroyed so many Iraqi defensive installations that many of their gunners were afraid to respond at all. Doubtless, this was the most effective use of artillery in any siege.

Three overriding reasons exist for the sweeping success of the ground campaign, dubbed Operation Desert Storm. One was the meticulous planning, timing, and execution of the coalition's ground movements that resulted in carefully controlled advances so that no flanks were left exposed and no single unit outran any others. The second was the coordination between air and ground forces, some accidents and some poor communications notwithstanding. The third reason was that most of the high technology equipment worked better than expected under battle conditions in the desert. That enabled the coalition forces to overwhelm the Iraqis with such firepower and speed that they did not have time to react. The Iraqi defenses, not very deep for an age of offensive mobility and long-range weapons, were over-flown, dominated, penetrated, and effectively defeated in a 100-hour ground campaign.

Thus, Saddam made two closely related errors: He underestimated both the will to combat and the technological sophistication of his enemy.

True, the coalition fielded a very heterogeneous force. But too many Arab states wanted to put Saddam in his place for fear his territorial ambitions might grow beyond Kuwait, and Western powers needed relative stability in the region to secure a reasonably predictable political climate for their oil supplies. Saddam tried to split the coalition by firing Scud missiles into Israel in hopes they would respond because, once the Jewish nation was in the war, Arab forces would probably back out. But the Israelis stood firm, took their losses, and did nothing, depending on U.S. anti-missile units to protect them. That was enough to keep them out of the war and allowed the Arab nations to remain committed to the coalition without compromising their traditional ideological stand against Israel.

Saddam underestimated the impact of the coalition's firepower on his defensive positions, for never in the history of warfare had air power so completely destroyed a defensive line. He obviously overestimated his own army's ability to respond and the degree to which his troops were committed to his goals.

Yet, firepower, although vitally important, was not the key factor in victory for the coalition. Without imaginative and cooperative leadership the coalition's power would have been very compromised. That is a contrast to the personal control exerted by Saddam Hussein over his forces. As Robert Leonhard points out in his study *The Art of Maneuver*, once that control was disrupted, there were no subordinate Iraqi commanders with enough fortitude and imagination to respond to changing local battlefield conditions.

The re-conquest of Kuwait was, then, very much a siege. But Desert Storm represented a significant change in siege warfare: Unlike all the other sieges previously discussed, it ranged over considerable distances, reaching 200 miles inland from the Gulf and as far north as Baghdad. The zone of the siege was enlarged not so much by the placement of the fortifications, as of old, but by the character of the communications network and the range of the weapons, particularly air power and guided missiles. These elements enlarge any modern battlefield and make a fair target of anything between the frontlines and the communications and command center.

The enlargement of siege battle zones could alter in the future the entire definition of siege warfare that has been traditionally predicated on the notion of constricted space. But such a re-definition contains an obvious conditional clause: The opponents, or certainly one of them, must possess the weapons and the technology that make spatial enlargement of the battle zone possible. In a time period characterized by the emergence or re-emergence of many new nations, that possibility fades because such technology comes at a very high price, and the new nations, even Russia, at present, have marginal economies.

But the Kuwait siege—the Gulf War—not only began with ambiguity, it also ended with ambiguity. For all the rhetoric about how nasty Saddam Hussein was—Bush called him another Adolf Hitler—the war did not end his power or completely destroy his military capacities. The war was abruptly stopped—allegedly because the mandates of the U.N. resolutions were met. What remained of Iraq's army, including large contingents of the Republican Guard and 700 of their tanks that were never engaged in battle, was turned on those civilians who openly rebelled against Saddam's regime during the days immediately following the surrender. These included Islamic fundamentalists in the Basra area and the Kurds in the north. Another forty-eight hours of incessant attack by the coalition forces would have completely destroyed the Iraqi army, turning the siege into yet another battle of annihilation. Lacking that (the Western powers in fact proclaiming that such devastation was not among the mandates of the war), the "Hitler" of the Near East continued in power, purchasing arms from Russia, China, and North Korea within a year after the war as he simultaneously tried to wriggle free from continued U.N. sanctions. Ironically, President Bush, who so impatiently called for an end to sanctions in 1990 and for the start of war, supported sanctions after the war as the only way to bring Saddam to heel. A dilemma was left hanging over the Near East: Was it of greater value to keep Saddam's regime intact and have a buffer against the spread of Islamic fundamentalism from Iran, or was it better to be rid of him and risk the ethnic fracturing of Iran and a potential destabilization of the Near Eastern power balance?

FINAL THOUGHTS

Massive firepower worked for the coalition forces in Kuwait as certainly as it had failed the French at Dien Bien Phu. From that viewpoint, the two sieges seem incomparable. But, forgetting good guys and bad guys, if we think of the French as the Iraqis and the Viet Minh as the coalition, then things begin to make sense. In both instances, the offenses—the Viet Minh and the coalition—took away defensive mobility and maneuverability and neutralized defensive air power. The offense established domination, they attacked the perimeter with artillery at Dien Bien Phu and with air power in Kuwait, and they rapidly penetrated the perimeters. Both the French army and the Iraqis were dug into static defenses. Both were surrounded, cut off, and killed. Because the Viet Minh were a peasant army, it is easy to accept Bernard Fall's conclusion that they used eighteenth-century siege methods to go under, through, and over the French perimeter. What is a little harder to appreciate, because they used such sophisticated weapons, is that the coalition forces used the same methods to crack the Iraqi lines. Thus, the methods of siege remain constant: Escalation, penetration, and ruse were used, as they have been since earliest times. The specific tools by which those were accomplished changed. Thus, again, it is changing weapons technology that provides so many of the variables in siege warfare.

What remains clear from the sieges at Dien Bien Phu and Kuwait is that the army that remains static is doomed to lose. What alters that comfortable formula is the potential of the defensive leadership to respond imaginatively to the offense under the specific conditions of the siege. Tragically at both Dien Bien Phu and Kuwait, the defensive leaders were guilty of negligence bordering on criminal stupidity. As usual, the troops were the ones who were made to suffer.

The destruction wrought in these last two sieges invites the additional conclusion that sieges may have at last become a military anachronism. But, at the risk of having put up a straw man, I cannot accept that. First, a general's calculation of the probable levels of destruction does not materially affect the decision to offer or accept a siege. Second, there were too many changes in the world scene in the early 1990s that suggest traditional sieges will persist.

The Soviet Union dissolved in 1991, its republics forming a loose confederation of independent states, all filled with historic precedent and bristling with long-submerged ethnic, religious, and nationalistic pride. Yugoslavia, glued together after World War I from the patchwork quilt of independent Balkan states that were constantly battling one another and from the shambles of the Austro-Hungarian and Turkish empires, also fell apart. Names buried for seventy-five years—Croatia, Serbia, Bosnia-Herzegovina among them—symbolized the fracturing and the very complex ethnic co-mingling that made quick solutions difficult and added to the savagery of the ensuing fighting. Nationalist and separatist movements also surfaced in Sri Lanka, among the Sikhs in India, in Ireland, northern Spain, Moldavia, the former Czechoslovakia, and among the French-Canadians and the Scots. Many of these people argued their cases in the courts of public opinion and along the halls of government. Others, exemplified by the conflicts within Armenia and among Croatia, Bosnia, and Serbia, have opted for violent solutions.

There are three characteristics common in those regions where armed conflict arose. First, the hate level was very high. Ancient wounds were uncovered as people in the streets cried out against generations of oppression and for freedom. A second characteristic is that, in the crying out, history sometimes took a beating as the pre-oppression days were romanticized or re-written to fit current ideological necessities. Thus, however justified the independence movements by the Croatians or any other ethnic/nationalistic group in what was Yugoslavia, the epoch prior to World War I was hardly "the good old days." Most of the common people were poor, autocracy ran high, inter-ethnic hatred was common, and warfare was a constant. Third, the level of weapons technology in use was rather on the conventional side. Certainly enough blood was shed to satisfy everyone's honor, but aircraft were few and helicopters and tanks only somewhat more frequent. Artillery and hand-held rocket launchers were common enough, but most of the weapons were rapid fire rifles and machine guns. Many of these armed conflicts were street wars, battles between civilians and hastily organized militia or between a militia and a regular army. They sometimes increased in intensity and the areas of violence spread, very much as they did under similar circumstances in Spain in 1936, or, indeed, in Viet Nam in 1953. Within such low technology wars, sieges within constricted spaces have again surfaced. Thus, for example, during 1992, the Bosnian capitol of Sarajevo was besieged by the Serbs, the city bombarded by artillery, mortars, and tanks located in surrounding hills, the only accesses to the city being a single road and an airfield, both vulnerable to Serbian fire—in short, a physical setting not unlike Dien Bien Phu. The purpose of the siege, according to Serbian ideology, was less to actually take the city than to annihilate its largely Moslem population in an act of "ethnic cleansing."

Similar low technology sieges can be expected wherever violence is seen as a necessary course by which to redress wrongs and where the contending forces are more like urban guerrillas than formal armies. And so long as any commander announces "We shall hold at any cost," or "They shall not pass," or "Since those people are different from us, we must take what they have," and as long as egos, despair, stupidity, pride, and greed accompany soldiers into battle, then sieges will be offered and sieges will be accepted, familiar warts on the face of battle.

Selected Bibliography

MANUSCRIPT SOURCES

London: National Army Museum, 6807/720, Anthony Sterling, Letters from the Crimea.

NEWSPAPERS

London:	*Examiner*, 1854–58
	Illustrated London News, 1854–58
	Times, 1854–58, 1991–93
New York:	*Times*, 1990–93
San Francisco:	*Chronicle*, 1990–91
Washington, DC:	*Washington Post*, 1990–91

NEWS MAGAZINES

Life, 1940–41
Newsweek, 1990–91
Time, 1940–41, 1990–91
U.S. News and World Report, 1990–91

BOOKS AND PERIODICALS

Adock, F. *The Greek and Macedonian Art of War*. Berkeley, CA: University of California, 1957.
Adye, J. "The Battle of the Alma: A Contemporary Account." *Journal of the Society for Army Historical Research* 17 (1938): 223–226.

Allen, T., et al., eds. *War in the Gulf*. Atlanta, GA: Turner Publishing, 1991.

Attwill, K. *Fortress: The Story of the Siege and Fall of Singapore*. New York: Doubleday, 1960.

Balbi di Coreggio, Francisco. *The Siege of Malta, 1565*. Tr. E. Bradford. London: Folio Society, 1965.

Baldwin, M., ed. *The First Hundred Years*. Vol. 1, *A History of the Crusades*. Ed. K. Setton. Philadelphia, PA: University of Pennsylvania Press, 1958.

Barber, N. *A Sinister Twilight: The Fall of Singapore, 1942*. Boston: Houghton-Mifflin, 1968.

Barker, A. *The Bastard War: The Mesopotamian Campaign of 1914–1918*. New York: Dial, 1967.

Barnett, C. *Britain and Her Army, 1509–1970*. London: Murrow, 1970.

Baynes, J. *Morale*. Wayne, NJ: Avery, 1988.

Bell, J. *Besieged: Seven Cities Under Siege*. New York: Chilton Books, 1966.

Biddulph, R. "The Assault on the Redan," *Journal of the Society for Army Historical Research* 21 (1942): 52–54.

Braddon, R. *The Siege*. New York: Viking, 1970.

Bradford, E. *The Great Siege, Malta, 1565*. New York: Harcourt, Brace, and World, 1961.

————. *The Sword and the Scimitar*. New York: Putnam's, 1974.

Brockman, E. *The Two Sieges of Rhodes*. London: Murray, 1969.

Brodie, B., and F. Brodie. *From Crossbow to H-Bomb*. Bloomington, IN: Indiana University Press, 1973.

Cadogan, G., and S.J.F. Calthorpe. *Cadogan's Crimea*. Ed. W. Luscombe. Abbrev. ed. New York: Atheneum, 1980.

Chapman, F. S. *The Jungle Is Neutral*. New York: Norton, 1949.

Churchill, W. *The Grand Alliance*. Vol. 3, *The Second World War*. Boston: Houghton Mifflin, 1950.

————. *Hinge of Fate*. Vol. 4, *The Second World War*. Boston: Houghton Mifflin, 1950.

Cohen, E., and J. Gooch. *Military Misfortunes*. New York: Free Press, 1990.

Contamine, P. *War in the Middle Ages*. Tr. M. Jones. Oxford, England: Blackwell, 1986.

David, P. *Triumph in the Desert*. Ed. R. Cave and P. Ryan. New York: Random House, 1991.

Dewar, M. *Brush Fire Wars: Campaigns of the British Army Since 1945*. New York: St. Martin's, 1984.

Duffy, C. *Fire and Stone: The Science of Fortress Warfare, 1660–1860*. Newton Abbot, England: David and Charles, 1975.

————. *Siege Warfare: The Fortress in the Early Modern World, 1494–1660*. London: Routledge and Kegan Paul, 1979.

Dupuy, T. *Understanding Defeat*. New York: Paragon House, 1990.

Fall, B. *Street Without Joy: Indo-China at War*. Harrisburg, PA: Stackpole, 1961.

Finucane, R. *Soldiers of the Faith*. New York: St. Martin's, 1983.

Fromkin, D. *A Peace to End all Peace*. New York: Avon, 1989.

Fulcher of Chartres. *A History of the Expedition to Jerusalem, 1095–1127*. Tr. F. Ryan. Ed. H. Fink. Knoxville, TN: University of Tennessee Press, 1969.

Fuller, J.F.C. *A Military History of the Western World*. 3 vols. New York: Funk and Wagnalls, 1954–56.

Gabrieli, F., ed. *Arab Historians of the Crusades*. Tr. E. Costello. Berkeley, CA: University of California Press, 1969.

Gibbs, P. *Battle of the Alma*. New York: Lippincott, 1963.

Goure, L. *The Siege of Leningrad*. Stanford, CA: Stanford University Press, 1962.

Grauwin, P. *Doctor at Dienbienphu*. Tr. J. Oliver. New York: John Day, 1955.

Halder, F. *The Private War Journals of Colonel General Franz Halder*. Ed. and tr. A. Lissance. Boulder, CO: Westview Press, 1976.

Hale, J., ed. *Europe in the Late Middle Ages*. Evanston, IL: Northwestern University Press, 1965.

Hibbert, C. *The Destruction of Lord Raglan*. Boston: Little, Brown, 1961.

Hill, J., and L. Hill. *Raymond IV, Count of Toulouse*. Syracuse, NY: Syracuse University Press, 1962.

Hogg, I. V. *A History of Artillery*. New York: Hamlyn, 1974.

———. *Fortress: A History of Military Defense*. New York: St. Martin's, 1977.

———. *History of Fortification*. London: Orbis, 1981.

Horne, A. *The Fall of Paris: The Commune and Siege, 1870–1871*. New York: Penguin, 1965.

Hughes, J. *Fortress: Architecture and Military History in Malta*. London: Humphries, 1969.

Kearsey, A. *A Study of the Strategy and Tactics of the Mesopotamian Campaign, 1914–1917*. Aldershot, England: Gale and Polden, 1934.

Keegan, J. *The Face of Battle*. New York: Viking, 1976.

———. *The Mask of Command*. New York: Viking, 1987.

———. *The Second World War*. New York: Viking, 1989.

———, and J. Darracott. *The Nature of War*. New York: Holt, Rinehart, and Winston, 1981.

———, and R. Holmes, with J. Gau. *Soldiers: A History of Men in Battle*. New York: Viking, 1986.

Kinglake, A. *The Invasion of the Crimea*. 4th ed. 6 vols. Edinburgh, Scotland: Blackwood, 1877 et seq.

Kirby, W., ed. *The War Against Japan*. Vol. 1, *Official History of the Second World War*. London: HMSO, 1957.

Krey, A., ed. *The First Crusade: The Accounts of Eye-Witnesses and Participants*. Gloucester, MA: Peter Smith, 1958.

Leasor, J. *Singapore: The Battle That Changed the World*. New York: Doubleday, 1968.

Leonhard, R. *The Art of Maneuver*. Novato, CA: Presidio, 1991.

Mesopotamian Commission. *Report*. London: HMSO, 1917.

Millard, R. *The Death of an Army: The Siege of Kut, 1915–1916*. Boston: Houghton Mifflin, 1970.

Moberly, F., ed. *The Campaign in Mesopotamia, 1914–1918*, Vols. 1 and 2, *Official History of the Great War*. London: HMSO, 1923–27.

Morrison, I. *Malayan Postscript*. London: Faber and Faber, 1942.

Myatt, F. *British Sieges of the Peninsular War*. New York: Hippocrene Books, 1987.

O'Connell, R. *Of Men and Arms*. New York: Oxford University Press, 1982.

Oman, C. *The Art of War in the Sixteenth Century*. New York: Dutton, 1937.

———. *The Art of War in the Middle Ages*. Ithaca, NY: Cornell University Press, 1960.

O'Neil, B. H. *Castles and Cannon: A History of Artillery Fortifications in England*. Oxford, England: Clarendon, 1960.

Palmer, A. *The Banner of Battle*. New York: St. Martin's, 1987.

Pemberton, W. *Battles of the Crimean War*. New York: Macmillan, 1962.

Roy, J. *The Battle of Dienbienphu*. Tr. R. Baldick. New York: Harper and Row, 1965.

Runciman, S. *The First Crusade*. Vol. 1. *A History of the Crusades*. Rev. ed. Cambridge, England: Cambridge University Press, 1962.

Russell, W. H. *Despatches from the Crimea*. Ed. N. Bentley. London: Deutsch, 1966.

Salisbury, H. *The 900 Days: The Siege of Leningrad*. New York: Harper and Row, 1969.

Schermerhorn, E. *Malta of the Knights*. London: Heinemann, 1929.

Seeman, M. "On the Meaning of Alienation." *American Sociological Review* 24 (December 1959): 783–791.

Seymour, W. *Great Sieges of History*. London: Brassey's, 1991.

Southern, R. W. *The Making of the Middle Ages*. New Haven, CT: Yale University Press, 1961.

Steele, M. *American Campaigns*. 2 vols. Washington, DC: United States Infantry Association, 1943.

Strachan, H. "Soldiers, Strategy and Sebastopol." *Historical Journal* 21 (1978): 303–325.

Swayne, M. *In Mesopotamia*. London: Hodden and Stoughton, 1917.

Tanham, G. *Communist Revolutionary Warfare: The Vietminh in Indo-China*. New York: Praeger, 1961.

Taylor, F. *The Art of War In Italy, 1494–1529*. Cambridge, England: Cambridge University Press, 1921.

Townshend, C. *My Campaign in Mesopotamia*. New York: McCann, 1920.

Tsuji, M. *Singapore: The Japanese Version*. Ed. H. Howe. Tr. M. Lake. New York: St. Martin's, 1960.

Vauban, S. *A Manual of Siegecraft and Fortifications*. Ed. G. Rothrock. Ann Arbor, MI: University of Michigan Press, 1968.

Viollet-le-Duc, E. *Military Architecture*. 3rd ed. Tr. M. MacDermott. Novato, CA: Presidio, re-issue 1990.

Watson, B. A. *The Great Indian Mutiny: Colin Campbell and the Campaign at Lucknow*. New York: Praeger, 1991.

Watson, B. W., et al., eds. *Military Lessons of the Gulf War*. Novato, CA: Presidio, 1991.

Wolseley, G. *The Story of a Soldier's Life*. 2 vols. New York: Scribner's, 1903.

Young, P., and W. Emberton. *Sieges of the Great Civil War*. London: Bell and Hyman, 1978.

Index

Adhémar of Le Puy: death of, 17, 22; at Dorylaeum, 21, 29; as a leader, 12, 28; vision of, 26; volunteers for First Crusade, 12

Alexius I, emperor of Byzantium: fears Frankish knights, 17; imperial police of, 17; relations with Raymond of Toulouse, 18; requests western aid, 12; and surrender of Nicaea, 20, 27

Antioch, siege of. *See* Jerusalem, siege of

armor: Russian armor in Kuwait, 160; in Singapore campaign, 114, 123–24; U.S. and British armor in Kuwait, 159; U.S. Marine Corps armor in Kuwait, 160; in World War I, 5; in World War II, 6–8

arquebus/harquebus: against Ft. St. Elmo, 46, 54, 74; introduced, 2, 39; use by Janissaries on Malta, 40, 45

artillery: attack on Ft. St. Elmo, 43–47; attack on Senglea, 47–48, 49, 53–54; at Battle of the Alma, 63–64; at Battle of Balaclava, 65; bombardment of Sebastopol, 68–70, 71–72, 73; as breaching mechanisms, 4; British abandon guns, 116; British artillery in Malaya, 114–15; British and Japanese uses of, compared, 139; evaluation of role in Mesopotamia, 100–101; French artillery at Dien Bien Phu, 150; ineffective use by

British, 142; against infantry at Sebastopol, 75–76; introduction of cannon, 2; Japanese bombard Singapore Island, 117; Japanese bombers as flying artillery, 124; at Jerusalem, 29–30; number of guns on Malta, 40; Sebastopol as end of gunpowder era, 74–75; shortage of, in Mesopotamia, 88; and Tigris Corps, 97; U.N. coalition artillery in Kuwait, 160; Viet Minh artillery at Dien Bien Phu, 151

Australian Army at Singapore: 8th Division on Singapore Island, 119; 22nd Brigade, 110; 22nd Brigade in island defense, 120; 27th Brigade, 110; 27th Brigade stalls Japanese attack, 120; size of, 110. *See also* British Army at Singapore; Indian Army at Singapore; Japanese Army at Singapore

Balbi di Corregio, Francisco: as chronicler of Malta siege, 8, 9; description of incendiary devices, 46; estimates of Moslem artillery, 40

Baldwin, brother of Godfrey of Bouillon: elected king of Jerusalem, 32; in First Crusade, 21

Barbarossa, Operation, 6–8. *See also* Leningrad, siege of

Barrett, General Sir Arthur: early suc-
    cesses against Turks, 85; takes
    Poona Division to Mesopotamia, 84
battles of attrition; in Kuwait, 160; on
    Malta, 55; in Mesopotamia, 101–2,
    105, 130, 142; at Sarajevo, 164; at
    Sebastopol, 72–73, 81; and sieges, 5
Baynes, John: *Morale* and generalship
    in Mesopotamia, 103; morale in
    relation to casualties, 133
Bell, J. B., *Besieged*, 6, 9
Bohemund of Taranto: abandons
    Crusade, 22, 131; and Alexius I, 18–
    19; ambitions of, 19; defeats Yaghi-
    Siyan, 21–22; at Dorylaeum, 20–21;
    joins First Crusade, 18; takes An-
    tioch by ruse, 22
British Army brigades in the Crimea:
    at Battle of the Alma, 64; charge of
    Heavy Brigade, 65–66, 74; charge
    of Light Brigade, 65, 74, 80; decima-
    tion of Guards, 66, 79; Guards, 60,
    61; Highlands Brigade, 60, 61;
    Light Brigade at the Alma, 64
British Army in the Crimea: ad-
    ministration of, 59; army organiza-
    tion, 59; in Battle of the Alma,
    63–64; in Battle of Balaclava, 64–66;
    in Battle of the Inkerman, 66;
    casualties, 77–78; leadership of, 60–
    63; purchase system, 59–60;
    reforms of, 80; size, 57; will to com-
    bat in, 78–79. *See also* Sebastopol,
    siege of
British Army divisions in the Crimea,
    61; at Battle of the Alma, 64
British Army in Kuwait, 157; 7th Ar-
    mored Brigade, 159
British Army regiments in
    Mesopotamia, 1915–1916: Black
    Watch, 98, 100–102; Oxfordshire-
    Buckinghamshire Light Infantry,
    95; Seaforth Highlanders, 98, 101;
    2nd Dorsetshire, 88. *See also* Kut-al-
    Amara, siege of
British Army at Singapore: Argyll and
    Sutherland Highlanders, 110, 123;
    artillery deficiencies of, 111; blunts
    Japanese attack, 120; 18th British
    Division, 119; ineffectiveness of ar-

tillery, 114–16, 120, 124; size, 110.
    See also Australian Army at Sin-
    gapore; Indian Army at Singapore;
    Japanese Army at Singapore; Sin-
    gapore, siege of
British regiments, cavalry, and the
    Crimea: Inniskilling Dragoons, 66;
    Scot Greys, 66; 17th Lancers, 61
British regiments, infantry, and the
    Crimea: Coldstream Guards, 61;
    Grenadier Guards, 66; 42nd (Black-
    watch), 64, 76; 79th (Cameron
    Highlanders), 64; 88th, 78; 93rd
    (Sutherland Highlanders), 64, 65,
    74, 79, 80, 138; 95th (Rifle Brigade),
    78; 98th, 61
Brooke-Popham, Sir Robert, com-
    mander-in-chief, Far East: back-
    ground of, 113; blame for defeat,
    128; failure of Matador, 114; on pos-
    sible Japanese attack on Singapore,
    108; judgement questioned, 113;
    creates Operation Matador, 109;
    relieved of command, 112
Brown, General Sir George: advice on
    attacking Great Redan, 72; com-
    mands Light Division in Crimea, 61
Buller, Sir George, 61; at the Battle of
    the Alma, 64
Bush, George, president of the United
    States: changes position on sanc-
    tions, 162; impatient with U.N.
    sanctions against Iraq, 154–55

Calthorpe, Major Somerset: on effec-
    tiveness of Russian artillery, 76; es-
    timates Inkerman casualties, 66;
    estimates of Sebastopol defenses,
    68; on second bombardment of
    Sebastopol, 70
Cambridge, George, 2nd duke of: at
    Battle of the Alma, 64; commands
    1st Division in Crimea, 61; made
    commander-in-chief of the British
    Army, 80
Campbell, Brigadier General Sir
    Colin: at Battle of the Alma, 64;
    commands army in Great India
    Mutiny, 80; commands Highland
    Brigade in Crimea, 61; critiques

Sebastopol assaults, 76; and the Thin Red Line at Balaclava, 65, 68, 74, 79; and will to combat, 138

Canrobert, General Francois: resigns, 70; takes command of French army in Crimea, 66

Cardigan, James Thomas Brudenell, 7th earl of: blame for charge, 80; in the Crimea, 57; leads charge of the Light Brigade, 65; sets example of bravery, 138

castles. *See* fortresses

Castries, Colonel Christian de, commander in Dien Bien Phu, 150; conceals death of Colonel Piroth, 151–52; led astray by General Navarre, 150; surrenders Dien Bien Phu, 153

cavalry: charge of Heavy Brigade, 65; charge of Light Brigade in Crimea, 65; charges by, 21, 28–29; medieval knights as, 14; in Mesopotamia, 84, 97; poor use of in Crimea, 74; raid against Turks on Malta, 48–49

Chamberlain, Joseph Austin, secretary of state for India, sanctions British advance to Kut-al-Amara, 88

Chapman, Frederick Spencer: chronicles Singapore defeat, 8; observes Japanese soldiers, 114; wants to establish a guerrilla force, 112

Charles V, king of Spain: grants Malta to Knights of St. John, 36; sees strategic position of Malta, 38

Charles VIII, king of France, sieges in Italy, 2

Churchill, Winston, British prime minister: instructions to General Wavell, 119; reaction to unconditional surrender of Singapore, 121; surprised at state of Singapore defenses, 111

Codrington, Major General Sir William, brigade commander in the Crimea, 61; assumes command in the Crimea, 80; at Battle of the Alma, 64

Crimean War. *See* Sebastopol, siege of

Delamain, Major General W. J.: at Battle of Ctesiphon, 91; protests Turkish treatment of British prisoners, 104; on withdrawal to Kut-al-Amara, 94

Dien Bien Phu, siege of, 10; aerial supply, 152; ambiguities behind siege, 153; background to, 147–48; defenses of, 150–51; as an epiphany of battle, 152; French assumptions about Viet Minh, 149; and Kuwait siege, 162–63, 164; plans for, 149; Viet Minh operations against, 151–52

Dobie, Major General W.G.S., theory of Singapore defense, 109

Dragut/Torghud, Moslem corsair: and attack on Ft. St. Elmo, 45; background of, 43; killed, 46; sent to Malta by Suleiman, 43

Duff, Sir Beauchamp, Indian commander-in-chief in 1915, urges Indian Army forces to move up Tigris River, 84, 85

Duffy, Christopher: *Fire and Stone*, 4; *Siege Warfare*, 2–4, 55

Enver Pasha, demands humiliation of British forces in Mesopotamia, 99

Evans, Major General Sir George de Lacy: at Battle of the Alma, 64; commands division in Crimea, 61

First Crusade. *See* Jerusalem, siege of

fortresses: bastions, 2–3; caponiere, 5, 71; conditions for withstanding a siege, 3; demise of the castle, 1–2; the Great Redan, 71; and history of siege warfare, 13; Jerusalem fortifications, 24; Malta fortifications, 38; and mobile warfare, 4; Sebastopol fortifications, 68, 70

French Army in the Crimea: in Battle of the Alma, 63–64; in Battle of the Inkerman, 66; condition of at end of the war, 80; in siege of Sebastopol, 68–74; size of, 57. *See also* British Army in the Crimea; Sebastopol, siege of

French Army in Kuwait, 157; 6th Armored Division, 159
Fulcher of Chartres: belief in miracles, 27, 28; as chronicler of First Crusade, 8, 22

German Army: morale of, 133; in Operation Barbarossa, 5–8
Giap, Vo Nguyen: commands Viet Minh forces, 147; infiltrates his army around Dien Bien Phu, 149; supplies his army, 150
Godfrey of Bouillon: given title of Advocate of Holy Sepulcher, 32; at Jerusalem, 26, 31; joins First Crusade, 18; outflanks Jerusalem defenders, 140
Gorringe, Major General Sir George: commands 12th Indian Division in Mesopotamia, 84; ordered up Tigris River, 97; at Second Battle of Hanna, 101
Gortchakoff, Prince Mikhail: takes command in the Crimea, 70; withdrawal from Sebastopol, 80
Gulf War. See Kuwait, siege of; United States Armed Forces in Kuwait

Hardinge, Charles, 2nd viscount: announces limited military resources, 87; India's viceroy in 1915, 84
Hardinge, Henry, 1st viscount: commander-in-chief of British Army in 1854, 59; and purchase system, 60
Hussein, Saddam: disruption of his command, 161; misjudgments of, 155, 161; rise to power in Iraq, 154, 155; survives the war, 161–62

Iftikhar-ad-Dawla: creates a defensive dead zone, 134; expels Christians from Jerusalem, 132; governor of Jerusalem, 24; guaranteed safe passage, 26
Indian Army brigades, cavalry, in Mesopotamia: as part of Tigris Corps, 97; 6th Brigade, 84; 16th Brigade at Sheikh Sa'ad, 97

Indian Army corps in Mesopotamia, 2nd, 84; battle casualties of, 96–98; Tigris Corps, 97
Indian Army divisions in Mesopotamia: 6th (Poona), 84, 88, 90–91, 92–99, 104; 7th, 101; 13th, 101
Indian Army in Mesopotamia, 1915–1916: army unprepared, 87–88; Force D embarks for, 84; poor generalship of, 103–4; as prisoners of Turks, 104. See also British Army in Mesopotamia, 1915–1916; Kut-al-Amara, siege of; Turkish Army in Mesopotamia, 1915–1916
Indian Army regiments, infantry, in Mesopotamia: Dogras, 101; Gurkhas, 102; 6th Jats, 100; 66th Punjabs, 104th Rifles, 117th Mahrattas as part of 16th Brigade, 88; 92nd Punjabs, 97; 103rd Mahrattas, 95
Indian Army at Singapore: in defense of Singapore Island, 119; 11th Division at Jitra Line, 116, 121, 124; 45th Brigade at Muar, 121; 6th Brigade counter-attack at Gurun, 121; size of, 109
Iraq. See Kuwait, siege of
Iraqi Army in Kuwait: divisions destroyed, 159; immobility of, 157, 162; Republican Guard, 154; as a special target, 156, 160; troops surrender, 160. See also Kuwait, siege of; United States Armed Forces in Kuwait

Japanese air force: aerial superiority of, 125–26; in Singapore operations, 114; sinking of Prince of Wales and Repulse, 116 See also Royal Air Force at Singapore; Singapore, siege of
Japanese Army at Singapore: atrocities committed by, 127–28; attacking Jitra Line, 116; battles on peninsula, 116–17; landing on Malayan coast, 114–15; planning campaign, 113–14; and samurai code, 126–27; siege of Singapore Is-

land, 117–20. *See also* British Army at Singapore; Indian Army at Singapore; Singapore, siege of

Jerusalem, siege of, 22–26; breaching the defenses, 139; campaign leading to, 20–22; cavalry in, 28–29; defensive domination, 136; escalation of defenses, 140; First Crusade, 11–20; in-depth defenses of, 134; role of infantry in, 31; slaughter of city's survivors, 31–32, 132; use of artillery in, 29–31; will to combat during, 27–28

Keegan, John: agreement to conduct battle, 131; battle as moral disintegration, 130; bombers as flying artillery, 125; categories of combat, 9–10; and the comparative approach, 142; *The Face of Battle*, 9; impact of tanks, 124–25; *Nature of War*, 138; opting-out, 132–33; panic, 31; on the samurai ideal, 125; *The Second World War*, 7

Kerbogha, 13; declares Crusaders unstoppable, 27; governor of Antioch, 22

Khalil Pasha: at Battle of Bait Isa, 101; takes surrender of Kut, 99

Kilij Arslan: governor of Nicaea, 20; routed at Battle of Dorylaeum, 21

knights: as heavy cavalry, 29; as heavy infantry, 31, 39; as a military elite, 14

Knights of St. John/Hospitallers. *See* Malta, siege of

Korniloff, Vice Admiral Vladimir, and Russian will to combat at Sebastopol, 79

Kut-al-Amara, siege of: artillery versus infantry, 100–101; background and early campaigning, 84–94; British leadership, 131, 132–33, 139, 140, 141, 143; December 1915 operations, 95–96; decline of British forces in, 98–99; infantry versus infantry, 102; infantry versus rifles and machine guns, 101–2; operations of relief force, 96–99; town and its defenses, 92–95; as an

unintended siege, 105, 129; will to combat, 102–4; wounded and prisoners, 104. *See also* British Army regiments in Mesopotamia, 1915–1916; Indian Army in Mesopotamia, 1915–1916; Turkish Army in Mesopotamia, 1915–1916

Kuwait, siege of: coalition air attacks, 156–57; coalition maneuvering, 157–59; the continuing dilemma with Iraq, 162; and Dien Bien Phu, 163; Iraq and, 154; Iraqi invasion of, 154–55; Iraq on defensive, 155–56; operations against Iraqi forces, 159–60; operations as a siege, 160; reasons for coalition success, 160–61; U.N. coalition formed, 155. *See also* United States Armed Forces in Kuwait

Leningrad, siege of, 78, 144. *See also* Barbarossa, Operation

Lucan, George Charles Bingham, 3rd earl of: blamed for charge, 80; and charge of Light Brigade, 65; commands Cavalry Division in Crimea, 61

Malaya. *See* Singapore, siege of

Malta, siege of: artillery versus infantry, 53; assault force, 40–41; attempted escalation, 140, 141, 142; as a battle of attrition, 55, 131, 132; causes, 35–37; collapse of Turkish resolve, 138; defending army, 38–40; defensive perimeter of, 133; defensive shaping of battlefield, 143; in-depth defense, 134; infantry versus infantry, 53–54; leadership, 41–43; mining, 139; operations on Malta, 43–50; surrender of defensive domination, 136; will to combat, 50–53; wounded and prisoners, 54–55. *See also* Moslem army on Malta

Melliss, Major General Sir Charles: at Battle of Ctesiphon, 91; protests Turkish treatment of British prisoners, 104

Menschikoff, Prince Alexander: at Battle of the Alma, 63–64; and Battle of Balaclava, 65; and Battle of the Inkerman, 66

Mesopotamia. *See* Kut-al-Amara, siege of

Moslem armies in First Crusade: artillery at Jerusalem, 30; compared to Frankish knights, 28, 29, 31; lack of unity among, 27

Moslem army on Malta: artillery, 53; character of, 40–41; divided leadership, 42–43; infantry, 54; operations against Malta, 43–50; prisoners, 55; will to combat, 51–52; wounded, 54. *See also* Malta, siege of

Mustapha Pasha. *See* Moslem army on Malta

Napoleon III: and causes of Crimean War, 58; intimidates General Canrobert, 70

Navarre, General Henry: assumes Indo-China command, 147; plans for Dien Bien Phu, 149; warned to limit operations, 149, 153

Nicaea, siege of. *See* Jerusalem, siege of

Nicot, Colonel Jean, commander of French air transport: on supplying Dien Bien Phu, 149; transports of, under fire, 152

Nixon, General Sir John: assumptions regarding Kut-al-Amara, 94–96; background of, 85; and Battle of Ctesiphon, 92; commands in Mesopotamia, 84; disbelieves intelligence reports, 85–86; estimations of medical facilities, 92; the goal of Baghdad, 84; relinquishes command, 99

Nur-ud-Din. *See* Turkish Army in Mesopotamia

Pélissier, General Aimable: assumes French command in the Crimea, 70; on effectiveness of allied artillery, 75; plan for 18 June assault on

Sebastopol, 71–72; plan for September assault, 73, 74

Percival, Lieutenant General Sir Arthur: blame for defeat, 128, 131; commanding army in Singapore, 112; defense zones on Singapore Island, 119, 120, 126; tactics for Malayan defense, 116

Peter the Hermit: ambushed, 15; as a charismatic leader, 12; and Peasant Crusade, 15; preaching, 26

Piali Bassa. *See* Moslem army on Malta

Pulford, C.W.A., R.A.F. commander, Far East, 112; and air cover for Royal Navy, 116

Raglan, Fitzroy Somerset, 1st baron, 57; at Battle of the Alma, 64; death of, 72; decision to invade Crimea, 58; demise of the army, 66; on effectiveness of allied artillery, 75, 131; given command, 60–61; and siege of Sebastopol, 70–72

Raymond of Toulouse, 12, 15; and Alexius I, 18, 19; desire to lead First Crusade, 17; at Dorylaeum, 21, 29; leads Crusade to Jerusalem, 22; march to Constantinople, 17–18; at Nicaea, 20; in siege, 23, 131, 140

Royal Air Force, in Kuwait, 156

Royal Air Force, at Singapore, 107, 198; deficiencies in, 111; and Japanese air superiority, 125–26; number and types of aircraft, 110. *See also* Japanese air force; Singapore, siege of

Royal Navy: arrival of *Prince of Wales* and *Repulse*, 109, 110; naval base at, 108; role at Singapore, 107; and Singapore defensive perimeter, 133; sinking of *Prince of Wales* and *Repulse*, 116

Russell, William Howard: on Raglan's role in Crimea, 60; and the Thin Red Line, 64

Russian Army in the Crimea: at the Alma, 63–64; at Balaclava, 64–65; and first bombardment of Sebastopol, 68; at Inkerman, 66; and

Malakoff and Great Redan, 73; in the Mamelon and Quarries, 71; repulsion of 18 June assault, 71–72; will to combat, 79; withdrawal from Sebastopol, 80–81. *See also* Sebastopol, siege of

St. Arnaud, Marshal Le Roy de. *See* Sebastopol, siege of

Schwarzkopf, General Norman, shapes battlefield in Kuwait, 157

Sebastopol, siege of, 5, 55, 68–74; allied attempts at escalation, 140; artillery versus artillery, 74–75; as a battle of attrition, 72–73, 81; British Army in, 58–60; British leadership, 60–63; campaign leading to, 63–67; causes of, 57–58; and defensive domination, 136; and defensive perimeter, 133; and effectiveness of artillery, 136; and in-depth defense, 135; infantry versus infantry, 76–77; and invitation to battle, 131; prisoners and the wounded, 77–78; will to combat, 79–80, 138. *See also* British Army in the Crimea; French Army in the Crimea; Russian Army in the Crimea

sieges: as battles of attrition, 55, 72–73, 81, 101–2, 105, 130; comparative method for study of, 9–10; as defense, 132–37; as a form of battle, 129–31; in gunpowder era, 1–5; heuristic conclusions about, 141–44; and mobile warfare, 4–5; modern sieges, 5–8; as offense, 137–41; persistency of, 147–53; physical space and, 55; writing about, 8–9. *See also names of specific sieges*

Simpson, General Sir James: assumes command in Crimea, 72; plans for second assault on Sebastopol, 73, 74; resigns, 80

Singapore, siege of: air power, 125–26; artillery, 123–24; British illusions about, 108; British and Japanese artillery compared, 139; British leadership in, 111–13; defense of Singapore, 109–11; in-depth defense of, 135–36; infantry versus infantry, 121–23; Japanese

atrocities, 127–28; Japanese campaign, 113–17; Japanese escalation, 140–41; loss of defensive domination, 137; mis-judgements of Japanese, 108–9; siege operations, 117–21; Singapore as myth, 128, 129, 131; tanks, 124–25; the three Singapores, 108; will to combat, 126–27. *See also* British Army at Singapore; Indian Army at Singapore; Japanese Army at Singapore

Stalingrad, siege of, 6, 144

Steele, Major Matthew, *American Campaigns*, and futility of frontal attacks, 5, 55

Sterling, Major Anthony: on British Army purchase system, 60; on reinforcement in Crimea, 68

Suleiman the Magnificent: advised to attack Malta, 38; death of, 50; invading army of, 40–41; miscalculations of, 51; and siege of Rhodes, 35. *See also* Malta, siege of

Tancred, nephew of Bohemund: goes raiding, 21; at siege of Jerusalem, 26, 32; takes Edessa, 32

Tanks. *See* armor

Thomas, Sir Shenton, governor general of Singapore: background of, 112; blame for defeat, 128; as an obstructionist, 112–13, 119, 125

Todleben, Colonel Franz Eduard, 64; enlists civilians in Sebastopol defense, 70, 79

Townshend, Major General Charles, 83; advance to Ctesiphon, 90; assumes command of Poona Division, 85; background of, 86–87; surrender of Kut, 99; treatment by Turks, 104, 132, 143; views on siege at Kut-al-Amara, 94, 96, 98–99; withdrawal from Ctesiphon, 91–92

Tsuji, Lieutenant Colonel Masonobu: cites Japanese casualties, 127; comments on tanks, 124–25; at Jitra Line, 123; planning Singapore campaign, 113–14; regrets atrocities, 127; *Singapore: The Japanese Version*, 126

Turkish Army in Mesopotamia, 1915–
1916: atrocities committed by, 104;
attacks against Kut-al-Amara, 95–
96; Battle of Sheikh Sa'ad, 97–98; at
Ctesiphon, 90–91; regrets
atrocities, 127; quality of troops,
85; will to combat in, 102–3;
withdraws up Tigris River, 84

United Nations, sanctions against
Iraq, 154; and Soviet Union, 155,
162; U.N. coalition build-up, 154
United States Armed Forces in
Kuwait: U.S. Air Force and Naval
air attacks, 156–57; U.S. Army
corps, 157, 159, 160; U.S. Army
divisions, 159, 160; U.S. Marine
Corps, 157–58, 159, 160
Urban II, Pope: calls for First Crusade,
12–13; does not name a leader, 17,
19, 26, 27

Valette-Parisot, Jean de la: background of, 42; challenges Moslems,
36–38; and defense of Ft. St.
Michael, 49; and defense of
Senglea, 47–48; defensive force of,
38–40; invites siege of Malta, 38;
kills prisoners, 47, 55; leads Order of
St. John, 36, 42; shaping the battle
zone, 51, 131. See also Malta, siege of
Vauban, Sébastien le Prestre de, 4;
theory of sieges, 9
Viet Minh. See Dien Bien Phu, siege of

Wavell, General Sir Archibald: assumes Far East command, 112;
communication to Churchill, 111;
instructions from Churchill, 119
Windham, Colonel Charles: on character of Pélissier, 70; discounts effects
of Sebastopol bombardment, 68;
evaluation of assault on Great
Redan, 72; evaluation of second assault, 74, 80
Wolseley, Captain Garnett: and attack
on Great Redan, 73; charac-
terization of British Army, 59;
evaluation of second assault, 74, 80
World War I: armor in, 5; Britain
declares war on Turkey, 84, 100;
collapse of Turkish power, 145,
154; compared to Sebastopol siege,
73; in Mesopotamia, 83; Western
Front, 102–3, 133
World War II: armor in, 6, 8; post-war
world changes, 145–47; and technological change, 140–41; use of
atom bomb, 144

Yamashita, General Tomoyuki: commands Malay invasion force, 113;
executed for war crimes, 127–28;
reduces his force, 117, 120; siege of
Singapore a bluff, 126, 136; takes
Percival's unconditional surrender,
121
Yugoslavia: breakup of, 163; siege of
Sarajevo, 164